Bogardus does an excellent job of explaining and dispelling the confusion behind current thinking about sex. He takes his opponents seriously, engaging in a clear, comprehensive, and compelling way. The book is perfectly positioned to make a timely intervention on the current debate, and to reorient conversations about what sex is, how it relates to gender, and what our obligations are when it comes to pronouns. Bogardus brings ideas from philosophy of biology, philosophy of language, ethics, and more together into a forceful argument that it will be hard for critics to ignore. A must-read for students and academics alike.

Holly Lawford-Smith, *Associate Professor in Political Philosophy at the University of Melbourne, Australia*

THE NATURE OF THE SEXES

How complex is sex? According to this book, not nearly as complex as we're often told these days.

Author Tomás Bogardus first critically evaluates varieties of a complex view of sex—supported by Anne Fausto-Sterling, Sarah Richardson, and others—in which sex is a constellation of traits related to chromosomes, hormones, gonads, and phenotypes. Bogardus then considers several gamete-based accounts of sex, to which he is more sympathetic, including those from Alex Byrne, Laura Franklin-Hall, and Paul Griffiths. Shortcomings of these views are described, and an improved account is proposed: the sexes are *activated higher-order functions*. In short, to be male is to have the function of producing sperm, and to be female is to have the function of producing eggs. Bogardus develops this view, all while untangling the various meanings and definitions of 'gender' and 'gender identity', and while examining whether all of them are ultimately defined in terms of the sexes.

The author then defends his methodology of deferring to biologists when figuring out the nature of the sexes and concludes with practical questions about whether we should revise the meanings of our sex terms for the sake of social justice. He asks whether pronouns like 'he' and 'she' track biological sex, and whether they should continue to do so.

The Nature of the Sexes: Why Biology Matters expands current philosophical debate on sex and gender, and is essential reading for curious students and academics alike.

Tomás Bogardus is Professor of Philosophy at Pepperdine University, USA. He works mainly in metaphysics and epistemology, as well as philosophy of language, and has been publishing on the philosophy of sex and gender since 2019.

THE NATURE OF THE SEXES

Why Biology Matters

Tomás Bogardus

NEW YORK AND LONDON

Designed cover image: The Met / *Joan of Arc*, by Jules Bastien-Lepage (1879). Gift of Erwin Davis, 1889

First published 2026
by Routledge
605 Third Avenue, New York, NY 10158

and by Routledge
4 Park Square, Milton Park, Abingdon, Oxon, OX14 4RN

Routledge is an imprint of the Taylor & Francis Group, an informa business

© 2026 Tomás Bogardus

The right of Tomás Bogardus to be identified as author of this work has been asserted in accordance with sections 77 and 78 of the Copyright, Designs and Patents Act 1988.

All rights reserved. No part of this book may be reprinted or reproduced or utilised in any form or by any electronic, mechanical, or other means, now known or hereafter invented, including photocopying and recording, or in any information storage or retrieval system, without permission in writing from the publishers.

Trademark notice: Product or corporate names may be trademarks or registered trademarks, and are used only for identification and explanation without intent to infringe.

ISBN: 978-1-041-02954-0 (hbk)
ISBN: 978-1-041-02953-3 (pbk)
ISBN: 978-1-003-62159-1 (ebk)

DOI: 10.4324/9781003621591

Typeset in Sabon
by SPi Technologies India Pvt Ltd (Straive)

Non nobis, Domine.

CONTENTS

Acknowledgments		*x*
1	Introduction	1
2	What the Sexes Could Not Be: The Complex View	10
3	What the Sexes Could Be: The Gamete View	49
4	Gender is Defined in Terms of the Sexes	92
5	When Biology Meets Politics	110
6	A Defense of the Sex-Tracking View of Pronouns	130
7	Conclusion	155
Index		*157*

ACKNOWLEDGMENTS

I'm grateful to Kathleen Stock for blazing this trail and for graciously helping me along the way back in 2018. Thanks also to Holly Lawford-Smith, whose humor and wit remain undimmed despite repeated injustices against her. Thanks to Alex Byrne for thoughtful comments and encouragement dating back several years now. The integrity and grit of these three are a credit to Philosophy. Thanks to all the participants (and now friends) at the top-secret Gender-Critical workshops in 2020, 2024, and 2025. Thanks to my many interlocutors on these issues, including Emma Hilton, Colin Wright, Jon Pike, Jane Clare Jones, Anne Fausto-Sterling, Justin Garson, and others who may wish to remain anonymous. Thank you to the folks at Routledge, for having the courage to publish these ideas. Most of all, I'm grateful to T & M, for bearing with me through all this.

1
INTRODUCTION

One winter morning as an undergraduate in La Jolla, California, I crawled out to the surf across a carpet of copulating squid. I grew up surfing, bodyboarding, and thinking about marine biology in Southern California, so nobody was surprised when I went to UC San Diego after high school. That morning, my friends and I drove up to a reef called Horseshoes and to some of the best waves we'd ever seen. My feet barely touched the sand as I rushed to the water, but while paddling out, I immediately noticed that, each time my hands plunged into the water, they pushed against something about the size and shape of a small baguette. *Squid*: mottled brown, some dead or dying, the live ones with chromatophores still firing hypnotically. They were all around us, too many to count, like a pulsating, psychedelic crowd at Burning Man with tentacle dreadlocks. Off-putting, for sure, but the waves were too good to pass up. So, I dragged myself through that sprawling squid bouquet.

All along the California coast, we later learned, hundreds of thousands of these squid—*Doryteuthis opalescens*, formerly known as *Loligo opalescens*—meet up each winter for grand festivals of reproduction. When all goes to plan, the male holds the female from below, and spreads his arms around her mantle, transferring a bundle of spermatophores from his mantle cavity to near the female's oviduct, or in the bursa copulatrix (Hurley 1977, 196). Females later secure the fertilized egg capsules into the sand in giant egg beds until the hatchlings begin the cycle anew. Many of the adult squid expire directly after mating, their brief lives devoted to love and the abyss. The romance might smite my Californian heart if these animals weren't so very ugly.

I remember the waves that day, including one of the best of my life. But being up to my neck in the swirling life and death of those squid left a deeper impression on me. The productive power of living things fills the world with wonder. Living things assemble and grow their bodies; they secrete organic matter like silk, ink, and resinous lac.[1] They metabolize and excrete waste. Most notably, for our purposes, they multiply themselves. They produce new individuals from pre-existing individuals, in this process known as *reproduction*. Sometimes, reproduction is a solo act: asexual reproduction. Among multicellular organisms, reproduction is more often a collaboration: sexual reproduction. And the most familiar version of sexual reproduction is a duet, involving two complementary types of mates: male and female.

Many questions about sexual reproduction have puzzled biologists. For example: Why do organisms reproduce sexually at all, as opposed to asexually?[2] After all, a solo is less complicated than a duet, logistically. For those species that reproduce sexually, why the dominance of a strategy involving only *two* mates and *two* sex cells of different sizes (anisogamy), as opposed to one size (isogamy) or some other number?[3] And given that a species settles on two types of mates, why do so many organisms adopt a strategy in which individuals are genetically determined to exemplify only one of exactly two sexes (gonochorism), as opposed to the less popular two-for-one strategy in which each individual exemplifies *both* sexes at the same time? Your nearest garden snail, for example, is both male and female at the same time, and it works well for them. Why isn't that a more common strategy?[4]

These and others are interesting questions about *why* the sexes are the way that they are. But this book is about a more fundamental question: *what* are the sexes? What is it to be male, and what is it to be female? To appreciate the meaning of the question, consider that humans thought and spoke about water, light, gold, life, genes, rainbows, the Sun, and much else, for many years before scientific investigation uncovered in each case the deeper truth of what it is that we had been thinking and speaking about. We discovered that water is H_2O, that our genes are realized by DNA, that the Sun is an enormous nuclear fusion reactor, and so on. Can we, in a similar way, discover the deeper truth of what it is we've been referring to all these years with words like 'male' and 'female'?

Some biologists find the question surprising. The field is so replete with talk of males and females that the biologist is like a squid who doesn't know it's wet. We're all familiar with ordinary animals like lions, tigers, and bears described using 'male' or 'female', and, of course, humans as well. But biologists describe even very simple organisms using 'male' or 'female'. For example, nematodes are described in this way (e.g. Martin and Lee 1980), as are the extremely simple Placozoa (Eitel et al. 2011). Biologists also describe gametes using 'male' or 'female' (e.g. Takeuchi et al. 2008)—male gametes are those produced by males, female gametes by females—and they commonly describe embryos and blastocysts using 'male' or 'female' (e.g. Moutos et al. 2021). Cosexual plants have male and female flowers on the same plant, either hermaphroditically within the same flower or in separate flowers on so-called monoecious plants. Dioecious plants, on the other hand, segregate the sexes (Ohya et al. 2017): these plants come in two varieties, exclusively male and exclusively female.

I mention this because I believe Maximiliana Rifkin and Justin Garson (2023, 2) are correct when they suggest that biology has special authority to shape our ontology of sex: the way that biologists talk and think about sex should inform our understanding of what sex is. I will repeat that, since it is a cornerstone of this project: if we want to know what 'male' and 'female' refer to, when used as adjectives and said of organisms, we should pay special attention to how biologists use those words. I will defend this claim at length in Chapter 5; until then, we will take it as a working assumption. And, according to Rifkin and Garson (2023, 1), there is "an emerging consensus" that the nature of sex has to do with anisogamy, with the ability to produce large gametes (female) or small gametes (male). They call this "a very standard view in the sexual selection literature" (2023, 2).[5]

Consider this early statement of the view, from Charles Sedgwick Minot (1885, 437):

> As evolution continued hermaphroditism was replaced by a new differentiation, in consequence of which the individuals of a species were, some, capable of producing ova only; others of producing spermatozoa only. Individuals of the former kind we call females, of the latter males, and they are said to have sex.

Here's another early statement of the view, from Robert Payne Bigelow (1904, 144):

> The ability to produce a macro- or microgamete constitutes the essential distinction of sex. The individual which produces the latter is said to be of the *male* sex, the individual producing the former is said to be of the *female* sex.[6]

More recently, Jussi Lehtonen and Geoff Parker (2014, 1161–2) put it this way: "males are those individuals that produce smaller gametes (e.g., sperm), while females are defined as those that produce the larger gametes."[7] Laura Franklin-Hall (2021, 180) agrees: "From a creature's anatomy, to its behavior and genetics, biologists have uncovered no feature–save gamete size–perfectly distinctive of either sex." John Dupré (1986, 446, reproduced nearly verbatim in 1993, 68) as well: "What it is to be male or female... is a property at a higher level of structural organization, that of producing relatively large, or small, gametes."[8] Or take Joan Roughgarden (2004, 23), who said:

> To a biologist, *'male' means making small gametes, and 'female' means making large gametes*. Period! By definition, the smaller of the two gametes is called a sperm, and the larger an egg. Beyond gamete size, biologists don't recognize any other universal difference between male and female.[9]

Even Simone de Beauvoir ([1949] 1956, 39) would have no quarrel with these gamete-based definitions: "In the vast majority of species male and female individuals co-operate in reproduction. They are defined primarily as male and female by the gametes which they produce—sperms and eggs respectively."

Roll credits? Case closed? Not so fast. In a popular and culturally influential article in *Nature*, Claire Ainsworth (2015, 288) hoists the flag of a competing line of thought that we have to take seriously: "Sex can be much more complicated than it at first seems." Let's call any gamete-based analysis of the sexes "the Gamete View," and we'll call any rival analysis a species of "the Complex View." Anne Fausto-Sterling (2012, 4) has done much to propagate the idea that sex is complex, that in fact there are several kinds of sex in metaphorical spirals and layers, like "multilayered phyllo dough." More on her view below. Here's another recent statement, from Kristina Smiley et al. (2024, 2): "sex is a multifaceted, complex phenomenon that consists of many intersecting variables and can be approached from different perspectives." These authors propose that 'sex' refers to "a group of traits that are often, but not always, associated with reproduction" (Kristina Smiley et al. 2024, 3). As another example, McLaughlin et al. (2023, 891–2) tell us that "sex is not a single trait," and that the word 'sex', used in the way relevant to our purposes, "encompasses a broad collection of gametic, genetic, hormonal, anatomic, and behavioral traits." Below, we'll distinguish between four sub-species of this view and evaluate each one.

This debate is no trifle, and indeed has taken center stage in the popular culture's discussion of sex and gender. It turns out that talk of the sexes pervades law and culture, and so *what the sexes are* has deep implications for spaces and activities we've long segregated by sex: sports, prisons, military service, restrooms, dormitories, scholarships, entire colleges, and the like. For example, trans-identifying philosopher Veronica Ivy, then going by the name "Rachel McKinnon" (2019), appealed to sex in order to justify racing in the women's division: "The rules require me to race in the women's category. That's exactly where I belong: I am a woman, after all. I am female as well… Trans women are women. We are female." The Complex View has been recruited to argue that *sex is not binary* (e.g. Fausto-Sterling 2018). Others use the Complex View to argue that, among the constellation of things that 'male' and 'female' might refer to are what they call "gender identities." And so, they conclude, having a "male gender identity" is a legitimate way of being male, even if the person is male in no other alleged sense of the word.[10] Lawyers from the American Civil Liberties Union (2025, 6), for example, recently endorsed the Complex View, expressing it like so: "The concept of 'sex' refers to multiple physiologic attributes, such as chromosomes, gonads (glands that produce hormones and gametes), and anatomy (internal and external reproductive parts), secondary sex characteristics that usually develop during puberty, and gender identity."

Everyone agrees that the stakes are high. Philosopher Katharine Jenkins (2016, 396), for example, says that "[f]ailure to respect the gender identifications of trans people is a serious harm and is conceptually linked to forms of transphobic oppression and even violence." Insofar as failure to respect the *sex* identifications of trans-identifying individuals (e.g. Ivy/McKinnon, above) is also "conceptually linked" to transphobic oppression and violence, one might think the same goes for respecting those identifications as well. It is worth investigating, therefore, whether some version of the Complex View is true, and whether sex really is as complex as these thinkers say it is.

Notes

1 Cf. Derby 2014, Jadoun and Riaz 2022.
2 See Hill (2019, 96): "Explaining the evolution of sexual reproduction is among the most significant and long-standing problems in evolutionary biology (Williams, 1975; Maynard Smith, 1978). Sexual reproduction has proven so formidable a challenge for evolutionary biologists that it is commonly spoken of as 'the paradox of sex' (Otto and Lenormand, 2002)."
3 This is another longstanding problem. See Fisher (1930), and more recently Lessells and Snook (2009), and Parker (2011, 18), who offers a "survey of all theories relating to the evolution of anisogamy (including gamete competition)."
4 See Tomlinson (1966), Ghiselin (1969), Williams (1975), Déprés and Maurice (1995), and Leonard (2013).
5 As examples, they cite Roughgarden (2004, 23), Paul Griffiths (2020), Muhammad Khalidi (2021), Franklin-Hall (2021), Marlene Zuk and Leigh Simmons (2018), and Ryan (2018).

6 The Nature of the Sexes

6 Thanks to Colin Wright, who brought these early statements from Minot and Bigelow to my attention. And thanks to Jerry Coyne for directing me to this statement from Douglas Futuyma's (2005, 417) standard textbook, *Evolution*: "Most sexually reproducing species have distinct female and male sexes, which are defined by a difference in the size of their gametes (ANISOGAMY)."

7 See also the gamete-based definitions offered by Robert Hine (2019). Parker (2011, 17), citing Parker et al. (1972), says the same: "in an anisogamous population, males produce microgametes and females produce macrogametes." See also Wolfgang Goymann et al. (2023, 2) who say, "With a few exceptions, all sexually reproducing organisms generate exactly two types of gametes that are distinguished by their difference in size: females, by definition, produce large gamete (eggs) and males, by definition, produce small and usually motile gametes (sperm)." The exceptions, according to Goymann, include isogametic species, who reproduce sexually but using gametes of roughly the same size, some species of *Drosophila*, the males of which make sperm of three sizes, and some protozoans at the boundary of single-celled and multicellular organisms, which reproduce using a variety of large, small, and intermediately sized gametes (cf. Roughgarden 2004, 24–5).

8 It's true that, more recently, Dupré (2019, 232) says that, "Organisms in general and sex in particular must be understood developmentally," and proceeds (Dupré 2019, 233) to give a list of what may look to be various kinds of sex, while explicitly acknowledging his gratitude to Anne Fausto-Sterling. However, it is clear in that context (Dupré 2019, 233) that he's exploring "the processes through which differentiated sexes in humans develop," and earlier (Dupré 2019, 228) he continues to maintain that "Sex is a biological distinction grounded in reproductive physiology." Presumably, this is an application of his "processual philosophy of biology" (cf. Nicholson and Dupré 2018) to biological sex, though evidently that processual philosophy is consistent with sex being grounded in reproductive physiology. So, while he doesn't explicitly reiterate his 1986/1993 view, I believe it's a mistake to read him as abandoning that view in his more recent work.

9 This is particularly noteworthy given that Roughgarden, a trans individual who identifies as a woman, is "as ardent a critic of traditional sex and gender binaries as any," according to Franklin-Hall (2021, 177).

10 See, for example, the Advocates for Trans Equality: "Note: A4TE uses both the adjectives 'male' and 'female' and the nouns 'man' and 'woman' to refer to a person's gender identity." https://transequality.org/trans-101/about-transgender-people. So did the CDC, that is, the US Centers for Disease Control and Prevention, apparently, when they said that gender identity is a person's "inner sense of being a boy/man/male, girl/woman/female, another gender, or no gender." Notice that the term 'male' allegedly named a gender, there. https://www.cdc.gov/healthy-youth/lgbtq-youth/terminology.html (In the event that the current administration removes that website, an archived version is here: https://web.archive.org/web/20250120234629/https://www.cdc.gov/healthy-youth/lgbtq-youth/terminology.html). Question 32 of a New York Times/Ipsos public poll, conducted in January of 2025, asks respondents about "transgender female athletes—meaning athletes who were male at birth but who currently identify as female." Notice the use of 'female' to describe these athletes who identify as female. https://static01.nyt.com/newsgraphics/documenttools/f548560f100205ef/e656ddda-full.pdf. And Dea (2016, 21) does the same, saying "If I think of myself as female, that is my gender identity."

References

Ainsworth, Claire (2015). "Sex Redefined," *Nature* 518: 288–91.
American Civil Liberties Union (2025). Orr v. Trump, "Class Action Complaint for Declaratory and Injunctive Relief." https://www.aclu.org/cases/orr-v-trump
Bigelow, Robert Payne (1904). "Sex," in *A Reference Handbook of the Medical Sciences Embracing the Entire Range of Scientific and Practical Medicine and Allied Science*, Vol. 7, Alfred H. Buck (ed.) (New York: William Wood and Company), 144–7.
de Beauvoir, Simone [1949] (1956). *The Second Sex*, translated by H.M. Parshley (New York: Vintage Books).
Dea, Shannon (2016). *Beyond the Binary: Thinking about Sex and Gender* (Peterborough, Canada: Broadview Press).
Deprés, Laurence and Sandrine Maurice (1995). "The Evolution of Dimorphism and Separate Sexes in Schistosomes," *Proceedings: Biological Sciences* 22 (262): 175–80.
Derby, Charles (2014). "Cephalopod Ink: Production, Chemistry, Functions and Applications," *Marine Drugs* 12 (5): 2700–30.
Dupré, John (1986). "Sex, Gender, and Essence," *Midwest Studies in Philosophy* 11 (1): 441–57.
Dupré, John (1993). *The Disorder of Things* (Cambridge, MA: Harvard University Press).
Dupré, John (2019). "A Postgenomic Perspective on Sex and Gender," in *How Biology Shapes Philosophy: New Foundations for Naturalism*, David Livingston Smith (ed.) (Cambridge: Cambridge University Press), 227–46.
Eitel, Michael, Loretta Guidi, Heike Hadrys, Maria Balsamo, and Bernd Schierwater (2011). "New Insights into Placozoan Sexual Reproduction and Development," *PLoS One* 6 (5): e19639.
Fausto-Sterling, Anne (2012). *Sex/Gender: Biology in a Social World* (New York: Routledge).
Fausto-Sterling, Anne (2018). "Why Sex is Not Binary," *New York Times Opinion*, October 25th, 2018, https://www.nytimes.com/2018/10/25/opinion/sex-biology-binary.html
Fisher, Ronald A. (1930). *The Genetical Theory of Natural Selection* (Oxford, UK: Clarendon Press).
Franklin-Hall, Laura (2021). "The Animal Sexes as Historical Explanatory Kinds," in *Current Controversies in Philosophy of Science*, S. Dasgupta, R. Dotan, B. Weslake (eds.) (New York: Routledge), 177–97.
Futuyma, Douglas (2005). *Evolution* (Sunderland, MA: Sinauer Associates, Inc.).
Ghiselin, Michael T. (1969). "The Evolution of Hermaphroditism among Animals," *The Quarterly Review of Biology* 44 (2): 189–208.
Goymann, Wolfgang, Henrik Brumm, and Peter Kappeler (2023). "Biological Sex is Binary, Even Though There is a Rainbow of Sex Roles," *BioEssays* 45 (2): 2200173.
Griffiths, Paul (2020). "Sex is Real," *Aeon*. https://aeon.co/essays/the-existence-of-biological-sex-is-no-constraint-on-human-diversity, accessed May 23, 2023.
Hill, Geoffrey (2019). *Mitonuclear Energy* (Oxford: Oxford University Press).
Hine, Robert (2019). *A Dictionary of Biology*, Eighth Edition (Oxford, UK: Oxford University Press).
Hurley, Ann C. (1977). "Mating Behavior of the Squid Loligo Opalescens," *Marine Behaviour and Physiology* 4 (3): 195–203.

Jadoun, Sapana, and Ufana Riaz (2022). "Polymer-based Green Composites and their Applications," in *Green Sustainable Process for Chemical and Environmental Engineering and Science*, Inamuddin Tariq Altalhi (ed.) (Amsterdam: Elsevier), 123–45.

Jenkins, Katharine (2016). "Amelioration and Inclusion: Gender Identity and the Concept of Woman," *Ethics* 126: 394–421.

Khalidi, Muhammad Ali (2021). "Are Sexes Natural Kinds?" in *Current Controversies in Philosophy of Science*, S. Dasgupta, R. Dotan, and B. Weslake (eds.) (New York: Routledge), 163–76.

Lehtonen, Jussi, and Geoff Parker (2014). "Gamete Competition, Gamete Limitation, and the Evolution of the Two Sexes," *Molecular Human Reproduction* 20 (12): 1161–8.

Leonard Janet L. (2013). "Williams' Paradox and the Role of Phenotypic Plasticity in Sexual Systems," *Integrative and Comparative Biology* 53 (4): 671–88.

Lessells, C. (Kate) M., Rhonda R. Snook, and David J. Hosken (2009). "The Evolutionary Origin and Maintenance of Sperm: Selection for a Small, Motile Gamete Mating Type," in *Sperm Biology*, Tim R. Birkhead, David J. Hosken, and Scott Pitnick (eds.) (Amsterdam: Elsevier), 43–67.

Martin, Jean and D. L. Lee (1980). "Observations on the Structure of the Male Reproductive System and Spermatogenesis of Nematodirus battus," *Parasitology* 81 (3): 579–86.

Maynard Smith, J. (1978). *The Evolution of Sex* (Cambridge, UK: Cambridge University Press).

McKinnon, Rachel (2019, December 5). "I Won a World Championship. Some People Aren't Happy," *The New York Times*. https://www.nytimes.com/2019/12/05/opinion/i-won-a-world-championship-some-people-arent-happy.html

McLaughlin, J. F., Kinsey M. Brock, Isabella Gates, Anisha Pethkar, Marcus Piattoni, Alexis Rossi, and Sara E. Lipshutz (2023). "Multivariate Models of Animal Sex: Breaking Binaries Leads to a Better Understanding of Ecology and Evolution," *Integrative and Comparative Biology* 63 (4): 891–906.

Minot, Charles Sedgwick (1885). "Sex," in *A Reference Handbook of the Medical Sciences Embracing the Entire Range of Scientific and Practical Medicine and Allied Science*, Vol. 6, Alfred H. Buck (ed.) (New York: William Wood and Company), 436–8.

Moutos, Christopher P., William G. Kearns, Sarah E. Farmer, Jon P. Richards, Antonio F. Saad, and John R. Crochet (2021). "Embryo Quality, Ploidy, and Transfer Outcomes in Male Versus Female Blastocysts," *Journal of Assisted Reproduction and Genetics* 38 (9): 2363–70.

Nicholson, Daniel and John Dupré (2018). "A Manifesto for a Processual Philosophy of Biology," in *Everything Flows: Towards a Processual Philosophy of Biology*, Daniel Nicholson and John Dupré (eds.) (Oxford: Oxford University Press), 3–45.

Ohya, Itsuki, Satoshi Nanami, and Akira Itoh (2017). "Dioecious Plants are More Precocious than Cosexual Plants: A Comparative Study of Relative Sizes at the Onset of Sexual Reproduction in Woody Species." *Ecology and Evolution* 7 (15): 5660–8.

Otto, Sarah P., and Thomas Lenormand (2002). "Resolving the Paradox of Sex and Recombination," *Nature Reviews Genetics* 3: 252–61.

Parker, Geoff A. (2011). "The Origin and Maintenance of Two Sexes (Anisogamy), and their Gamete Sizes by Gamete Competition," in *The Evolution of Anisogamy: A Fundamental Phenomenon Underlying Sexual Selection*, Tatsuya Togashi and Paul A. Cox (eds.) (Cambridge, UK: Cambridge University Press), 17–74.

Parker, G. A., R. R. Baker, and V. G. F. Smith (1972). "The Origin and Evolution of Gamete Dimorphism and the Male-Femal Ephenomenon," *Journal of Theoretical Biology* 36: 529–53.
Rifkin, Maximiliana, and Justin Garson (2023). "Sex by Design," *Biology and Philosophy* 38 (13): 1–17.
Roughgarden, Joan (2004). *Evolution's Rainbow* (Berkeley, CA: University of California Press).
Ryan, Michael J. (2018). *A Taste for the Beautiful* (Princeton, NJ: Princeton University Press).
Smiley, Kristina O., Kathleen M. Munley, Krisha Aghi, Sara E. Lipshutz, Tessa M. Patton, Devaleena S. Pradhan, Tessa K. Solomon-Lane, and Simón(e) D. Sun (2024). "Sex Diversity in the 21st Century: Concepts, Frameworks, and Approaches for the Future of Neuroendocrinology," *Hormones and Behavior* 157: 105445.
Takeuchi, Takumi, Queenie V. Neri, and Gianpiero D. Palermo (2008). "Male Gamete Empowerment," *Annals of the New York Academy of Sciences* 1127: 64–6.
Tomlinson, Jack T. (1966). "The Advantages of Hermaphroditism and Parthenogenesis," *Journal of Theoretical Biology* 11: 54–58.
Williams, George C. (1975). *Sex and Evolution* (Princeton, NJ: Princeton University Press).
Zuk, Marlene, and Leigh W. Simmons (2018). *Sexual Selection: A Very Short Introduction* (Oxford: Oxford University Press).

2
WHAT THE SEXES COULD NOT BE

The Complex View

Introduction

Cards on the table: I don't think sex is all that complex. I favor the Gamete View over the Complex View. To go some way toward supporting that claim, I will distinguish four species of the Complex View: the Ambiguity Hypothesis, the Contextualist Hypothesis, the Indeterminacy Hypothesis, and the Property-Cluster Hypothesis. I will then critically evaluate each of these hypotheses.

Let me first say something about 'males' as opposed to males, something about *words* as opposed to *objects*, representations as opposed to reality. This is a book about the sexes: what it is to be male, and what it is to be female. But already and in what follows, I will often frame this investigation in terms of *what words refer to*, words like 'sex', 'male', and 'female'. One may find it confusing that, though I intend to answer a question about biological properties, in doing so, I discuss the *terms* used to designate those properties. I believe this is innocuous and dialectically useful. Innocuous because something is a male if and only if the word 'male' applies to it. This follows from a more general disquotational principle, and it's true of 'female' and 'sex' as well.[1] And it's dialectically useful, since many of the theorists and theories we'll discuss below focus on the meanings of our sex terms, and possibly the revision of those meanings. So, bear with me as I frame the issue in those two equivalent ways, sometimes as an inquiry into the nature of the *sexes*, and other times as an inquiry into the nature of what our sex *terms* refer to.

Now, according to the Ambiguity Hypothesis, the word 'sex' is ambiguous—more precisely, polysemous[2]—in that it refers variously to so-called "chromosomal sex," or "hormonal sex," or "phenotypic sex," and so on (and on). The hypothesis says the same of 'male' and 'female', that, for example, a creature may be hormonally male, yet chromosomally female. The Contextualist Hypothesis says that "the definition of sex and sex-related variables, and whether they are relevant in biomedical research, depends on the research context" (Sarah Richardson 2022, 9). According to the Indeterminacy Hypothesis, it is indeterminate what biologists refer to when they use 'sex' (and 'male' and 'female'), and so-called chromosomal sex, hormonal sex, phenotypic sex, etc. are roughly equally eligible candidates. So, on this view, more work must be done by us to precisify or operationalize talk of 'sex' (and 'male' and 'female') depending on our research or social goals. On the Property-Cluster Hypothesis, there is no single property that is necessary and sufficient to be a female, or to be a male. Rather, for each of the sexes, there is a *set* of properties that "cluster" in that they encourage one another's presence. And to be male or to be female is to have enough (perhaps most) of the properties in the relevant cluster.

I will now argue against all of these views in turn, and we'll thereby learn what the sexes could not be. In the following chapter, we'll learn what the sexes could be, and which version of the Gamete View is true. We'll begin the negative phase of my project with a preliminary point about social construction.

The Sexes Are Not Social Constructs

Speaking of what the sexes are not, let me begin by explaining why the sexes are not social constructs. You've no doubt heard the claim that *gender* is a social construct. Believe it or not, some people say the same thing about the sexes.[3] Judith Butler, for example. Butler is notoriously difficult to understand, and the following passage's meaning is obscured by rhetorical questions, hedged suggestions, and conditional statements. But Butler is widely taken to have endorsed the claim that sex is a social construct. The sexes are real, on this view, but they are established by our thought, our language, our discourse, and therefore are not a "prediscursive" given: they do not exist outside our discourse. The sexes exist by *convention*, the way in which it may seem that, for example, touchdowns and Texas exist by convention. Butler asks (2006 [1990], 9):

> [W]hat is 'sex' anyway? Is it natural, anatomical, chromosomal, or hormonal, and how is a feminist critic to assess the scientific discourses which purport to establish such 'facts' for us?... Is there a history of

how the duality of sex was established, a genealogy that might expose the binary options as a variable construction?

And Butler seems to answer affirmatively (Butler 2006, 9–10),

> If the immutable character of sex is contested, perhaps this construct called 'sex' is as culturally constructed as gender; indeed, perhaps it was always already gender, with the consequence that the distinction between sex and gender turns out to be no distinction at all.

Butler concludes (2006, 10):

> Gender ought not to be conceived merely as the cultural inscription of meaning on a pregiven sex (a juridical conception); gender must also designate the very apparatus of production whereby the sexes themselves are established. As a result, gender is not to culture as sex is to nature; gender is also the discursive/cultural means by which 'sexed nature' or 'a natural sex' is produced and established as 'prediscursive', prior to culture, a politically neutral surface on which culture acts.

As far as I can tell, these passages mean to communicate the following: the sexes are a cultural construct, just as the genders are. The sexes are not "pregiven," they are created, by us and our conventions, yet in such a way as to *appear* as though they're prior to culture.

Amia Srinivasan offers an argument inspired by Butler's. Citing that very passage of Butler, Srinivasan says (2021, xi), "We inspect this supposedly natural thing, 'sex', only to find that it is already laden with meaning," for example, expectations about appropriate appearance and fitting social roles. From this, she quickly concludes (2021, xii) that "Sex is, then, a cultural thing posing as a natural one. Sex, which feminists have taught us to distinguish from gender, is itself already gender in disguise."

Yet these arguments are distinct and fall short in unique ways. Let's take them in turn. Butler asserts that there is a "history of how the duality of sex was established," and concludes on that basis that sex was made by us, by our classificatory practices, and therefore is not "pregiven" or "prediscursive." The problem is that Butler's premise admits of two interpretations. On one reading, the premise is true, but the conclusion doesn't follow, and so the argument is unsound. On the second reading, the premise is false, in which case the argument is again unsound. Either way you go, then, the argument is unsound. Let me explain.

Butler's premise trades on a difference between 'sex' and sex, a difference between the *word* 'sex' and what the word *refers* to. Butler starts with a question about the word: "what is 'sex' anyway?" Next, there is an assertion that sex has a history, that our cultural practices are "an apparatus of production" by which sex is established. Now, what is it that has a history? What is it that culture has established? The word 'sex'? Our concept of sex? Our ideas, practices, expectations, and norms of sex? True enough, *these* all have cultural histories; *these* were constructed by us, developed by us. On this reading, Butler's premise is true. But from the fact that we made the *word* 'sex', it hardly follows that we made *sex*, just as from the fact that we made the word 'stars', it hardly follows that we made the stars. We developed a concept of the stars, we invented myths and stories about the stars, but the stars themselves are beyond our reach; we didn't make *them*. In a similar way, we may have invented the word 'sex', and the concept of sex, and various ideas, practices, expectations, and norms about the sexes. But none of this suggests that we made sex *itself*, or the sexes themselves.[4] So, on this interpretation of Butler, the premise may be true, but the conclusion doesn't follow. If we instead interpret the premise as a claim about *sex itself*, then what Butler is asserting is that the sexes themselves were produced by some cultural apparatus of ours. This, however, is difficult to believe, given how very ancient the sexes are. More on this in a moment.

Let's now consider Srinivasan's argument. Though she cites Butler, Srinivasan's argument looks to be distinct from Butler's, though no less hasty. What Srinivasan points out is that "'sex'… is already laden with meaning." And what she concludes is that sex is a cultural thing, posing as a natural one. As with Butler, it's not clear whether Srinivasan, in her premise, means to assert something about sex itself or about *the word* 'sex'. But given the flexibility of her "laden" metaphor, it doesn't seem to matter: both sex and the word 'sex' are plausibly "laden with meaning." Either way, though, it doesn't follow that sex is a cultural thing, not a natural one. Think about gold and 'gold'. Both the word and the object are plausibly "laden with meaning." Both are culturally significant, making substantial appearances in art, music, myth, social norms, and the like. Yet who would doubt that gold is a natural thing, and not culturally constructed? In the same way, even if sex and 'sex' are "laden with meaning," it hardly follows that sex is a social construction, that sex or the sexes were made by us. Rather, it looks as though we loaded meaning onto *reality*, both in the case of gold and in the case of the sexes.

And here's one good reason to believe that the sexes are not social constructions, alluded to before: the sexes vastly predate human societies. As Alex Byrne (2018) put it:

> If a category is socially constructed, then in order for an object to belong in that category, the object must exist (or have existed) within a society or social organization. Clearly many animals have belonged to the

category *female* (or *male*) without existing within a society of any kind... *Female* and *male* are therefore not socially constructed categories; that is, sex is not socially constructed.

Unfortunately, there has been some misunderstanding about what a category is, and an argument featuring that term invites confused readers to balk at Byrne's second premise, that animals belonged to the category *female* (or *male*) prior to societies. A reader sympathetic to social construction may well think of categories as mental or linguistic entities, something like a word or a concept. Burdened with that confusion, such a reader may stumble over Byrne's second premise, making the same mistake Ian Hacking (1999, 29) admitted to making when he said child abuse is a social construct: the mistake of switching from object (child abuse) to idea (the concept of child abuse). Only the *concept* of child abuse is socially constructed, Hacking admitted. In a similar way, a reader of Byrne's argument may mistake talk of *the sexes*, those categories, for our *ideas* or *concepts* of the sexes, and thereby deny the second premise in error.

To forestall this misunderstanding, I recommend Paul Boghossian's version of the argument (2001, cf. also 2006, 38):

> [A]nything that could have – or that did – exist independently of societies could *not* have been socially constructed: dinosaurs, for example, or giraffes, or the elementary particles... How could they have been socially constructed if they existed *before* societies did?

Notice that Boghossian speaks of dinosaurs and giraffes, instead of the categories *dinosaur* and *giraffe*, thereby focusing the reader's mind on the things out there in the world, and not our words, concepts, or ideas of those things. Surely dinosaurs existed before human societies, even if nobody was there to call them "dinosaurs," or to think of them in any way at all. In a similar way, we might run the following argument:

a   The sexes predate any society.
b   If something predates any society, then it cannot be a social construction.
c   Therefore, the sexes are not social constructions.

I have encountered people who deny premise (a), even after being alerted to the distinction between word and object, or between mental/linguistic categories and things out there in the world. In defense of (a), we might offer this argument:

d   We humans evolved only if anisogamous sexual reproduction via sperm and eggs predates any society.
e   We humans did evolve.

f   So, anisogamous sexual reproduction via sperm and eggs predates any society.
g   If anisogamous sexual reproduction via sperm and eggs occurred at some time, then the sexes existed at that time.
h   Therefore, the sexes predate any society.

What the predating argument shows is that, just as a rose by any other name would smell as sweet, so too the sexes by any other name would be sexes, and would multiply. And they would do so even if they had no name at all, as was the case for ages of ages before the existence of any society capable of constructing names for them.

The Ambiguity Hypothesis

Let's turn now to the first species of the Complex View: the Ambiguity Hypothesis. The word 'mouse' is ambiguous. It has more than one meaning. One may have a live pet mouse, and one may have a computer mouse. The word 'sex' is also ambiguous. One can discern the sex of a chicken, and thereby be said to *sex* a chicken. One can sex up a book to make it more engaging, by opening with a story of a squid "group encounter," say. As a noun, 'sex' refers to coitus, but also to the genus of males and females, the general type of which being male and being female are subtypes. This is the sense of 'sex' that concerns us in this book. But even in that case, 'male' and 'female' are themselves ambiguous, having both nominal and adjectival senses. And, even when used as adjectives, there is ambiguity. There are male and female organisms, of course, but also male and female hairstyles, and male and female pipe fittings. In this book, we will be concerned with 'male' and 'female' in their characteristic use as adjectives to describe organisms, and 'sex' as the generic for these. Our current question is, when used in *this* way, are 'male' and 'female' still ambiguous?

Some thinkers seem to believe so, and the resulting Ambiguity Hypothesis has had a colossal influence, both among scientists and at the popular level. Here, for example, is Anne Fausto-Sterling (2016, 193):

> The big problem with the term *sex* in both common and scientific usage is that it has many meanings. These are usually not clearly defined in discussion or in print, which leads to people talking at cross purposes, applying conclusions based on the idea of sex in one sense to the idea of sex in some totally other sense.

Now, Fausto-Sterling doesn't seem to have in mind the uncontroversial ambiguities of 'sex' mentioned above (coitus, sexing chickens, etc.).

She means something more substantial, something having to do with what it means to be male or female. She says (2016, 198) that there are independent "types of sex (chromosomal, hormonal, and so on)," and, again (2016, 195), that there are "different levels (chromosomal, genital, hormonal, etc.) of sex." Elsewhere (2018), she calls these "layers of sex."

This talk of "types" or "levels" or "layers" of sex traces back to John Money, Joan G. Hampson, and John L. Hampson (1955, 302), who distinguish "six variables of sex": assigned sex and sex of rearing; external genital morphology; internal accessory reproductive structures; hormonal sex and secondary sexual characteristics; gonadal sex; and chromosomal sex.[5] Now, it's not clearly stated by Money et al. that this is a claim of *semantic ambiguity*. But those authors do often talk of "contradiction" and "inconsistency" between these variables of sex. For example (1955, 304): "Among the 76 patients, there were 20 in whom a contradiction was found between gonadal sex and the sex of assignment and rearing." Of course, this cannot be a literal contradiction, since contradictions are impossible, and these patients actually existed. One plausible interpretation of what Money et al. are asserting here is that 'male' and 'female' are ambiguous, and that some patients were male in one sense of 'male' (e.g. gonadally), but not male in another sense of 'male' (e.g. assignment and rearing). This produces a *prima facie* contradiction, but the apparent contradiction is resolved upon disambiguation. (Compare: "There's a mouse near my computer, but no mouse near my computer." Disambiguation resolves the apparent contradiction.)

Around the same time, Harry Benjamin was making similar distinctions between "kinds of sex," which he eventually published as "7 Kinds of Sex" in *Sexology* in 1961. These ideas appeared again in his 1966 book, *The Transsexual Phenomenon*, as the chapter titled "The Symphony of the Sexes." There, Benjamin says:

> Instead of the conventional two sexes with their anatomical differences, there may be up to ten or more separate concepts and manifestations of sex and each could be of vital importance to the individual. Here are some of the kinds of sex I have in mind: chromosomal, genetic, anatomical, legal, gonadal, germinal, endocrine (hormonal), psychological and—also—the social sex, usually based on the sex of rearing.

Benjamin speaks of "kinds of sex," and "separate concepts" of sex, which is suggestive of the Ambiguity Hypothesis. Later in that same chapter, we get a clearer claim that 'male' and 'female' are ambiguous. He says, "it can well be said that, actually, we are all 'intersexes', anatomically as well as endocrinologically. But we are male or female in the anatomical or endocrine sense, according to the predominant structures or hormones."

For Benjamin, evidently, these multiple kinds of sex, these multiple concepts of sex, are different *senses* of 'male' and 'female'.

As for what these senses are, Benjamin defines chromosomal sex like so: "The mother's egg cell always carries an X chromosome and therefore the normal male chromosomal constellation is XY; the normal female, XX." These, apparently, give us the (alleged) chromosomal senses of 'male' and 'female'. And he clarifies the (alleged) anatomical sense 'male' as you might expect: "The secondary organs of the male are the penis, scrotum, prostate, masculine hair distribution, a deeper voice, and so on, and a masculine psychology…" And similarly for the (alleged) anatomical sense of 'female'.[6]

Citing John Money, Andrea Dworkin (1974, 183) says, "We are, clearly, a multisexed species which has its sexuality spread along a vast continuum where the elements called male and female are not discrete."[7] Believe it or not, Janice Raymond ([1979] 1994, 6–8) also seems to uncritically accept Money's list of sexes, in her (in)famous book, *The Transsexual Empire*. More recently, Sally Haslanger (2016, 134) said, "Because there are different frameworks of social meaning, different ways of drawing sex differences will be adequate to those frameworks." And, should people need to communicate while employing different frameworks, "there are mechanisms available to disambiguate their terms." She also provides a now-familiar list of "relevant kinds," or "multiple candidate kinds" (2016, 139–40), having to do with chromosomes, gametes, primary and secondary sex characteristics, the internal sense of one's sex, and social role.[8] Most recently, and in a different vein, Marcus Arvan (2023, 374) asserts that,

> in ordinary usage, the literal meaning of *female* is ambiguous, having both a biological interpretation (classifying individuals by reproductive biology) and a gendered interpretation, referring to individuals who satisfy socially constructed gender norms (such as norms for gendered traits and performance, as well as self-identification).[9,10]

We're also told, by Beans Velocci (2024, 1345), that "sex [sic] is neither static nor unitary in its meaning," and that "scientists have used multiple meanings of sex [sic] for a long time."[11] Are these thinkers correct?

Against the Ambiguity Hypothesis

The Ambiguity Hypothesis is that there are several distinct senses of 'male' and of 'female' used to describe organisms: for each, a chromosomal sense, a gonadal sense, a hormonal sense, and so on. But what is ambiguity? A serviceable, pre-theoretical definition of ambiguity goes like this: an expression is *ambiguous* if and only if it has more than one meaning (cf. Gillion 1990,

394). If an expression has exactly one meaning, we say that it's *univocal*, that there's univocity, not ambiguity. So, we can call the view on which 'male' and 'female' each have exactly one meaning, when used as adjectives and said of organisms, "The Univocity Hypothesis." For our purposes, we are interested in cases where ambiguity arises due to the meanings of individual words in the expression, rather than the structure of the expression itself, and it would be nice if we could run 'male' and 'female' through tests for ambiguity, to see if the Ambiguity Hypothesis is true. A test for this sort of ambiguity is a semantic test, an attempt to construct environments or contexts where the two alleged readings of a target sentence are made explicit.

Such tests exist; so, we will run them in order to evaluate the Ambiguity Hypothesis. And we'll run them in order of increasing plausibility, of increasing power. We'll first use the test of contradiction (cf. Arnold Zwicky and Jerrold Sadock 1975, 7–8). According to Bryan Pickel (2010, 200), "[t]he contradiction test works as follows: if [a sentence] S has two readings, then speakers should agree that an utterance of a sentence of the form S&(not S) can be true." We'll also consider a test of redundancy, which Pickel (2010) describes in this way: "if S has two readings, then speakers should agree that an utterance of a sentence of the form S&S can provide non-redundant information." And, as Pickel says, if a sentence fails both of these tests, this gives us reason to doubt that the sentence is ambiguous.

Take, for example, this sentence:

(1) "I saw her duck."

You may already detect an ambiguity here, owing to "duck."[12] We can bring out this ambiguity with the contradiction test:

(2) "I saw her duck, but I didn't see her duck."

It's easy to interpret (2) in a way that isn't a contradiction, for example, as expressing the proposition that, while I did see her bow/dip/dodge, I didn't see her waterfowl. So, (1) passes the contradiction test, as expected. We can also bring out the ambiguity with the redundancy test:

(3) "I saw her duck. Also, I saw her duck."

Again, it's easy to interpret (3) in a way that isn't redundant, for example, as the claim that I saw her waterfowl, and also I saw her bow/dip/dodge. So, here too, (1) passes the test, which is further evidence that (1) is ambiguous, as we already knew.

Now let's try it with 'male', used in its characteristic way of describing organisms. Suppose 'Joe' names Joe Biden.

(4) "Joe is male."

Does sentence (4) pass the contradiction test? If 'male' is ambiguous between chromosomal maleness, hormonal maleness, and the like, then it should. Let's check:

(5) "Joe is male, but he isn't male."

All it would take for (5) to be true on the Ambiguity Hypothesis is for Joe to change his hormone levels, or social role, etc., so that he would count as male in one alleged sense of 'male', but not in another. But I struggle to interpret (5) in any natural way that isn't a contradiction. If you think the problem is it's well known that Joe Biden is actually male in all these alleged senses of 'male', and therefore it's difficult to entertain possibilities in which (5) is true, then name the nearest male nematode 'Neville'. Neville is such a simple organism that he fails to satisfy at least one of these alleged senses of 'male'. In that case, there should be a true reading of "Neville is male, but he's not male." Still, I cannot but hear this as a contradiction, and perhaps the same goes for you. If so, this is evidence against the Ambiguity Hypothesis. Similarly with the redundancy test:

(6) "Joe is male. Also, Joe is male."

To my ears, this sounds plainly redundant. If that's right, then 'male' fails both the contradiction test and the redundancy test, which is evidence that 'male' is not ambiguous.

I admit that these tests are not conclusive, especially among philosophers, skilled as they are at finding possibilities where the naïve may hear only contradiction (or redundancy). Fortunately, there are other ambiguity tests that produce better evidence. So, let's try a third test, which I think is more definitive: conjunction reduction. According to Adam Sennet (2021), "A standard test for ambiguity is to take two sentences that contain the purportedly ambiguous term and conjoin them by using the term only once in contexts where both meanings are encouraged." He gives this example:

(7) "The colors are light."

(8) "The feathers are light."

But, when we conjoin these, the result "sounds weird," you might say. It's infelicitous, or "zeugmatic" as linguists say:

(9) "The colors and the feathers are light."

And this is due to an ambiguity in the adjective 'light'. In one sense, featured in (7), it means not dark. In another sense, featured in (8), it means not heavy. When we form this conjunction, by reducing one instance of 'light', in a context where 'colors' encourages one meaning of 'light' but 'feathers' encourages another, the result is infelicity, weirdness.

Or consider this example, from John Martin (1982, 252), but adapted from Zwicky and Sadock (1975, 18):

(10) "I saw her duck."

(11) "I saw her swallow."

(12) "I saw her duck and swallow."

Of this example, Martin says:

> (10) and (11) are each open to two readings, one verbal and the other nominal, but their abbreviation (12) admits readings in which both must be verbal or both nominal; so-called cross-readings are rejected... The rejection of cross-readings is thus taken as a mark of ambiguity.

In other words, it's easy to hear (12) as expressing the proposition that I saw her *perform* two actions, and it's easy to hear (12) as expressing the proposition that I saw two birds that belong to her, but it's difficult to hear "cross-readings" of (12), for example, to hear (12) as expressing the proposition that I saw her bow/dip/dodge and her bird (a swallow). As above, it's the infelicity of the cross-reading that's evidence of ambiguity here.[13]

Does the same thing happen with 'male'? Consider Gene, a chicken across the street from my house, who crows at all hours regardless of my feelings. Gene is of the homogametic sex in chickens, bearing ZZ sex chromosomes, typical of roosters. Now consider Envo, a Nile crocodile. According to John St. John et al. (2012, 2), "Unlike organisms with genetic sex-determination systems, crocodilians are not thought to have sex chromosomes. Instead sex is determined by incubation temperature of the egg." And according to Woodward and Murray (1993, 149), "In crocodilians the temperature of egg incubation is the environmental factor determining sex. If the temperature is cool, around 30 °C, the hatchlings are all female.

Warmer temperatures, around 34 °C, hatch all males." Envo was incubated at 34 °C.

Consider this sentence:

(13) "Gene is male."

Given the information you received, on the Ambiguity Hypothesis, sentence (13) should encourage a chromosomal reading of 'male'. Next, consider this sentence:

(14) "Envo is male."

Given the information you received, on the Ambiguity Hypothesis, sentence (14) cannot encourage a chromosomal reading of 'male'. Envo is a crocodile, and the sex of crocodiles is not determined by genetics. Envo has no sex chromosomes at all.

Now, let's run the conjunction reduction test. If (13) plus the information given about Gene encourages an alleged chromosomal sense of 'male', but 'male' in (14) expresses a distinct sense of that word, then this conjunction reduction test should produce an infelicitous, weird, zeugmatic sentence:

(15) "Gene and Envo are male."

If 'male' were ambiguous in the way Benjamin, Fausto-Sterling, and those others seem to think, then a cross-reading of (15) should be rejected. It should be unavailable, just as it was with (12) above. We shouldn't find a univocal reading of (15) natural. But on the contrary, as far as I can tell, sentence (15) is perfectly felicitous, perfectly natural, not even slightly weird. Gene and Envo are indeed both male. So, this is yet more evidence against the Ambiguity Hypothesis.

And we can go even further. Following Zwicky and Sadock (1975, 18), we can import contextual information in order to promote a cross-reading, to increase the odds of producing a zeugmatic sentence, which would be evidence of ambiguity:

(16) "Gene, who has the sex chromosomes typical of roosters, and Envo, who has no sex chromosomes at all, are male."

Yet even here, the resulting sentence seems natural and felicitous. So, even with the deck stacked in favor of the Ambiguity Hypothesis, we fail to find evidence for the hypothesis where we'd expect to, and, therefore, we have here evidence *against* the hypothesis instead. Again, I wouldn't go so far as to say that this is *conclusive* evidence, since it relies on us making unbiased linguistic judgments, and each of us is saddled with biases. But after three tests, we're building a formidable cumulative case against the Ambiguity Hypothesis.

I believe a final test is the most compelling. Sennet (2021) tells us that "Aristotle offers a test for ambiguity: try to construct a definition that encompasses both meanings and posit an ambiguity only if you fail." And Sennet gives the example of someone who proposes that 'uncle' is ambiguous, having a sense in which it means brother of a father and another sense in which it means brother of a mother. The fact that both proposed meanings are encompassed by—that is, entailed by—the definition *brother of a parent* suggests that, as Sennet says, "the phrase is not ambiguous but unspecified with respect to parent."

I don't believe there's an ordinary sense of 'male' that *entails* the alleged other senses of 'male', and likewise with 'female'. But I believe we can do something similar enough with the proposed meanings of 'male' and 'female'. Perhaps what happens in the case of 'uncle' is this: we tend to think a hypothesis of univocity is *simpler* than a hypothesis of ambiguity—at least, when the proposed univocal sense is natural and plausible. And if we come to see that the relevant linguistic data we'd like to have explained can in fact be explained on such a Univocity Hypothesis, we should favor it over an Ambiguity Hypothesis. So, for example, if we come to see that some core set of linguistic judgments concerning 'uncle' can be explained by the one natural and plausible definition of 'uncle', we should favor that over a hypothesis on which there are two definitions of 'uncle'. This is what I believe we can see with respect to 'male' and 'female'. In fact, I believe we can go further and explain away a substantial portion of the motivation for the Ambiguity Hypothesis. If we can do those two things, then we will have an additional, strong reason to reject the Ambiguity Hypothesis.

To do this, begin by noticing that whenever advocates of the Ambiguity Hypothesis spend the time to clarify what they mean by 'chromosomal male', 'hormonal male', and the like, they themselves rely on a more fundamental sense of 'male'.[14] A so-called chromosomal male is an organism with chromosomes typical of *male* members of that species. A so-called hormonal male is an organism with hormone levels typical of *male* members of that species. An organism with a so-called male gender role occupies a social position typical of *male* members of that species. And so on for the other alleged senses of 'male'.[15] In other words, being hormonally male is defined partly in terms of being male, and so if there had been no males, there would be no hormonal males. It begins to look as though 'male' is not ambiguous in all these cases, but rather used univocally to describe a variety of sex-related traits. It looks as though we are confusing sex-*related* traits for sex *itself*; that is, we're confusing *markers* of sex for sex *itself*.

And isn't this what's happening? After all, there are many ways that human males typically are. Human males have typical patterns of dress and typical vocal patterns, to name just two. Is anyone tempted to say that here too we have distinct *senses* of 'male', perhaps sartorially male and vocally male? Isn't it obvious, rather, that 'sartorially male' simply picks out ways males of our species typically dress, and 'vocally male' picks out ways the voices of males of our species typically sound? But all this can easily be explained on the Univocity Hypothesis; there's no need to posit ambiguity. And likewise with 'chromosomally male', 'hormonally male', and the like.[16]

This becomes even clearer when we consider again the list of alleged senses of 'male': a particular chromosome structure, hormone levels, large or small gamete production, external genitalia, social role, brain structure, legal status, psychology, sex assigned at birth, sex of rearing, etc. Setting aside facts about gamete production, not one of these is necessary, nor individually sufficient, nor are they even jointly sufficient for an organism to be male. Doesn't it strike us as quite obvious that being hormonally male, for example, is not sufficient to actually *be* male? Couldn't a female have hormone levels that are typical of male members of her species? It seems equally clear that being hormonally male is not necessary for being male, since a male may fail to have hormone levels *typical* of males. And it seems clear that a female may also have a male gender role, while remaining female (and not male), which shows that the alleged gender role sense of 'male' is not sufficient for being male. And neither is it necessary, since males can fail to play the role typical of males.

This can all be explained by the hypothesis that 'male' and 'female', in their typical use as adjectives said of organisms, are univocal, and that the sexes are comparatively simple. As we saw above, Lehtonen and Parker (2014, 1161–2) say that

> males are those individuals that produce smaller gametes (e.g., sperm), while females are defined as those that produce the larger gametes. Of course, in many species, a whole suite of secondary sex characteristics exists, but the fundamental definition is rooted in this definition of gametes.

Even an advocate of the Contextualist View (see below) like Richardson (2013, 26) agrees: "the subclass of a species that produces the larger gamete is always considered female, regardless of its chromosome complement or its mating and offspring-rearing behaviors."[17]

This simple Univocity Hypothesis is, it seems to me, natural and plausible. And it explains a range of core linguistic intuitions. It explains any inclination we have to think that sentence (5) is a contradiction ("Joe is male, but Joe isn't male"), and that sentence (6) is redundant ("Joe is male, and also Joe is male"). It explains any inclination we have to think that sentence (15) above—"Gene and Envo are male"—is natural and felicitous. What's more, it explains various judgments we might have been inclined to make a few paragraphs up concerning the various alleged kinds of sex. For example, sentences like this:

(17) "An organism with the hormone levels typical of males of that species may not be male at all."

(18) "An organism may not have the hormone levels typical of males of that species, and yet nevertheless be male, and not female at all."

On the Ambiguity Hypothesis, (17) and (18) should be unnatural and infelicitous: if we're told, for example, that an organism has hormone levels typical of males of that species, then on the Ambiguity Hypothesis this guarantees that the organism *is* male, in one sense of "male." In that case, (17) should be infelicitous, and similarly with (18). Insofar as you're inclined to judge that (17) and (18) are natural and felicitous—along with similar constructions concerning so-called chromosomal sex, anatomical sex, social sex, etc.—then this is evidence in favor of the Univocity Hypothesis.

Here's another consideration. As the Ambiguity Hypothesis would have it, each of these alleged additional senses of 'male' is sufficient to be male, and similarly with 'female'. If so, then, surprisingly, many of us would be *both* male *and* female, or *both* male and also *not* male, in different alleged senses of these words. Consider Envo again, the Nile crocodile. Envo has no chromosomal sex, since crocodiles have no sex chromosomes. Let's suppose further that Envo has the anatomy typical of males of his species and produces sperm. Envo never has and never will produce any eggs. But, let's also suppose, due to environmental pollution, or a genetic mutation, or whatever, Envo has the hormone levels typical of female crocodiles. Now consider this sentence:

(19) "Envo is male, and female, and not male."

On the Ambiguity Hypothesis, (19) has a true reading (allegedly, that Envo is gametically male, hormonally female, and not hormonally male). On the

Univocity Hypothesis (19) doesn't have any true reading. Speaking for myself, this is evidence for the Univocity Hypothesis. I can hear no true reading of (19).

This is just a minor elaboration of the contradiction test that we ran above. Notice, though, that similar considerations reveal that the Ambiguity Hypothesis would have worrisome implications from the perspective of trans activists, that is, those who actively advocate for the additional legal rights demanded by trans-identifying individuals. A trans individual who identifies as a female, for example, may not be anatomically female, and indeed may be anatomically male. On the hypothesis that 'male' and 'female' are ambiguous in the way we're considering, it would follow that this trans individual may be male *and* not male, female *and* not female, male *and* female, etc. *All in different senses*, according to the Ambiguity Hypothesis.[18] I have in mind sentences like this, where 'Jess' names a trans individual who identifies as a woman:

(20) "Jess is male, and female, and not male."

On the Ambiguity Hypothesis, this sentence has a true reading. Insofar as you find this result unwelcome (politically, morally), that counts against the Ambiguity Hypothesis.

The humble transparent nematode *Caenorhabditis elegans* comes in two varieties: male and hermaphrodite. The males have chromosomes, hormones, genitals, social roles, neural structures, etc., that are very different from those of human males. Yet they and I are all male. The only relevant thing we have in common is this: *C. elegans* males produce sperm, and human males produce sperm.[19] On the Univocity Hypothesis, this is the basic, fundamental sense of 'male'—used as an adjective to describe organisms—that is featured in and used to pick out sex-specific traits in the definitions of 'chromosomal male', 'hormonal male', and the like. So, according to our fourth and final ambiguity test, we have here some final evidence that 'male' and 'female', used as adjectives to describe organisms, are not ambiguous. According to the Univocity Hypothesis, those who say otherwise are mistaken. They've confused species-specific *typical features* of males, for what it means to be male *simpliciter*. They've confused different property profiles between males and females for different "kinds" or "levels" of males and females. They've confused differences of sex-linked traits for differences of sex.

The idea behind this final test, recall, was this: we may come to see that some core set of linguistic judgments concerning 'male' can be explained by one natural and plausible definition of 'male'. (Likewise with 'female'.) I believe we have seen this. But we may also go further, and explain away a substantial part of the motivation for the Ambiguity Hypothesis. If we do those two things, then we will have an additional, strong reason to reject the Ambiguity Hypothesis and to favor the Univocity Hypothesis. Let's now explain away at least some motivation for the Ambiguity Hypothesis.

It's fairly standard to distinguish between what a speaker literally says and what he actually conveys. And, sometimes, as François Recanati (2005, 177) puts it, a pragmatic process "takes place in order to make sense of the communicative act performed by the speaker," modulating what a speaker literally says into the intuitive content of the utterance. For example, what a waiter literally says with "The ham sandwich left without paying" is absurd. But, through a pragmatic process Recanati calls "transfer," the sentence may convey information to his audience about *the customer* who ordered the sandwich. That's what the audience may come to understand, even though it's not what the waiter literally said.

In a similar way, the literal interpretation of the noun phrase 'a stone lion' is a lion made of stone. In almost all cases, this is not what a speaker intends to convey. In those cases, a pragmatic process delivers the correct interpretation to the hearers: *(a representation of a lion) that is made of stone* (Recanati, 2005, 179). Importantly, we don't need to posit any ambiguity in these cases. 'Ham sandwich' continues to mean ham sandwich; it is just that a pragmatic process modulates (absurd) literal content about a ham sandwich to (sensible) conveyed content about a customer. 'Lion' continues to mean lion; it is just that a pragmatic process modulates literal content about a lion (made of stone) to convey content about a stone statue (of a lion).

In that same way, it seems to me that the *literal* interpretation of "Jess is hormonally male and socially male" is the proposition that Jess is male in a hormonal way, male in a hormonal sense of 'male', and also male in a social way, male in a distinct, social sense. That's what's literally said with such a sentence. Yet, according to the Univocity Hypothesis, there is only one relevant way to be male—as opposed to a variety of ways a male can be. And, it's evidently the case, as we've seen above, that neither this hormonal way of being nor this social way of being entails actually being male. If that's right, then the literal interpretation of "Jess is hormonally male and socially male" is clearly false. And yet, a pragmatic process plausibly delivers the correct interpretation: *Jess has hormone levels typical of male members of that species, and also plays a social role typical of males of that species*. In this way, 'male' may be univocal just as 'ham sandwich' and 'lion' are univocal in their uses above, despite the use of 'male' in constructions like 'hormonally male' and 'socially male'. And likewise with 'female'.

I believe this helps explain away at least some of the attraction of the Ambiguity Hypothesis, since we see that some degree of that attraction may well be due to an error. The literal meaning of "Jess is hormonally male and socially male"—taking 'male' to be ambiguous—is clearly false. The *conveyed* meaning of that statement—namely that **Jess has hormone levels typical of male members of that species and plays a social role typical of male members of that species**—is not absurd, and it may well be true. *But that meaning may be conveyed even if 'male' is not ambiguous.* Accepting that this boldfaced proposition is conveyed does not require that 'male' be ambiguous. And someone may muddle these two meanings together, and mistakenly think that the true meaning and the meaning that requires ambiguity are one and the same. But, in fact, they're not. What's more, when pressed on the apparent falsity of the literal meaning, advocates of the Ambiguity Hypothesis may be tempted to retreat to the more modest and plausible conveyed meaning, convincing themselves that, anyway, this is all it really means to say that Jess is hormonally male and socially male. They may thereby mistakenly think that the plausible (conveyed, boldfaced) meaning is the one that requires the Ambiguity Hypothesis. But that's not correct; the conveyed meaning does *not* require the Ambiguity Hypothesis. Those who think otherwise are plausibly the victims of proposition confusion.

So, our contradiction test, our redundancy test, our conjunction reduction test, and that final Aristotelian test all count against the Ambiguity Hypothesis. What's more, we've explained away at least some degree of the attraction of the Ambiguity Hypothesis. I myself conclude that 'male' and 'female' are not ambiguous in the way that Benjamin, Fausto-Sterling, and those others would have us believe. And I hope you do as well.

To say that this is an important result would be a prodigious understatement, given the profound influence that the Ambiguity Hypothesis has had in a large number of academic fields. But, if the arguments of this section are sound, the sober fact of the matter is that those fields have long been weighed down by a grave misunderstanding of the sexes. Yet this is not the only misunderstanding in this area. Let us now turn to the other species of the Complex View: the Contextualist Hypothesis, the Indeterminacy Hypothesis, and the Property-Cluster Hypothesis.

The Contextualist Hypothesis

Another species of the Complex View of the sexes is the Contextualist Hypothesis. Sarah Richardson (2022, 9) expresses the hypothesis this way: "sex contextualism is the view that the definition of sex and sex-related variables, and whether they are relevant in biomedical research, depends on the research context." As Rifkin and Garson (2023, 2) understand it, Richardson's view is that there is no single, universal definition of, e.g., maleness, but that scientists must 'operationalize' maleness in different ways in different research contexts. In some contexts, maleness will be operationalized in terms of hormones; in others, genetics; in still others, behavior.

Other examples may help illuminate this proposal. In psychology, motivation and intelligence are operationalized differently for different research projects. Some psychologists may construe intelligence as general cognitive ability and measure it using a standardized intelligence test. Others may construe intelligence as academic achievement and measure it using grade point average. Some psychologists may construe motivation as performing a task for the satisfaction it brings, and quantify it using behavioral measures, such as how long a subject engages with a task. Other psychologists may construe motivation as job satisfaction and measure it using a job satisfaction survey.

Another statement of the Contextualist Hypothesis comes from Katrina Karkazis et al. (2012, 6), who say that "the demarcation between male and female categories depends on context… In the context of reproduction, the presence of a uterus may categorize someone as female." This isn't maximally clear, but it does read as though Karkazis et al. think that the conditions for 'female' to apply vary by context. In some contexts, having a uterus is sufficient for 'female' to apply. In other contexts, it isn't.

But, one might wonder, what exactly is it to be female, or to be male? Here and now, in this very context, if you like. And what exactly does the Contextualist Hypothesis have to say about this? Richardson (2022, 10) puts it another way: "According to sex contextualism, there is no 'sex itself'. There is only sex as pragmatically constituted in an observational frame." This is a rather striking thing to say, since it seems to entail that, before there were any observational frames (or research contexts), there were no sexes. As we mentioned above when discussing claims of social construction, this raises questions about how, for example, dinosaurs managed to multiply for so many years, if there were no males or females among them. Could this really be what Richardson means? Perhaps not since, on the same page, she stresses that "sex contextualism neither denies the reality of sex as an evolved developmental pathway with many implications for biology nor the possibility that male-female comparisons may at times be an apt research design for studying sex." So, there is no sex itself according to Richardson, and yet this is consistent, she says, with the reality of sex, and that it may be apt to compare males and females. But how could this be? Obviously, saying there is no sex itself is not consistent with the claim that there is such a thing as sex itself, but *perhaps* it's consistent with the claim that sex exists *as* a developmental pathway. I say "perhaps" because, depending on the details, you might have thought *sex as a developmental pathway* just is sex itself. What's more, we're told the meaning of 'sex' depends on the research context. And yet here, in Richardson's article, independent of any particular research context, we're told that comparisons between *males* and *females* may be apt, and that some researchers study *sex*. Richardson's reader is left to untangle these tortuous threads, if he can.

Richardson (2022, 9) explicitly draws inspiration from Haslanger's project of "ameliorative" inquiry in developing what she (Richardson) calls a "real theory, i.e., 'here's what people say sex is, and here's how we can tweak that to be more like what we think it ought to be'." But even for Haslanger, there are limits to our conceptual engineering, limits to what we could excusably say 'sex' refers to. As Haslanger puts it (2000, 35),

> the proposed shift in meaning of the term would seem semantically warranted if central functions of the term remain the same, for example, if it helps organize or explain a core set of phenomena that the ordinary terms are used to identify or describe.

So, a researcher couldn't reasonably declare that, for the purposes of his research, 'sex' refers to diet, and carnivores and herbivores are two sexes. And that's because this would be too much of a departure from the "core set of phenomena" that 'sex' is used to identify or describe. But what *is* that core set of phenomena that 'sex' identifies? And wouldn't that count as "sex itself," which Richardson denies exists? Unfortunately, Richardson's statements on these matters offer little by way of clarification.

Against the Contextualist Hypothesis

I propose that there are four things Richardson might be up to here, parading beneath the banner of 'sex contextualism'. The first interpretation we've already begun talking about, and, unfortunately, it is irrelevant, wide of the mark, and not about sex at all. Rather, it's a thesis about *sex-related* variables, the unremarkable thesis that different researchers will focus on different sex-related variables for different purposes. Sometimes, it sounds like this is just what she's up to. For example, Richardson (2022, 10) says that "[a] helpful analogy can be made here between 'sex' and 'age'." She says that "age contextualism" is how she proposes that we think of sex, where age contextualism is presumably the view that the definition of age and age-related variables, and whether they are relevant in biomedical research, depends on the research context.[20] About age contextualism, she admits that "[e]veryone has an unchanging year of birth; everyone has an age." That's true, there is such a thing as age, and everybody has one. But it's puzzling for her to say there is such a thing as age itself, as we might put it, for how is this analogous to her claim, with respect to sex contextualism, that there is no "sex itself"? Yes, there are many "age-related variables" that one might research, for example, telomere length or graying hair. But these variables *related* to age are not themselves age. It's true, as she says, that one commonly hears a distinction between chronological age and biological age. But it's clear that biological age is defined in terms of the more fundamental notion of chronological age: to say someone has the "biological age" of a 20-year-old is an abbreviated way of saying that this person has certain characteristics typical of people who are *actually that age*, that is, people who are actually 20 years old. And that's the reason Richardson (2022) can say things like "[t]he telomeres of a 20-year-old's DNA can show the weathering of a 50-year-old [sic]": because age is a real thing, and this is the DNA *of a 20-year-old*. In a similar way, there are sex-related variables, for example, hormone levels. But variables *related* to sex are not themselves sex. We might say someone is "hormonally female," but this is an abbreviated way of saying this person has the hormone levels typical of people who are *actually female*. That's why we can say things like "this male has the hormone-levels of a 50-year-old female." Because sex is a real thing, and these are the hormone levels *of a male*.

So, on this interpretation of sex contextualism, it's not about sex at all, but rather about variables *related* to sex. Researchers have the right to choose which *sex-related variables* they choose to study, as a psychologist has a right to choose which motivation-related variables to study. But while psychologists might operationalize motivation in different ways for different studies, in order for these studies to be about the same thing, 'motivation' must have some shared meaning, a shared referent. In just the same way, though researchers may operationalize sex in different ways for different studies, in order for these studies to be about the same thing, 'sex' must have some shared meaning, a shared referent.And unfortunately this interpretation of Ricahardson tells us nothing about this shared referent of 'sex' across research contexts. That is, it tells us nothing about sex itself, and is therefore irrelevant to the main questions of this book, namely what the sexes are, and whether their natures have to do with gamete production or not.

The second interpretation of Richardson's project takes seriously those quotations that say there is no "sex itself," and that the meaning of 'sex' is "constituted in an observational frame." On this second interpretation, Richardson is offering a modest addendum to the Ambiguity Hypothesis, saying merely that 'sex', 'male', and 'female' refer to different things in different contexts, in just the same way that an ambiguous word like 'mouse' can refer to different things in different contexts. And, in that case, the

Contextualist Hypothesis entails the Ambiguity Hypothesis. So, the arguments against the Ambiguity Hypothesis in the previous section count against this second interpretation of the Contextualist Hypothesis.

But this second reading would be contextualism in name only. I think Mark Schroeder (2020) was right when he said, "In general, appeals to semantic context-dependence are illuminating when they appeal to a common core meaning." Think of the relevant common core meanings revealed by David Kaplan's (1989) treatment of the "character" of indexicals, for example, as 'I' refers to whomever is *the speaker in the context*.[21] Think also of Saul's (2012, 201) contextualist definition of 'woman': "X *is a woman* is true in a context C iff X is human and relevantly similar (according to the standards at work in C) to most of those possessing all of the biological markers of female sex." Whether or not this account is true—and Saul herself does not endorse it—Saul here proposes a core meaning held common across contexts, namely: sufficient similarity to those possessing all the biological markers of female sex. What varies across contexts, on this proposal, are the *standards* for what counts as sufficient similarity.

Hewing closely to Saul's contextualist account of 'woman', we might venture a third guess as to what Richardson is trying to say, using 'female' as an example. Perhaps Richardson means to say that there is a core meaning held common across contexts, and it's something like this: Some organism is *female*, in a context C, if and only if it is *relevantly* similar (according to the standards at work in C) to most females of this type of organism. And *relevant* similarity may be "operationalized" based on our interests or instruments: perhaps similarity with regard to (female sex) chromosomes, or (female sex) hormone levels, or gametes (female sex cells), etc. On this third interpretation of Richardson, the word 'female' shows up in the definiens, presumably in its fundamental sense.[22] And the biconditional describes what 'female' refers to in its various uses, in various research contexts. ('Male' would receive a similar treatment.) If so, then this third interpretation of the Contextualist Hypothesis entails the Ambiguity Hypothesis: there's one fundamental meaning of 'female' and of 'male' operating behind the scenes, as it were, to generate a variety of other meanings across research contexts. And, therefore, arguments we gave against the Ambiguity Hypothesis in the previous section could easily be repurposed to count against this third interpretation. From a linguistic perspective, it just doesn't seem that this is how 'male' and 'female' function.

For example, recall Gene the rooster and Envo the crocodile, and suppose that, while situated in a research context with a squad of geneticists, we're concerned with patterns of sex chromosomes. In that context, on this third interpretation of Richardson's view, the following sentence would express something true:

(21) "Gene is male."

And that's because Gene the rooster has the sex chromosomes typical of males of his species, so he meets the "relevant similarity" requirement to be a male in this context. But in that same context, according to this interpretation of Richardson, this sentence would express something false:

(22) "Envo is male."

And that's because Envo the crocodile has no sex chromosomes at all, and therefore does not have the sex chromosomes typical of males of his species, and is not "relevantly similar" to males in this research context. So, on this third interpretation of Richardson, 'male' functions in such a way that, in this geneticist-dense research context, Envo is not male. (Neither is he female. He has no sex at all in this context, according to this version of the Contextualist Hypothesis.) But could that really be true? Insofar as you think Envo is simply male, no matter who studies him (or why), this is evidence against a version of the Contextualist Hypothesis that makes such claims about the semantic content of words like 'sex', 'male', and 'female'.

Here's another implausible implication of this third interpretation of Richardson's project. Say Alan is a geneticist who has operationalized 'male' in a chromosomal way, and Bob is a physiologist who has operationalized 'male' in a way having to do with external genitals. Each is ensconced in his respective research context, and each is thinking about Gene and Envo. If so, then, if this third interpretation of Richardson is right, Alan can truthfully say:

(23) "I know that Gene is male and Envo is not male."

And Bob can truthfully say:

(24) "I know that Gene is not male and Envo is male."[23]

If this third interpretation of Richardson's Contextualist Hypothesis were correct, then this should all sound totally fine, just as we can construct similar sentences with words that seem to require a contextualist interpretation. For example, we can make perfect sense of how, in one context, Alan can truthfully say "I know my brother is here," and, in a different context, Bob can truthfully say "I know my brother is not here." Because

Kaplan was right about indexicals like 'I', 'my', and 'here'. But we do *not* feel similarly inclined to accept the felicity of the situation surrounding (23) and (24). If you agree, then this is a strike against Richardson's contextualist view of words like 'sex', 'male', and 'female'.

Trans activists may find this view troubling for a third reason (see Saul 2012, 207). Namely, it will turn out that there are many contexts in which trans individuals who identify as women, for example, are male. And that's because there are many contexts in which 'male' is operationalized in such a way that relevant similarity requires only having XY chromosomes, or producing sperm, etc. And, for similar reasons, this version of the Contextualist Hypothesis will entail that, in many contexts, individuals who identify as non-binary are in fact male (or female). So, trans activists should consider this another strike against this third interpretation of Richardson's project, this time from a specifically trans-activist direction.

We're presently considering a version of the Contextualist Hypothesis according to which the following biconditional expresses the *core meaning* held constant across contexts: Some organism is female, in a context C, if and only if X is *relevantly* similar (according to the standards at work in C) to most females of this type of organism. But we've seen reasons to reject this version of the Contextualist Hypothesis. So, consider finally a fourth interpretation of Richardson's view: what that biconditional describes may well be a pragmatic process of transfer. When 'female' has been operationalized in a hormonal way and a scientist says "this organism is female," what's *literally* said may well be false. But the biconditional purports to describe the content that is *conveyed pragmatically*, perhaps that *this organism has hormone levels typical of females of its species*. Positing pragmatic transfer is, in a way, simpler than positing semantic ambiguity, since only one sense is required of each term, and it sidesteps the argument we gave a moment ago involving Gene and Envo. Perhaps it is the case that, were we to hear a scientist researching sex chromosomes say "Envo is not male," we would *interpret* him as saying something not about Envo's *sex*, but about his lack of sex *chromosomes*. On this fourth interpretation, what the scientist says is literally false, the way it's literally false when the server says, "the ham sandwich left without paying." But, in both cases, the (quite different) proposition conveyed may well be true.

Despite its virtues, there are still problems for this fourth interpretation of Richardson's Contextualist Hypothesis: namely, *apparently* different meanings of words like 'sex', 'male', and 'female' are not *genuinely* different meanings. There is one fundamental meaning of those words, as applied to organisms. And that's the meaning featured in the propositions that are conveyed pragmatically from the literally false things that researchers might say. For example, Alan the geneticist might *say*, "Envo is not male."

But this is literally false, on this fourth interpretation. Given what 'male' means, Envo is in fact male. But, on this fourth interpretation, the proposition that is pragmatically conveyed is something like that *Envo does not have sex chromosomes typical of males of his species*, and this is true because there are no such sex chromosomes in crocodiles. And here, as I use an English sentence to express the conveyed proposition, 'male' is univocal. So, as with the first interpretation, this fourth interpretation is irrelevant to questions about the nature of the sexes.

I conclude, then, that every interpretation of Richardson's Contextualist Hypothesis is either false or irrelevant to the question of what sex is, the question of what 'sex' refers to, and likewise with 'male' and 'female'. Let's move on, then, to a third version of the Complex View: the Indeterminacy Hypothesis.

The Indeterminacy Hypothesis

The third species of the Complex View of the sexes is the Indeterminacy Hypothesis. According to this hypothesis, there are no facts that clearly determine the reference of 'male' and of 'female'. Instead, for each of these words, there is a range of things that it may refer to, when used as an adjective and said of organisms, and each of the candidates is equally eligible to be the referent.[24] But, in such cases, there's simply no fact of the matter as to what the term refers to, or at least no fact that we can (easily) know. Here's a quick example, based on a true story. A family houses a rabbit in the backyard. Unbeknownst to them, the rabbit is pregnant and gives birth deep in her burrow. To their surprise and delight, the family observes on several occasions an adorable bunny emerge cautiously from the burrow. Thinking there is only one bunny, the family introduces the name 'Buns', using this as a reference-fixing description: the bunny in our backyard.

But suppose that, again unbeknownst to them, there are *two* identical-looking bunnies that they've been seeing, each on different occasions. Which is named 'Buns'? Each is equally eligible, so it seems arbitrary to pick one. But it's difficult to see how the one name could refer to both bunnies,[25] and also difficult to accept that the name is empty, that it refers to nothing at all. Here, it seems to me quite natural to say that it is indeterminate what 'Buns' refers to. The reference of this name has not been clearly settled by the family's name-using practice. It's not *clear* which option is correct: that 'Buns' refers to one bunny, or to the other, or to both, or to neither. Perhaps there's simply no fact of the matter, but at least there's no fact that we can (easily) know. All that's obvious is the path forward for the family upon discovering the truth: to decide which bunny, if either, will be named 'Buns', by a clearly effective linguistic baptism ceremony, or to introduce two entirely new names, in order to avoid ambiguity.[26]

I believe some theorists working in this area think something like what happened with the name 'Buns' has happened with our words 'male' and 'female': biologists' practice of using these words has not clearly settled what they refer to. It's simply indeterminate what they refer to, among a range of equally eligible candidates. When biologists looked into the burrow, so to speak, they found several eligible candidates that might answer to 'sex' (and 'male' and 'female'). So, it's indeterminate what our sex terms refer to, just as it is with 'Buns'.

Sari van Anders may hold this view, given that she says (2024, 474) "sex is multiple and multifaceted, describing plural phenomena," and also "there is no 'getting sex right' and attempts to do so are a typological wild goose chase." Instead, she gives—you guessed it—a non-exhaustive list of "definitions of sex," as she calls them: genitals, internal sex, chromosomes, hormones, gametes, skull size, etc. Talia Bettcher (2020) may also subscribe to this view, saying that "once we recognize various features which go into sex determination (chromosomal sex, gonadal sex, genital sex, etc.) we see that sex is not a single, unitary, easily-determined feature." William Byne (2010, 102) says,

> The notion of 'true sex'… is problematic. When there is discordance among the biological variables of sex in an individual, there is no reason that one variable should hold precedence over the others as the indicator of that person's sex.

Claire Ainsworth (2015, 291) writes that the idea of two sexes is overly simplistic, culminating with this question: "So if the law requires that a person is male or female, should that sex be assigned by anatomy, hormones, cells or chromosomes, and what should be done if they clash?"[27] She concludes, as if exasperated by the sheer complexity of it all, that "if you want to know whether someone is male or female, it may be best just to ask."

Against the Indeterminacy Hypothesis

On this view, what happened with the word 'sex' (or its ancestor in an earlier language) is similar to what happened with the name 'Buns'. Biologists were confronted by several closely related phenomena—spirals and layers, to borrow Fausto-Sterling's metaphors—and biologists introduced the label 'sex' (or its ancestor). They took themselves to be naming one phenomenon—mistakenly, according to this view—then judged that there were two sub-types of this phenomenon, and introduced 'male' and 'female' (or their ancestors) to name those sub-types. But, from a third-person perspective of an interpreter of this linguistic practice, the use of these words and the judgments made with them are not unified; they're confused. *Sometimes*, the best interpretation seems to be that biologists are talking about dispositions to produce gametes, other times the genetic causes of those dispositions, other times the physiological and hormonal concomitants of those dispositions, still other times the various anatomical structures that facilitate reproduction, and so on. The use of these words is messy, on this view, to such a degree that there's simply no single most eligible candidate for *the* phenomenon that 'sex' refers to (and similarly for 'male' and 'female'). The reference of these words is indeterminate. The true answer to the question, "What trait does 'being male' refer to?" is: there is no such one trait, or at least none that we're in a position to know. The best we can do, then, is use our advanced knowledge of the underlying phenomena, and specify, or stipulate, what we wish 'male' to refer to for some purpose or project. And that's exactly what we ought to do, according to those who hold this view.

But this just isn't true. If we imagine ourselves to be interpreters of biologists' linguistic practice, we can see that there *are* indeed most eligible candidates for the referents of 'sex', 'male', and 'female'. Think of it like this. In the case of 'Buns', once we're fully informed of the rabbit situation in the backyard—namely, that there are two doppelganger bunnies—we are totally disinclined from using the name 'Buns'. We realize that there is no eligible candidate referent for the name 'Buns', and therefore either it doesn't refer at all, or it does, but we're not in a position to know what it refers to. We drop the name-using practice, and perhaps go on to initiate a new one, by clearly dubbing one of the rabbits with the name 'Buns', or just using completely new names. But this is decidedly *not* what happened with 'male' and 'female'. When biologists discovered gametes, sex chromosomes, sex hormones, and various systems of genitals, they did not drop the practices of using 'male' and 'female' as we would drop the practice of using 'Buns' in the backyard rabbit example. Rather, biologists continued to use 'male' and 'female' as adjectives to describe organisms across the plant and animal kingdoms, organisms with a kaleidoscopic diversity of chromosomal arrangements, hormone levels, genital systems, etc.

We've already seen that crocodiles are male or female, despite having no sex chromosomes, and that there are male birds, even those having no external genitalia. And consider organisms in the humble phylum Placozoa, whose bodies consist of just a few thousand cells, of only four types. These organisms are primitive indeed, and biologists openly investigate whether they feature males and females (cf. Eitel et al. 2011).[28] These organisms reproduce sexually (under certain lab conditions, at least), but in a very different way from us when it comes to chromosomes, genitalia, hormones, social roles, and the like. In dioecious algae species (e.g. the filamentous brown alga *Ectocarpus siliculosus*), individual gametophytes are either male or female (cf. Coelho et al. 2019). Here, too, there are evidently males and females, despite no relevant overlap with human males and females when it comes to chromosomes, hormones, genitals, brains, social roles, and the like.

This, therefore, is evidence against the Indeterminacy Hypothesis. That hypothesis predicts that, upon discovering these *allegedly* equally eligible candidates for referents for 'male' and 'female', the reasonable biologist would retire or suspend the practice of using those words, as we would with 'Buns' in the backyard rabbit example. Yet biologists manifestly did not do that, despite being reasonable. Why is that? I suggest it's for similar reasons that we saw above against the Ambiguity Hypothesis. For example, so-called chromosomal maleness is *not* a highly eligible candidate for the referent of 'male'. It is, rather, the chromosomal structure typical of *males* of the relevant species. And there 'male' refers to its actual most eligible candidate. And so-called hormonal femaleness is *not* a highly eligible candidate referent of 'female'. It is, rather, the range of hormone levels typical of *females* of whatever species we're talking about, where 'female' refers to the fundamental, most eligible candidate. And so on down the list. While biologists may coin terms to refer to these various markers of sex, sex itself remains a salient natural phenomenon, and eminently eligible for reference. The sexes cry out to be named, you might say, and it would be difficult for any biologist not to notice.

And what is that eminently eligible candidate? As I said above, I believe Rifkin and Garson (2023, 2) got it right when they said,

> To the extent that one believes that biology has some special authority to shape our ontology of sex – for example, the way that biologists talk and think about sex should inform our understanding of what animal sex is – then anisogamy seems to be the correct starting point.

To discern what biologists mean by 'sex', 'male', and 'female', we should very much like to accommodate this common and widespread use to describe organisms across the natural world. That use suggests there *are* most eligible candidates for the referents of those words, referents that would vindicate Joan Roughgarden's (2004, 23) dictum that there is no universal difference between male and female beyond *gamete size*. (Or, more carefully, gamete-*type*. More on this later.) Anisogamy is a widespread and very important biological phenomenon. It therefore provides highly eligible candidates for the referents of our sex terms. It would be astonishing if biologists did not name the phenomenon of sexual reproduction, or the sub-types of species that engage in sexual reproduction (males and females). So, it's reasonable to proceed on the hypothesis that they *did*.

Above, I said that when fully informed of the bunny lookalikes in the backyard, the rational response is to suspend use of the name 'Buns', though we may go on clearly to dub exactly one bunny with the name, or introduce two distinct names for the bunnies. A less useful strategy would involve dubbing each bunny with the name 'Buns', thereby originating two concepts, and living with the ambiguity. Another bizarre strategy would be to operationalize 'Buns' based on our interests. If one rabbit likes to burrow and the other is very social, we might operationalize 'Buns' to refer to the former on burrow-inspecting days, and operationalize 'Buns' to refer to the latter on days we feel like petting a rabbit. This would be strange, but possible. And these two strategies mirror the views discussed previously, namely the Ambiguity Hypothesis and the Contextualist Hypothesis. The advocate of the Indeterminacy Hypothesis may insist, for example, that upon discovering the indeterminacy of reference of our sex terms, we went on to embrace ambiguity: for example, 'male' is used in an alleged gametic sense when used to describe male humans and male gametophytes of brown algae, but in other senses when used to describe, for example, "hormonal males." Or he may insist that we went on to operationalize sex terms differently, depending on our interests, as the Contextualist Hypothesis would have it. But I have argued against those views already, above. Evidently, this is not what we did with our sex terms. So, I conclude that the Indeterminacy Hypothesis is false, and Roughgarden (2004, 23) is right: "To a biologist, 'male' means making small gametes, and 'female' means making large gametes. *Period*!" We will develop this view below, in the following chapter.

The Property-Cluster Hypothesis

We turn now to our fourth and final species of the Complex View: the Property-Cluster Hypothesis. As Alison Stone (2007, 43) expresses this hypothesis, there is no "single property that we can non-arbitrarily take to be necessary and sufficient for giving someone a particular sex." And she concludes (2007, 45) that to be female "is to have enough of a cluster of properties (ovaries, breasts, vagina, etc.), which cluster because they encourage one another's presence."[29] And similarly for being male, though in terms of having testes, penis, scrotum, etc. Kathleen Stock (2021, ch. 2) also considers a property-cluster account of sex. She says, "The 'cluster account' of sex first identifies a cluster of morphological characteristics relevant to identifying people as male or female in ordinary life." She goes on to say, "on the cluster account, no individual characteristic is treated as essential for being female or male. Equally, there's no requirement that an individual exhibit all of the features in a given cluster." This hypothesis draws from the work of Richard Boyd (1988, 1999), who defends a property-cluster account of natural kinds. On Boyd's account, when there is a family F of properties that co-occur in an important number of cases, the relevant kind term "is applied to things in which the homeostatic clustering of most of the properties in F occurs" (cf. Boyd 1988, 323).[30]

Against the Property-Cluster Hypothesis

There are at least three problems with this hypothesis. The first concerns the hypothesis' claim that there is no property that is necessary and sufficient for being a male, or for being a female. Instead, we're told, what it means to be female is to have enough (most?) of some particular set of properties. But, as Colin McGinn (2012, 18) points out, *this* then looks to be a property that is necessary and sufficient for being a female: having enough of some particular set of properties. In that case, the hypothesis is mistaken in claiming that there is no such property. We may, in our charity, interpret the hypothesis as the claim that there is no *natural* property that is necessary and sufficient for being male, or for being female, and that *having enough of some particular set of properties* is not a natural property. I'd prefer not to enter the sticky debate about what counts as natural, but below, I'll propose for each sex an analysis that I daresay names a natural property.

Second, this hypothesis is proposed as an account of what it is to be male, and of what it is to be female. Boyd (1988, 323) says that while this account offers no *analytic* definition of the relevant natural kind term, it is a *natural* definition. The problem is that this definition looks to be viciously circular.[31] This defect can't be missed in Esa Díaz-León's (2022, 233) proposed definition, which tells us that being a female is to be understood in terms of a cluster of features *associated with the female biological sex*. It's subtler when Stone (2007, 44) says "someone is female or male when they have the sufficient number of the relevant properties."[32] The problem is that, of course, the *relevant* properties are relevant because of their relationship to *being female*, as we saw in the Stock quotation above; when we define those relevant properties, we will refer to the property of being female, and we will thereby have gone in a circle. There must be, then, something that makes one a *female*, and therefore the typical bearer of these properties—*that* is the real definition of being female. In that case, there's a more fundamental property of being female that's making these features relevant to being female, and it's not these features that make an organism female. And it's *that* property of being female that we're interested in. The Property-Cluster Hypothesis does not tell us what this property is, but rather presupposes it.[33]

The third and final problem is like the first, but more substantial. Recall that the hypothesis claims there is no property that is necessary and sufficient for being a male. But reflecting on other species helps us see why this isn't correct.[34] As we said above, some *C. elegans* are male just as I am male. But *C. elegans* are different from me with regard to chromosomes (there is no sex-specific chromosome in this species, the males being XO), hormones, genitals, social position, etc. The only relevant thing we have in common relates to gametes: male *C. elegans* produce sperm, and male humans produce sperm. But as far as I can tell, this relation to gametes is, contra Stone, a single property that is necessary and sufficient for something's being male. If this relation to sperm production is absent—whatever exactly that relation turns out to be—then no amount or degree of other features in this cluster would be sufficient to be male. And if this relation to sperm production is present, no other features in this cluster are necessary to be male. So, reflection on other species gives us good reason to think that 'male' and 'female' do not name property clusters at all, but rather that 'male' and 'female' each pick out some specific—and, I'd say, quite natural—relation to producing a particular type of gamete. And that, my friends, is the Gamete View of the sexes. We turn now to evaluating a few proposals for what this relation to gamete production might be, the relation to gametes in virtue of which organisms are male or female.

Notes

1 See Esa Díaz-León (2025, 11): "If we can figure out what it takes for our term 'K' to refer to certain individuals, then we can make a lot of progress with respect to metaphysical questions about the nature of kind K." Yes, I agree.
2 A word is polysemous when it has multiple *related* senses. For example, the word 'mouse' refers to that common rodent, but also to a computer accessory so-named because it resembles that common rodent.
3 Pape et al. (2024, 1317) provide a recent example, saying that "sex is better understood as a system of classification." A system that, presumably, humans constructed. Similarly, Watkins and DiMarco (2025, 21) "emphasize that sex, like gender, is an organizing construct rather than a biological reality and many aspects of 'sex' [sic] in human biology are sensitive to gendered social relations…" I'm not sure why they put 'sex' in quotation marks, as though they were mentioning the word rather than using it, in order to talk about the many aspects of the *word* 'sex' in human biology.
4 Ian Hacking once wrote that child abuse is a social construct. Later (1999, 29), he realized this was, as he put it: a terrible equivocation; confused; a conflation

of two fundamentally different categories. He says that his "switch from object (child abuse) to idea (the concept of child abuse) is worse than careless." On the bright side, he said, some people found this confusion more helpful than clarity. Yet insofar as we're interested in the truth of the matter here, we should note that a similar mistake is being made here by Judith Butler, a conflation of word and object.

5 Money et al. (1955) add that patients showing various combinations and permutations of these six sexual variables may be appraised with respect to a seventh variable: Gender role and orientation as male or female, established while growing up.

6 Benjamin also defines the (alleged) hormonal senses of 'male' and 'female' as you might expect: "The abundant supply of androgen in a male would tend to make him more virile, a 'he-man', and the rich production of estrogen would insure—at least to some extent—the soft and lovely femininity of the typical woman…" None of these attempts at definitions from Benjamin is very clear or rigorous, but at least he tried. Even *attempts* at definitions for their "variables of sex" are surprisingly absent from Money et al. (1955). They seem to think it all goes without saying, though they do gesture toward a "female chromosomal pattern" and a "male chromosomal pattern" (Money et al. 1955, 302), as well as "estrogens" and "androgens" (Money et al. 1955, 304) with regard to hormonal sex, and a patient who "lived as a man" and three others, each of whom "lived as a woman" (Money et al. 1955, 305) with regard to gender role. Money et al. give similar clues for other variables of sex, but never a clear or careful definition.

7 Dworkin also echoes John Money when she says (Money et al. 1955, 176–7), "Chromosomal sex is not necessarily the visible sex of the individual. It happens that a person of one chromosomal sex develops the gonads of the other sex. *Gonadal sex and chromosomal sex can be in direct contradiction.*" As with Money et al., this talk of contradiction is suggestive of a view that 'male' and 'female'—used as adjectives and said of organisms—are ambiguous. Allegedly, one can be female and yet not female. This apparent contradiction is revealed to be *merely* apparent when we're told that, in this case, 'female' is used in two senses: the alleged gonadal and chromosomal senses. So, it may be best to understand Dworkin as also endorsing the Ambiguity Hypothesis, for the same reason it seems likely that Money et al. do as well.

8 But given her talk of frameworks and purposes, perhaps Haslanger means to endorse Contextualism, discussed below. I include her here because of her use of 'disambiguation' to describe the phenomena.

9 It's also interesting to note that Paul Griffiths, who advocates for a gamete-based understanding of 'male' and 'female' that we'll discuss below, does subscribe to a modest claim of ambiguity. Griffiths (2020) thinks there's an "extended sense" of 'male' and of 'female', which includes juvenile males and female worker bees, respectively. While Arvan and Griffiths propose ambiguity in 'male' and 'female', even as those words are used of organisms, it bears repeating that the typical form of the Ambiguity Hypothesis posits that 'male', used as an adjective and said of organisms, refers variously to being chromosomally male, being hormonally male, and so on down the list.

10 According to Arvan, an organism may be female in a biological sense, and yet not female in a social, gendered sense. So, someone who produces ova while flouting feminine gender norms would be female and not female, according to Arvan. And a human who produces sperm while abiding by feminine gender norms would not be female, but would be female. This strikes my ear as

infelicitous and implausible, and therefore counts as evidence against Arvan's claimed ambiguity here. But the reader must decide for himself. On top of all that, Arvan's view doesn't meet his goal of trans-inclusion, since it implies that a trans individual who identifies as a woman, yet who produces sperm and does not satisfy enough of the relevant feminine gender norms, is a male and not a woman. Remarkably, Arvan's view also entails that the female queen xenomorph from the movie *Aliens* would be a woman, since she is an "adult gendered female," that is, she "broadly satisf[ies] gender norms for [her] respective planetary race" (Arvan 2023, 378). This is a hard teaching; who can believe it?

11 Though Velocci appears to *use* the word 'sex' rather than *mention* it, I believe the charitable interpretation of this talk of "multiple meanings of sex" is that the word 'sex' has multiple meanings, that is, is ambiguous.
12 Those with more depraved minds may detect another, darker ambiguity, owing to 'saw'.
13 See David Liebesman and Ofra Magidor (forthcoming) for a nice response to recent concerns about these tests failing to find genuine ambiguity in cases of polysemy, concerns which fortunately don't affect our project here.
14 Alex Byrne (2018) makes this point. Emma Hilton and Colin Wright (2024, 28) do as well, when they say, "it would be impossible to claim that low and high testosterone levels are correlated with being female and male, respectively, unless the categories female and male already had established meanings that testosterone levels were being correlated with."
15 True, sometimes we're told only that, e.g., to be a chromosomal male (human) is to have XY chromosomes. And to be a chromosomal female (human) is to have XX chromosomes. But, if you ask why having XY chromosomes is called 'chromosomally male' and XX is called 'chromosomally female', and not vice versa, the answer is obvious: because XY chromosomes are typically had by human *males*, and XX chromosomes by human *females*. If we didn't already know that XY chromosomes are typically had by human *males*, then we wouldn't be in a position to know that 'chromosomal male' is the apt description of that condition.

To clarify, I don't mean to reason this way: because 'chromosomally male', 'hormonally male', etc., all feature 'male', there must be some fundamental sense of 'male' had in common by the definitions of these complex phrases. No, I don't mean to suggest that. I mean to say rather that, as a matter of fact, when you inquire as to what these folks mean by e.g. 'chromosomally male', they themselves tell you that they mean something like: has chromosomes typical of males (of this species). Recall the discussions of Money and the Hampsons, above, as well as Benjamin. So, as a matter of fact, though not as a matter of necessity, it looks like there is some fundamental sense of 'male' that features in all the definitions of these complex phrases.
16 I owe this point about 'sartorially male' to Alex Byrne, who suggested the idea to me in conversation, though any infelicities are my own.
17 Describing the bluehead wrasse, a species of fish that can change sex under certain environmental conditions, the 9th edition of *Campbell Biology* says this (Reece et al. 2011, 999): "a female wrasse undergoes sex reversal, a change in sex. Within a week, the transformed individual is producing sperm instead of eggs." Emma Hilton and Colin Wright (2024, 22) concur: sex is "reproductive role by reference to gamete type."
18 Many proponents of the Ambiguity Hypothesis add gender identity to the list of alleged senses of 'male' and 'female'. If so, then a trans individual who identifies as female would count as female in that (alleged) sense, and not male in that

same sense. But (likely) also male in the (alleged) chromosomal sense, and not female in that same sense. In that case, the Ambiguity Hypothesis would entail that very many trans individuals are male despite identifying as female, or female despite identifying as male, and both male and not male, or female and not female, and male and female at the same time. Of course, according to the Ambiguity Hypothesis, there is rampant ambiguity in these statements. Nevertheless, I suspect that many activists will think this is an unacceptable implication of the Ambiguity Hypothesis, that it even *apparently* cuts against self-identification in this way, and therefore it is a reason to reject that hypothesis. As philosopher Kate Manne (in)famously asserted on Twitter, trans women are "women in every sense of the term." See here: https://twitter.com/kate_manne/status/1188566795529211904 If you think they're also female in every sense of the term, then the Ambiguity Hypothesis must be false.

19 True, *C. elegans* hermaphrodites also produce sperm. In my view, that's because each of them is *both* male *and* female, a true *When Hermes Met Aphrodite* moment. (Hermaphroditus was, according to the Oxford English Dictionary [*OED Online*, 2023], the "son of Hermes (Mercury) and Aphrodite (Venus), who, according to the myth, grew together with the nymph Salmacis, while bathing in her fountain, and thus combined male and female characters." And, in that case, they are male just as I am male, though of course they are not *merely* male (and not also female), as I am *merely* male (and not also female). See also Giuseppe Fusco and Alessandro Minelli (2019, 112), who characterize hermaphrodites as both male and female, as does Parker (2011, 17), who says that a simultaneous hermaphrodite is "both male and female simultaneously." See also the 9th edition of *Campbell Biology* (Reece et al., 2011), the gold-standard undergraduate Biology textbook, which states that each simultaneous hermaphrodite is "both male and female." Rifkin and Garson (2023, 8) agree, saying that a simultaneous hermaphrodite is "an animal having both sexes at once." This seems to be old news: long ago, Bigelow (1904, 144) also agreed, saying that "In most of the higher plans and in a few of the lower animals both sexes are included in a single individual, which is then said to be *hermaphrodite*." The *Encyclopaedia Britannica* (1911, 746) says males produce sperm and females produce ova, and then says that "[an organism] producing both ova and spermatozoa is a true hermaphrodite."

Alternatively, if you prefer to avoid hermaphroditic species, the same point can be made using the male gametophyte of the dioecious brown alga *Ectocarpus siliculosus*. This species uses a UV system of haploid phase chromosomal sex determination, with the male gametophytes carrying the V sex chromosome (cf. Coelho et al. 2019). Yet these gametophytes are male just as I am male.

20 As Richardson (2022, 10) puts it, "When age is considered as a biological variable, it is operationalized in plural ways across research materials and disciplines."
21 See also Kratzer's (1977) treatment of modal verbs like 'must', and DeRose's (1992) theory of 'knows'.
22 This may help explain her claim (2022, 10) that her view does not deny "the reality of sex as an evolved developmental pathway with many implications for biology." Perhaps that's how we're meant to interpret 'female' as it appears in this interpretation: an organism that has gone some distance down a developmental pathway that results in the production of ova. And similarly for males with respect to sperm.
23 Roosters, like many other male birds, have no external genitalia.

24 Hartry Field (1998, 253) says, in such a case, that "the best we can say is that such a word 'partially refers' or 'indeterminately refers' to each of a range of things (viz., the eligible candidates for the referent)." I myself find talk of "partial reference" difficult to understand. I think David Lewis (1984, 223) put it better when he said,

> There might be two candidates that both fit perfectly; more likely, there might be two imperfect candidates with little to choose between them and no stronger candidate to beat them both. If so, we end up with indeterminate reference…: the new term refers equally to both candidates.

But here too, I have difficulty. If the term refers equally to both candidates, I can't see how it's indeterminate what the term refers to. Better to say, I think, that in such cases there's simply no fact of the matter as to what the term refers to (see Field 1973, 462), or at least no fact that we can (easily) know.

25 When one of the family members says, while looking at one of the bunnies, "Buns has two ears," that seems true. Yet if the name refers to *both* rabbits, what proposition is expressed there? That the first bunny and the second bunny (both, together) have two ears? But that's not true. Together they have four ears. So, on the hypothesis that 'Buns' refers to both bunnies, the proposition expressed by "Buns has two ears" seems to be false. And that's a perplexing result.

26 As Field (1973, 466) does with 'mass', using the new terms 'relativistic mass' and 'proper mass'.

27 As you can see, Ainsworth adds "cellular sex" to the list of kinds of sex that we've seen so far. To that list, these folks may also wish to add so-called brain sex. Daphna Joel (2021, 165) tells us that "the binary framework still dominates thinking about the relations between sex and the brain, and the 'male brain – female brain' or 'typical male brain – typical female brain' terminology still prevails." As a recent example, see Kim et al. 2022. It should also be noted that on July 21, 2017, Ainsworth was asked on Twitter whether in her article she meant to claim that there are more than two sexes, and in reply, she clarified her view: "No, not at all. Two sexes, with a continuum of variation in anatomy/physiology." You can view the question here: https://twitter.com/martian_munk/status/884395832962936832. And you can view Ainsworth's deleted (but archived) reply here: https://web.archive.org/web/20191119224848/https://twitter.com/tenin0/status/1196912570407571457.

28 According to Eitel et al. (2011, 1–2), "The question whether placozoans reproduce sexually in the field has not been answered yet," yet under certain laboratory conditions—high animal densities and with food scarceness—"female gametes (oocytes)" and "male gametocytes (sperm)" are observed, and "embryos grow inside the mother animal until the latter completely degenerates and releases the embryo."

29 Natalie Stoljar (1995, 283–4) gives a similar treatment of womanhood. She proposes that there are "four general elements in the concept 'woman'": being of the female sex, aspects of what it feels like to be a woman, various social roles and expectations (e.g. child rearing), and self-attributions of being a woman, together with the attributions of others. These features tend to cluster in individuals, she says, because "having a female sex causes the phenomenology, role, and attributions of womanness." She then uses these features to pick out paradigmatic examples of women, and suggests that "Any individual resembling any of the paradigms sufficiently closely… will be a member of the resemblance class 'woman'."

30 See also Esa Díaz-León (2022, 233), "In my view, the most useful understanding of biological sex is in terms of a cluster of biological and anatomical features that are associated either with the female biological sex or with the male biological sex." Hane Maung (2023, 45ff) also endorses this hypothesis, and even suggests adding "psychological and social properties in the clusters."
31 David Cooper (1972, 500) notices this problem, though he goes on to say that it's not insurmountable, since one could use a synonym in the definiens, or mention the definiendum instead of using it ("'Acid' =df. 'something having sufficient of the properties … for scientists to apply the word 'acid' to it'."). Clearly, he conceives of definitions as pragmatic, linguistic projects, focused on words and phrases instead of things and properties (the word 'acid' instead of acid). But if one is interested in the *real* definition of entities outside of language, a synonym in the definiens won't help us avoid circularity, and mentioning the definiendum introduces an English word into the definiens, which opens the definition up to counterexamples concerning times and places where English is not spoken. On real definitions, see Kit Fine (1994).
32 And when Boyd (1988, 323) says, "There is a family F of properties which are contingently clustered in nature in the sense that they co-occur in an important number of cases." In the case of being male, when we ask *in virtue of what* a property is a member of this family F, no doubt a more fundamental property of being male will figure into the explanation. And then, here too, we see that being male grounds or explains the cluster, and not the cluster that grounds or explains being male. So, the Property-Cluster Hypothesis does not offer us a real definition of being male, but rather presupposes one.
33 Just as attempts to define a feature in terms of "family resemblance" presuppose the feature to be defined, as a game is sometimes said to be anything bearing a family resemblance to… paradigm examples of *games*. Something is making those paradigm games instances of games, and *that* is the real definition of a game. It's not the paradigm games themselves that explain what it is to be a game, but the very reverse: the nature of games—whatever it may be!—grounds and explains why paradigmatic games are in fact games.
34 At least, taken as an account of *sex*, the account is incorrect. But notice how Stone speaks of "giving" someone a particular sex. And notice how Stock speaks of "identifying" people as male or female in ordinary life. Maung (2023, 45) says a virtue of the hypothesis is that it "captures the actual practices of scientists and clinicians who are involved in sex classification." As an account of how we come to *know* that an organism is male or female, or a *psychological* account of how we *apply* our concepts of the sexes, this may well be correct. But insofar as we're interested in what sex actually is, the account is mistaken. Compare: there may be a cluster of properties we use to *identify* gold—color, luster, malleability, etc. And perhaps none is necessary nor sufficient for something's actually being gold. True enough. But nevertheless, there is one thing that gold is: atomic number 79. Something similar goes with the sexes, I believe.

References

Ainsworth, Claire (2015). "Sex Redefined," *Nature* 518: 288–91.
Arvan, Marcus (2023). "Trans Women, Cis Women, Alien Women, and Robot Women Are Women: They Are All (Simply) Adults Gendered Female," *Hypatia* 38: 373–89.
Benjamin, Harry (1961). "7 Kinds of Sex," *Sexology* 27: 436–42.

Benjamin, Harry (1966). *The Transsexual Phenomenon* (New York: The Julian Press).
Bettcher, Talia (2020). "Feminist Perspectives on Trans Issues," in *The Stanford Encyclopedia of Philosophy*, Fall 2020 Edition, Edward N. Zalta (ed.), https://plato.stanford.edu/archives/fall2020/entries/feminism-trans/
Bigelow, Robert Payne (1904). "Sex," in *A Reference Handbook of the Medical Sciences Embracing the Entire Range of Scientific and Practical Medicine and Allied Science*, Vol. 7, Alfred H. Buck (ed.) (New York: William Wood and Company), 144–7.
Boghossian, Paul (2001). "What is Social Construction?" *Times Literary Supplement*, 5108.
Boghossian, Paul (2006). *Fear of Knowledge* (New York, NY: Oxford University Press).
Boyd, Richard (1988). "How to be a Moral Realist," in *Moral Realism*, G. Sayre McCord (ed.) (Ithaca: Cornell University Press), 181–228.
Boyd, Richard (1999). "Homeostasis, Species, and Higher Taxa," in *Species: New Interdisciplinary Essays*, R. A. Wilson (ed.) (Cambridge, MA: MIT Press), 141–85.
Butler, Judith (2006[1990]). *Gender Trouble* (New York, NY: Routledge Classics).
Byne, William (2010). "The Sexed and Gendered Brain," in *Principles of Gender-Specific Medicine*, M. J. Legato (ed.) (Amsterdam: Academic Press).
Byrne, Alex (2018). "Is Sex Socially Constructed?" *Arc Digital*, November 30th, 2018. https://medium.com/arc-digital/is-sex-socially-constructed-81cf3ef79f07
Coelho, Susana, Laure Mignerot, and J. Mark Cock (2019). "Origin and Evolution of Sex-Determination Systems in the Brown Algae," *New Phytologist* 222 (4): 1751–6.
Cooper, David (1972). "Definitions and 'Clusters'," *Mind* 81 (324): 495–503.
DeRose, Keith (1992). "Contextualism and Knowledge Attributions," *Philosophy and Phenomenological Research* 52 (4): 913–29.
Díaz-León, Esa (2022). "The Meaning of 'Woman' and the Political Turn in Philosophy of Language," in *The Political Turn in Analytic Philosophy*, David Plou, Víctor Castro and José Torices (eds.) (Berlin: De Gruyter), 229–56.
Díaz-León, Esa (2025). *The Metaphysics of Gender. Cambridge Elements in Metaphysics*, Tuomas E. Tahko (ed.) (Cambridge: Cambridge University Press).
Dworkin, Andrea (1974). *Woman Hating* (New York: Plume).
Eitel, Michael, Loretta Guidi, Heike Hadrys, Maria Balsamo, and Bernd Schierwater (2011). "New Insights into Placozoan Sexual Reproduction and Development," *PLoS One* 6 (5): e19639.
Encyclopaedia Britannica (1911). Volume 14, Eleventh Edition (Cambridge: Cambridge University Press).
Fausto-Sterling, Anne (2016). "On the Critiques of the Concept of Sex: An Interview with Anne Fausto-Sterling," *Differences* 27 (1): 189–205.
Fausto-Sterling, Anne (2018). "Why Sex is Not Binary," *New York Times Opinion*, October 25th, 2018. https://www.nytimes.com/2018/10/25/opinion/sex-biology-binary.html
Field, Hartry (1973). "Theory Change and the Indeterminacy of Reference," *Journal of Philosophy* 70 (14): 462–81.
Field, Hartry (1998). "Some Thoughts on Radical Indeterminacy," *The Monist* 81 (2): 253–73.
Fine, Kit (1994). "Essence and Modality," *Philosophical Perspectives* 8: 1–16.
Fusco, Giuseppe and Alessandro Minelli (2019). *The Biology of Reproduction* (New York: Cambridge University Press).

Gillion, Brendan (1990). "Ambiguity, Generality, and Indeterminacy: Tests and Definitions," *Synthese* 85: 391–416.
Griffiths, Paul (2020). "Sex is Real," *Aeon*. https://aeon.co/essays/the-existence-of-biological-sex-is-no-constraint-on-human-diversity, accessed May 23, 2023.
Hacking, Ian (1999). *The Social Construction of What?* (Cambridge, MA: Harvard University Press).
Haslanger, Sally (2000). "Gender and Race: (What) are They? (What) do We Want Them to be?" *Noûs* 34 (1): 31–55.
Haslanger, Sally (2016). "Theorizing with a Purpose: The Many Kinds of Sex," in *Natural Kinds and Classification in Scientific Practice*, Catherine Kendig (ed.) (New York: Routledge), 129–44.
"hermaphrodite, n. and adj." (March 2023). *OED Online* (Oxford University Press), Web. June 6th, 2023.
Hilton, Emma and Colin Wright (2024). "Two Sexes," in *Sex and Gender: A Contemporary Reader*, Alice Sullivan and Selina Todd (eds.) (New York: Routledge).
Joel, Daphna (2021). "Beyond the Binary: Rethinking Sex and the Brain," *Neuroscience & Biobehavioral Reviews*, 122: 165–75.
Kaplan, David (1989). "Demonstratives: An Essay on the Semantics, Logic, Metaphysics and Epistemology of Demonstratives and other Indexicals," in *Themes from Kaplan*, Joseph Almog, John Perry, and Howard Wettstein (eds.) (New York: Oxford University Press), 481–563.
Karkazis, Katrina, Rebecca Jordan-Young, Georgiann Davis, and Silvia Camporesi (2012). "Out of Bounds? A Critique of the New Policies on Hyperandrogenism in Elite Female Athletes," *American Journal of Bioethics* 12 (7): 3–16.
Kim, K., Y. Y. Joo, G. Ahn, H. H. Wang, S. Y. Moon, H. Kim, W. Y. Ahn, and J. Cha (2022). "The Sexual Brain, Genes, and Cognition: A Machine-Predicted Brain Sex Score Explains Individual Differences in Cognitive Intelligence and Genetic Influence in Young Children," *Human Brain Mapping* 43 (12): 3857–72.
Kratzer, Angelika (1977). "What 'must' and 'can' Must and Can Mean," *Linguistics and Philosophy* 1 (3): 337–55.
Lehtonen, Jussi, and Geoff Parker (2014). "Gamete Competition, Gamete Limitation, and the Evolution of the Two Sexes." *Molecular Human Reproduction* 20 (12): 1161–8.
Lewis, David (1984). "Putnam's Paradox," *Australasian Journal of Philosophy* 62 (3): 221–35.
Liebesman, David, and Ofra Magidor (forthcoming). "Ambiguity Tests, Polysemy, and Copredication," *Australasian Journal of Philosophy*, 102(3).
Martin, John (1982). "Negation, Ambiguity, and the Identity Test," *Journal of Semantics* 1(3): 251–74.
Maung, Hane Htut (2023). "Classifying Sexes," *DiGeSt: Journal of Diversity and Gender Studies* 10 (1): 36–52.
McGinn, Colin (2012). *Truth by Analysis* (New York: Oxford University Press).
Money, John, Joan G. Hampson, and John L. Hampson (1955). "An Examination of Some Basic Sexual Concepts: The Evidence of Human Hermaphroditism." *Bulletin of the Johns Hopkins Hospital* 97 (4): 301–19.
Pape, E., M. Miyagi, S. Ritz, M. Boulicault, S. Richardson, and D. Maney (2024). "Sex Contextualism In Laboratory Research: Enhancing Rigor And Precision In The Study Of Sex-Related Variables," *Cell* 187: 1316–26.
Parker, Geoff A. (2011). "The Origin and Maintenance of Two Sexes (Anisogamy), and their Gamete Sizes by Gamete Competition," in *The Evolution of*

Anisogamy: A Fundamental Phenomenon Underlying Sexual Selection, Tatsuya Togashi and Paul A. Cox (eds.) (Cambridge, UK: Cambridge University Press), 17–74.

Pickel, Bryan (2010). "There is No 'Is' of Constitution," *Philosophical Studies* 147: 193–211.

Raymond, Janice [1979] (1994). *The Transsexual Empire* (New York, NY: Teachers College Press).

Recanati, François (2005). "Literalism and Contextualism: Some Varieties," in *Contextualism in Philosophy: Knowledge, Meaning, and Truth*, Gerhard Preyer and Georg Peter (eds.) (Oxford: Oxford University Press).

Reece, Jane, Lisa Urry, Michael Cain, Steven Wasserman, Peter Minorsky, and Robert Jackson (2011). *Campbell Biology*, Ninth Edition (San Francisco, CA: Benjamin Cummings).

Richardson, Sarah (2013). *Sex Itself: The Search for Male and Female in the Human Genome* (University of Chicago Press).

Richardson, Sarah (2022). "Sex Contextualism," *Philosophy, Theory, and Practice in Biology* 14: 2, 1–17.

Rifkin, Maximiliana, and Justin Garson (2023). "Sex by Design," *Biology and Philosophy* 38 (13): 1–17.

Roughgarden, Joan (2004). *Evolution's Rainbow* (Berkeley, CA: University of California Press).

Saul, Jennifer (2012). "Politically Significant Terms and Philosophy of Language: Methodological Issues," in *Analytic Feminist Contributions to Traditional Philosophy*, Anita Superson and Sharon Crasnow (eds.) (Oxford University Press).

Schroeder, M. (2020). "Review of Semantics for Reasons," in *Dame Philosophical Reviews*, B. R. Weaver, and K. Notre Scharp (eds.). https://ndpr.nd.edu/reviews/semantics-for-reasons/, accessed May 10, 2023.

Sennet, Adam (2021). "Ambiguity," in *The Stanford Encyclopedia of Philosophy*, Fall 2021 Edition, Edward N. Zalta (ed.), https://plato.stanford.edu/archives/fall2021/entries/ambiguity/

Srinivasan, Amia (2021). *The Right to Sex* (London: Bloomsbury Publishing).

St. John, John et al. (2012). "Sequencing three crocodilian genomes to illuminate the evolution of archosaurs and amniotes," *Genome Biology* 13(1): Article 415, 1–12. https://genomebiology.biomedcentral.com/articles/10.1186/gb-2012-13-1-415

Stock, Kathleen (2021). *Material Girls* (London: Fleet).

Stoljar, Natalie (1995): "Essence, Identity and the Concept of Woman," *Philosophical Topics* 23: 261–93.

Stone, Alison (2007). *An Introduction to Feminist Philosophy* (Cambridge: Polity).

van Anders, Sari (2024). "Gender/Sex/ual Diversity and Biobehavioral Research," *Psychology of Sexual Orientation and Gender Diversity* 11 (3): 471–87.

Velocci, Beans (2024). "The History of Sex Research: Is 'sex' a Useful Category?" *Cell* 187: 1343–6.

Watkins, Aja and Marina DiMarco (2025). "Sex Eliminativism," *Biology and Philosophy* 40 (2): 1–30.

Woodward, D.E. and J.D. Murray (1993). "On the effect of temperature-dependent sex determination on sex ratio and survivorship in crocodilians," *Royal Society of London* 252: 149–55.

Zwicky, Arnold and Jerrold Sadock (1975). "Ambiguity tests and how to fail them," in J. Kimball (Ed.), *Syntax and semantics* (Vol. 4) (New York, NY: Academic Press), 1–36.

3
WHAT THE SEXES COULD BE
The Gamete View

Introduction

We've seen that there is much confusion about what the sexes are. "The only thing we can say for sure about what sex means," Paisley Currah (2022, 39) declares, "is what a particular state actor says it means." But no, let's not give in to despair. As Thomas Edison is said to have said, "Our greatest weakness lies in giving up. The most certain way to succeed is always to try just one more time." In this chapter, we'll try one more time.

The Gamete View of the sexes analyzes being male and being female in one way or another, ultimately in terms of gamete production. It eschews any notion that our sex terms—when used as adjectives and said of organisms—are ambiguous, or that what they refer to varies by context, or that they're semantically indeterminate, or that they refer to property clusters. Next, we'll evaluate three species of the Gamete View—the Developmental Pathway View, the Active Capacity View, and a Parts-or-Processes (PoP) Functional View. I will weigh the pros and cons of these, and then synthesize them into what I believe is the truth about the nature of the sexes: the Activated Higher-Order Functional account of the sexes

The Developmental Pathway View

First, a note about the development of human reproductive systems. Early human embryos have an undifferentiated bipotential gonad, which develops into either testes or ovaries, beginning around the fifth week of development (Aatsha et al. 2023). By around six weeks of development, both male and female human embryos have two pairs of genital ducts: the Müllerian and the Wolffian ducts (Aatsha et al. 2023). Up until this point, male and female embryos have undergone the same steps in reproductive development. But then a fork in the road occurs, under the influence of various genes.

The Y sex chromosome typically carries the sex-determining region Y gene, better known as the *SRY* gene. When this is expressed, the result is the SRY protein, also known as the testis-determining factor (TDF) (Aatsha et al. 2023). TDF transforms the bipotential gonad into testes, and also upregulates steroidogenesis factor 1 (SF1), which produces Sertoli and Leydig cells (Sadler 2004, 343). Sertoli cells then produce antimüllerian hormone (AMH), which causes the regression of the Müllerian ducts. Leydig cells produce testosterone (Sadler 2004), which is critical for the male sexual differentiation of the internal and external genitalia, including the differentiation of the Wolffian ducts into various parts of the male reproductive system. (Aatsha et al. 2023).

If the embryo has XX chromosomes, and the *SRY* gene is not present, or is not functioning properly,[1] then the *DAX1* gene, located on the X chromosome, downregulates *SF1* activity, thereby preventing the production of Sertoli and Leydig cells (Sadler 2004, 343–4). The early expression of growth factor WNT4 is maintained in females but downregulated in males, and contributes to ovarian differentiation (Sadler 2004, 344). Without Sertoli cells producing AMH, the Müllerian ducts are stimulated by estrogens to form the uterine tubes, uterus, cervix, and upper vagina, along with external genitalia (Sadler 2004). And without Leydig cells producing testosterone, the Wolffian ducts regress during sexual development (Aatsha et al. 2023).

Perhaps a picture would help summarize this process of early sexual development in humans (See Figure 3.1).

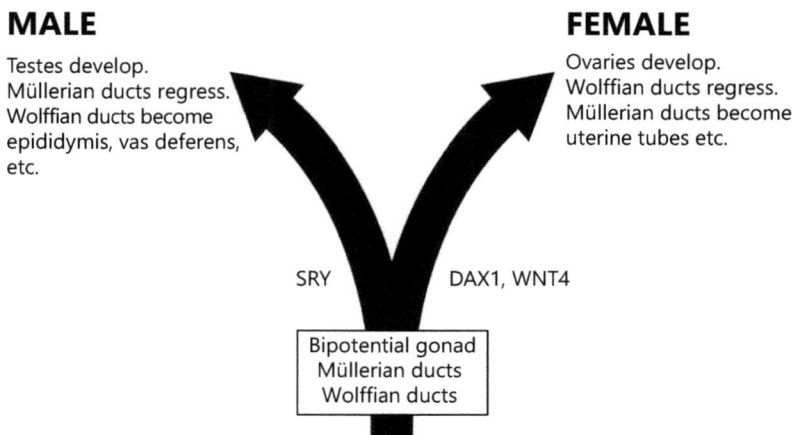

FIGURE 3.1 A common representation of diverging reproductive developmental pathways in humans.

Of course, so far we have discussed the reproductive developmental pathways only in humans. Other species do it differently, given their different reproductive systems. Invertebrates—like plants and algae, for example—and even vertebrates like birds and some reptiles do this all quite differently. Still, though, it has seemed to some thinkers like the nature of the sexes has something to do with these developmental pathways. We will look at two such examples now.

One version of the Developmental Pathway View comes from Laura Franklin-Hall (2021, 179–80), who thinks the nature of the sexes has to do with the *historical lineage* of these reproductive developmental processes. She says: "to be a male (or female) animal is to be one whose reproductive developmental process originates–in a way I will spell out–in that animal's earliest small (or large) gamete-producing animal ancestors." And later (Franklin-Hall 2021, 188), she says,

> An animal's sex, I want to suggest, is set by its reproductive developmental system, and in particular by whether that system is a variant–as determined by its sex developmental lineage–of the developmental process at work in its earliest male, or female, animal ancestors.

On the face of it, this proposal is circular. For example: x is a male if and only if its reproductive developmental system is a variant of the developmental process at work in its earliest...*male* ancestors. Franklin-Hall is sensitive to this concern (Franklin-Hall 2021, 188), saying:

> In making the case for a common origin in animal male and female reproductive developmental systems, I just implied that an animal's sex is set by some intrinsic feature – presumably the size of its gametes – which the sex developmental lineage happens to track. But what if we kick away the gametic ladder that we climbed to get here, and understand an animal's sex in terms of the history of the developmental system that produced it?

Suppose we do set out to understand an animal's sex in terms of the history of the developmental pathway that produced it. To avoid vicious circularity, we must eliminate any reference to the sexes of those earliest ancestors, and say only something like this: to be a male (or female) is to be one whose reproductive developmental process originates in that animal's earliest small- (or large-) gamete-producing ancestors. So, the sexes are a matter of having undergone a reproductive developmental process with the right ancestry. These are *historical* kinds, she says. The way that *being a Toyota* is a historical kind, or *being a Kennedy*. A perfect duplicate of a

Toyota would not be a Toyota if it didn't come from the right factory. And a perfect duplicate of a Kennedy would not be a Kennedy if it didn't come from the right family. Similarly, a perfect duplicate of a male would not be a male if it didn't have the right ancestry, on this proposal.

So, according to Franklin-Hall, an organism's sex is defined by the ancestry of its reproductive developmental process. Unfortunately, Franklin-Hall also seems to *deny* that an animal's sex is defined by that ancestry, when she says (Franklin-Hall 2021, 188), "It is only those earliest ancestors whose sex, male or female, was set by gamete size directly." But this is a problem, because nothing can have two natures. It cannot be that, for some organisms—our first sexually reproducing ancestors, for example—the nature of sex is gamete production, while for other organisms—us, for example—the nature of sex is historical, a matter of having a reproductive developmental process with a certain ancestry. Everything is what it is, and not something else. Sex *is* something. It has some nature, some real definition, which is true always and everywhere. And this real definition is either purely in terms of gamete production or in terms of ancestry, but not both. Having undergone a reproductive developmental process with a certain ancestry is either necessary for being male (or female), or it isn't. It cannot be both ways. Franklin-Hall's view seems to entail a contradiction—that this ancestry condition both is and is not necessary for being male (or female). It is necessary (for us), but it is not necessary (for our earliest sexed ancestors). This is a serious problem for the view.[2]

A second problem concerns some implications of Franklin-Hall's view that the sexes are historical kinds, as opposed to functional kinds defined solely in terms of gamete production. Consider this hypothetical scenario: everything is how it currently is, yet time stretches infinitely into the past, and life—indeed, sexual reproduction—has always been around. Yes, this is admittedly a far-out hypothetical scenario. But if it were so, then we humans would neither have *originated* sexual reproduction, nor would we have reproductive developmental processes that trace back to any *earliest* gamete-producing ancestors. For there would be no *earliest* ancestors in this scenario, only an infinite regress of *earlier* gamete-producing ancestors. Franklin-Hall's proposal entails that, in such a scenario, there would be no males or females, despite the prevalence of sexual reproduction. I submit this is not plausible. The sexes seem not to be historical kinds; they seem to be purely functional. This is why we are ready to describe organisms with different ancestries as male or female, depending solely on their reproductive functions, irrespective of their ancestries. Consider another thought experiment involving a microphysical duplicate of oneself formed by the random rearrangement of particles as lightning strikes a swamp. Swamp-person. My swamp duplicate would lack my historical properties: he would *believe* that he's a Bogardus, a Californian, a college graduate, but he really isn't. Yet... isn't he a vertebrate, just as I am a vertebrate? Yes, I'd say. And isn't he a male, just as I am male? I'd think so. And this too is evidence that the sexes are functional kinds, not historical kinds.[3]

A third problem has to do with sequential hermaphrodites. These are organisms with reproductive systems that have the capacity to produce one type of gamete at some stage of life, and later produce the other type of gamete at a different stage of life. If such an organism counts as having the *same* pluripotent reproductive system throughout its life, changing its structure to realize different functions, and this system traces its origins back both to male and to female ancestors, then, on Franklin-Hall's account, such organisms are both male and female *simultaneously*, not sequentially.[4] This unfortunate implication is a strike against the view; she has not put her finger on the kind that biologists have picked out with their thoughts and language about the sexes. Isn't it more plausible that Franklin-Hall is brushing up against the true, fundamental nature of the sexes, not as historical kinds, but as kinds "characterized by gamete size"? Or at least, if not gamete *size*, then gamete-*type*. (More on this below.) That's how things look to me.

Alex Byrne (2023, 63) proposes a different version of the Developmental Pathway View, giving this elaboration of Roughgarden's definition of the sexes:

> [F]emales are the ones who have advanced some distance down the developmental pathway that results in the production of large gametes. Similarly, males are the ones who have advanced some distance down the developmental pathway that results in the production of small gametes. That is better, if not completely right. It is accurate enough for our purposes.

Byrne offers this as a near-enough approximation, good enough for government work. But there are three reasons to think this isn't *precisely* what the sexes are. First, this Developmental Pathway View faces a dilemma concerning this question: When do the sexual differentiation pathways begin? Take humans, for example. Recall from above that, up to a certain point, the sexual development of both male and female embryos overlaps. For the period of time during that overlap, both Wolffian ducts and Müllerian ducts are present in each human embryo. Then begins a cascade of gene expression and hormone secretion that sends a male embryo onto a course that develops the indifferent gonads into testes, etc., and the Müllerian duct system disappears. In a female embryo, on the other hand, the lack of male-determining genes, together with a separate cascade of gene expression and hormone excretion, leads to the development of ovaries, etc., and the disappearance of the Wolffian ducts. So, as we saw above, in humans, the pathways of sexual differentiation are commonly depicted in the form of a capital "Y."

Beginning at the bottom, all embryos undergo the same early processes of sexual development, we're told. Later, as they move up the 'Y', male embryos journey along one path, and female embryos continue along the other. If this is correct, we can appreciate the dilemma for this Developmental Pathway View: When do the sexual differentiation pathways begin? Before the fork in the 'Y', or not? If before, then we have the unpalatable implication that every normal human embryo is both male and female, since every normal human embryo has, prior to the fork in the 'Y' of sexual differentiation, advanced *some* small distance down the developmental pathway that results in the production of large gametes, and also that same distance down the developmental pathway that results in the production of small gametes. If, on the other hand, we say that sexual differentiation pathways begin at the fork in the 'Y' or later, then we must accept the implication that every early human embryo is neither male nor female. Both of these implications run contrary to the common practice among biologists of describing embryos as either 'male' or 'female', and not both (e.g. Moutos et al. 2021). And this would be evidence against the proposal, at least if we were to take it as an account of the true nature of the sexes.

One plausible response on behalf of Byrne involves reconceptualizing these developmental pathways. True, in the early stages, all embryos undergo the same development of their reproductive systems. But why think this means there's *one* developmental pathway in the beginning, which forks into two distinct pathways, instead of thinking that there are *two* developmental pathways from the beginning, which happen to be exactly similar in their early careers? Consider how one factory producing aluminum cans and another factory producing aluminum foil may begin their respective processes in just the same way—using the Bayer process on bauxite ore to extract aluminum oxide, and then smelting the aluminum oxide to produce pure aluminum using the Hall–Héroult process—before treating the pure aluminum differently. Despite sharing these early sub-processes as components, still, it's *one* process that produces the cans and a *distinct* process that produces the foil. In the same way, it may well be one pathway that produces males, and a distinct pathway that produces females, even if those pathways begin in similar ways. If this is right, then

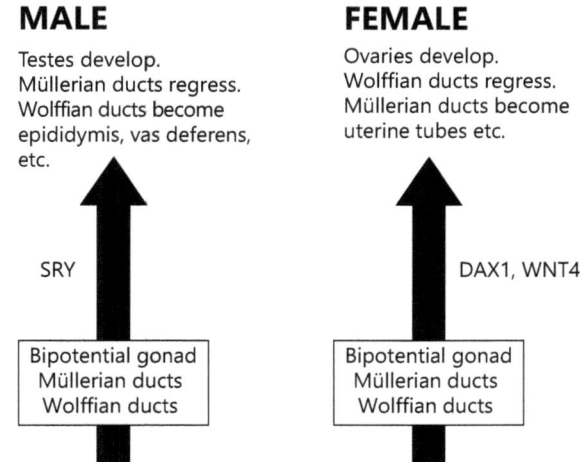

FIGURE 3.2 An alternative representation of the two reproductive developmental pathways in humans.

the 'Y' image commonly used to relay information about human reproductive developmental pathways has misled us. Really, there are just two pathways—one for males, the other for females—that happen to resemble each other in the early days, as depicted below.

Of course, if this is right, then the previous objection to Byrne's proposal fails, relying as it does on the developmental pathways having the shape of a 'Y.' Because Byrne might reply in this way: it's not the case that males and females both go down the *same* developmental pathway. Rather, males proceed down one pathway, and females proceed down another, so we needn't say that every embryo is neither male nor female, nor must we say that every human is both male and female.

But there remains one problem for Byrne's Developmental Pathway View, which is not so easily hurdled. This problem is similar to that facing Franklin-Hall's view, concerning the distinction between simultaneous hermaphrodites and sequential hermaphrodites. Simultaneous hermaphrodites, like the common garden snail, are both male and female at the same time.[5] Sequential hermaphrodites, on the other hand, can change sex during their lifetimes, but are never both male and female at the same time. The bluehead wrasse, for example. (That's a fish.) But now consider a bluehead wrasse after its reproductive transformation from female to male. At that point in its career, the organism has gone some way down both the developmental pathway leading to eggs *and also* (more recently) some way down the developmental pathway leading to sperm. On this Developmental Pathway view it follows that this organism is both female and male here and now, both sexes at the same time, and so we reach the unwelcome result that this wrasse is now a *simultaneous* hermaphrodite after all. Here again, this view would require us to revise ways in which biologists commonly use sex terms. Insofar as one believes the way that biologists talk and think about sex has a special authority on the subject, this is a cost. To repeat, though, Byrne has proposed this view only as a useful approximation of the truth. Below, we will develop a more exact understanding of the nature of the sexes.

The Active Capacity View

According to Paul Griffiths (2021, 19), "biological sexes are regions of phenotypic space that implement gametic reproductive strategies."[6] Which gametic reproductive strategies? Griffiths (2021, 2) says,

> Male phenotypes evolved as part of a reproductive strategy focused on the production of large numbers of small gametes, such as human sperm. Female phenotypes evolved as part of a reproductive strategy focused on the production of smaller numbers of larger, highly-provisioned gametes, such as human eggs.

Griffiths is keenly aware of sequential hermaphrodites, and concludes that it is not the *whole* organism that has a sex, but only a "life-history stage" of that organism (2021, 16). An organism may spend some of its life-history in the female region of its species' phenotypic space, and other parts of its life-history in the male region. Taken literally, this claim is quite revisionary: that organisms are not sexed, but only *life-history stages* of organisms are.[7] Presumably, Griffiths means to say at least that an organism is not necessarily of the same sex for its entire life, but may bear a sex for only a part of its life, and different sexes at different times, and no sex at all for some time. On this more charitable reading, it's only ever *the organism* that has a sex, and not a *duration* of its life that has a sex, whatever it might mean to ascribe a sex to a *period of time* in the life of an organism.

It is somewhat unclear whether Griffiths considers simultaneous hermaphroditism to be a sex distinct from male and female. He lists "hermaphrodite" as a sex (2021, 1 and also 19), and calls it a "mixed reproductive strategy" (2021, 2) and a "sexual form" (2021, 3). Indeed, simultaneous hermaphroditism does seem to fit Griffith's definition of a sex: a region of phenotypic space that implements gametic reproductive strategies. But in an earlier piece (Griffiths 2020), he says that "Males produce small gametes, and females produce large gametes," and that hermaphroditic *C. elegans* are male as larvae, and later become female (as well, i.e. in addition to being male). And speaking of simultaneous hermaphrodites in that 2020 piece, he explicitly says that such organisms "are both male and female."[8]

Griffiths thereby attempts to offer a simple, direct definition of the sexes: males produce sperm, females produce ova. And each must do so *now*, *actually*. I call this an Active Capacity View, since to be a male on this account, one must be actively producing sperm, and similarly with females and ova.[9] Griffiths (2021, 19) says that, "assigning a sex to a reproductively competent individual is straightforward": if the organism is actively producing sperm, it's a male, and if it's actively producing ova, it's a female.[10]

This promises to be a clear and simple view, fit to satisfy the staunchest empiricist. (You want to know what sex an organism is? Just *look*.) And yet Griffiths is sensitive to concerns about organisms that are not currently "reproductively competent," but which are commonly described by biologists as being male or female. Human embryos, for example, and juvenile males who do not yet produce sperm. Of juveniles, Griffiths (2020) says that they "are assigned to the sex they have started to grow into." Griffiths says (2021, 17) that if we label such organisms 'male' or 'female', then "we are engaging in 'prospective narration', labelling a current event by the future events that we predict will follow." So, Griffith's view seems to be that, in the primary senses of 'male' and 'female', embryos are neither male nor female, and neither are juvenile males who are not yet "reproductively competent" (i.e. do not yet produce sperm). Speaking of female worker bees, Griffiths (2020) says,

> The queen sends chemical signals that block the development of the worker bee's ovaries at an early stage. So worker bees are 'female' in the extended sense that they would develop into fertile females if they weren't actively prevented from doing so.

Again, the view seems to be that, in the primary sense of 'female', these worker bees are not female. But they are 'female' in "an extended sense." Griffiths (2020) also mentions postmenopausal women, who no longer produce ova. Though he offers no direct assessment of this situation, presumably he'd say something similar to what he said of juvenile males: postmenopausal women are 'female' only in an extended sense, assigned to the sex they had *previously* occupied for much of their life history.

You can see that, while the view may have appeared simple, things are getting rather baroque. 'Male' and 'female' have a central or primary sense, having to do with actively producing either sperm or eggs. Yet according to Griffiths, each word is polysemous, each word has a constellation of distinct but related senses: an embryo may be male in an extended sense of the word, in virtue of the fact that it *will* become male in the primary sense. Certain worker bees are female in an extended sense of the word because they *would* be female in the primary sense, but for the queen's pheromones. A postmenopausal woman is female in an extended sense of the word, in virtue of the fact that she *was* female in the primary sense. The appearance of biological simplicity has come at the cost of linguistic profligacy.

And one may rehearse our ambiguity tests above to tell against this alleged linguistic complexity. Griffiths is claiming that there is ambiguity where there doesn't seem to be any. Take the conjunction-reduction test: insofar as one believes that at least some embryos and I are both male, that postmenopausal women and Joan of Arc are both female, and that worker bees and queen bees are both female, then our words for the sexes are not ambiguous in the way that Griffiths proposes.[11] And all that seems quite clear to me. Recall also our fourth and final Aristotelian test for ambiguity: if the relevant linguistic data can be explained on a univocity hypothesis, we should favor that over an ambiguity hypothesis. Griffiths' theory entails that there are extended senses of our sex terms in order to explain the fact that biologists regularly apply those terms to organisms that do not exhibit the active capacity to produce the relevant gametes. But evidently that is not correct. If we were to abandon Griffith's Active Capacity view of the sexes and find a theory that confirmed the myriad ways in which biologists regularly apply our sex terms, then simplicity would favor a univocity hypothesis over Griffith's proposed ambiguity hypothesis. I believe there is such a theory of the nature of the sexes, and the next view is closer to that truth.

The Parts-or-Processes (PoP) Functional Account

Maximiliana Rifkin and Justin Garson (2023, 8) propose this account of the sexes:

> X is female if and only if X has biological parts or processes that have the (proximal or distal) biological function of producing eggs.
> X is male if and only if X has biological parts or processes that have the (proximal or distal) biological function of producing sperm.

And they understand function in terms of *selection history*, saying: "We think an individual is male if and only if that individual has a biological part or process that was *recently selected for producing sperm*, by evolutionary natural selection or some comparable selection process."

Now, the "parts or processes" bit of what we'll call this PoP Functional account is well suited to handle cases where an organism has had its testes or ovaries removed, or has a condition such that neither ovaries nor testes ever developed. Such an organism would presumably have *other* parts or processes that have the (distal, downstream) function of producing gametes. For example, in the case of females, they say (Rifkin and Garson 2023, 9), "hypothalamic estrogen receptors." And the "recently selected for" historical notion of function was added, according to Rifkin and Garson (2023, 8), because such a notion

> allows us to draw principled distinctions between parts and processes that merely enable versus realize the function in question. For example, while the heart enables the production of sperm, it lacks the distal function to produce sperm because it was not selected for it in our evolutionary history.

However, there are problems with the PoP Functional account. Rifkin and Garson feel pressured by their account to accept the implausible claim that genes have no function. And that's because (2023, 12) "[h]uman males and females both possess genes that contribute to the development of testes (like Fgf9 on autosomal chromosome 13), and genes that contribute to ovary development (like Wnt4 on chromosome 1)." If those genes do more than merely *contribute* to the development of gonads, but also have the *function* of doing so, then the worry is that every human would have a part or process with the function of producing sperm, and also a part or process with the function of producing eggs, and therefore every human would be both male and female, on their view. And that is a most unwelcome result. In response, Rifkin and Garson (2023, 13) say that "a gene as such doesn't have a function." This avoids the threat of entailing simultaneous hermaphroditism for every human, but at a great cost, since biologists commonly speak of gene functions.[12] This problem is especially acute for Rifkin and Garson, who, as you'll recall, say (2023, 2) that biology has special authority to shape our ontology of sex. In an effort to respect the authority of biology when it comes to sex, Rifkin and Garson end up denying its authority when it comes to the function of genes.

Rifkin and Garson say that it's only the *upregulation* of a gene that has a function (2023, 12–3), that is, when the gene is caused to be expressed ("read," and the protein it encodes produced) at higher rates. This has two troubling implications. The first is that embryos have no sex prior to the upregulation of the relevant genes, namely those with the function of producing gametes.[13] Here, again, the authors are at odds with how biologists commonly speak about sex. Second, Fgf9 is commonly upregulated in both male and female humans for a variety of purposes (cf. National Library of Medicine 2023). So, if upregulation of this gene is sufficient to be male, then virtually all humans are males, which is an implausible result. But even if there were a gene possessed by both males and females yet upregulated only in males, it would be simple enough to cause this gene to be upregulated in a female, via the introduction of the right transcription factors. Presumably, this would not necessarily make the female a simultaneous hermaphrodite. So, something has gone wrong with this account of the sexes.

Another problem concerns a type of sequential hermaphroditism—serial bidirectional hermaphroditism—as found in some members of the genus *Gobiodon*. (These, too, are fish.) Most sequential hermaphrodites change sex only once in their lifetime, but bidirectional sequential hermaphrodites can switch teams multiple times. Importantly, as Casas and Saborido-Rey (2021, 113) put it, "in bidirectional hermaphrodites ovotestis are permanent, but the gonad is unable to produce gametes simultaneously, and sex change means a mere shift in functionality where one tissue is capable to produce gametes and the other remains inactive." An ovotestis is a bisexual gonad, consisting either of dormant, proto-testicular tissue as well as functional ovarian tissue, or dormant, proto-ovarian tissue together with functional testicular tissue, depending on the situation. The account of the sexes from Rifkin and Garson plausibly rules that such an organism is a *simultaneous* hermaphrodite. Even if its ovotestis itself does not have the function of producing either gamete until it is elevated to functionality, nevertheless, it plausibly contains *parts or processes* with the (distal or proximal) function of producing each gamete-type. This, too, is contrary to the way biologists speak of these sequential hermaphrodites, as male or female but not both. So, we must look elsewhere for a true account of the nature of the sexes. And it's there, finally, that we now turn.

Developing the Activated Higher-Order Function (AHOF) Account

Griffith's Active Capacity view gets this right: being male (or female) is something that an organism *does*, something *active*. However, by requiring that this be an active first-order capacity—the production of sperm (or eggs)—the view rules that embryos, juvenile males, postmenopausal females, female worker bees, etc., are not male or female strictly speaking, but only in a linguistically suspect "extended sense." Byrne's Developmental Pathway view sidesteps most of those problems, but still rules that sequential hermaphrodites are really simultaneous hermaphrodites. Franklin-Hall's view is right to look toward the origin of an organism's reproductive system, but mistakenly concludes that an organism's sex is purely a matter of the ancestry of that reproductive system, rather than its function. By leaning heavily on the notion of function, Rifkin and Garson nicely account for malfunction and menopause, but the *parts-or-processes* bit of their view ultimately stumbles over embryos and sequential hermaphrodites, ruling that early embryos are sexless and that some sequential hermaphrodites are in reality simultaneous hermaphrodites.

A synthesis of these views is possible, namely, that the sexes are activated higher-order functions *of entire organisms*: AHOFs, for short. In this section, I will develop the AHOF view. In the next section, I will demonstrate its virtues by showing how well it handles difficult cases. As Roughgarden (2004, 23) puts it, "'Male' and 'female' are biological categories, and the criteria for classifying an organism as male or female have to work with worms to whales, with red seaweed to redwood trees."[14] Indeed, that's the goal. As I hope to show, the AHOF account meets those criteria for success.

Anyone who's taken a biology class can attest that the word 'function' blankets biology like cornfields in Kansas.[15] According to my Adobe Acrobat Reader, there are 1,820 instances of 'function' in the 9th edition of *Campbell Biology* (Reece et al., 2010), the standard undergraduate biology textbook. To pick just a few examples, one reads of how RNA regulates the functioning of protein-coding genes (Reece et al., 2010, 10), how one function of the stomach is to break down proteins (Reece et al., 2010, 855), how hearts Reece et al., 2010, 904), blood vessels (Reece et al., 2010, 905), red blood cells (Reece et al., 2010, 911), kidneys (Reece et al., 2010, 953), testosterone (Reece et al., 2010, 992), the uterus (Reece et al., 2010, 1002), eggs (Reece et al., 2010, 1005), and sperm cells (Reece et al., 2010, 1006) all have functions, and that males and females have sexual functions (Reece et al., 2010, 1011).[16]

Unless biologists are very badly mistaken, there are functions in nature. All this function-talk means *something*. One helpful way to interpret this function-talk is in terms of R.J. Nelson's (1975, 252) finite transducer, or sequential machine. Such a machine consists of a (finite, non-empty) set Q of internal states, a (finite, non-empty) set S of inputs, a (finite, non-empty) set O of outputs, a transition function M, taking ordered pairs of elements from Q and S to other elements of Q, and an output function N, taking ordered pairs of elements from Q and S to elements of O. These functions can be represented by so-called *machine tables*.

Let me give you an example. Consider a vending machine that dispenses bottles of soda (simplified from Nelson 1975, 253), which accepts nickels (worth five cents) and dimes (worth ten cents) as input, and which dispenses a soda in exchange for 15 cents. For such a sequential machine, the set of inputs S = {nickel, dime}, the set of internal states Q = {q1, q2, q3}, and the set of outputs O = {(∅, 0), (soda, 0), (soda, nickel)}, where the pair "(∅, 0)" means no soda and no change, "(soda, 0)" means soda and no change, and "(soda, nickel)" means soda and a nickel in change. We could represent the transition function M and the output function N on a machine table like so.

		M		N	
q	s	nickel	dime	nickel	dime
q1		q2	q2	(∅, 0)	(∅, 0)
q2		q3	q1	(∅, 0)	(soda, 0)
q3		q1	q1	(soda, 0)	(soda, nickel)

FIGURE 3.3   A simple machine table for our soda machine.

This machine has three *internal states*. The first state, q1, may be thought of as the initial state, where the machine has received no money. The second state, q2, may be thought of as a semi-primed state, where the machine has received five cents. While in q2, the input of a dime will release a soda, and the input of a nickel will move the machine into the third internal state. That third state, q3, may be thought of as a fully primed state, where the machine has received ten cents, and any further input (nickel or dime) will release a soda. We see that, when the machine is in state q1, then the input of a nickel moves the machine to the semi-primed state q2, according to the transition function M, and the machine produces no output, according to the output function N. And we see that when the machine is in the fully primed state q3, the input of a dime moves the machine to the initial state q1, according to M, and releases a soda and a nickel of change, according to N.

This table neatly displays for us the *functions* of this machine. For each function, there is a conditional, citing an internal state and an input in the antecedent, and then citing an internal state and an output in the consequent. I will call these *function-conditionals*. For example, one of the functions of this machine is to dispense a soda and a nickel, and to return to state q1, *if* it is in state q3 and receives a dime as input. Here's another function-conditional for the machine: *If* the machine is in state q3 and receives a nickel as input, *then* it dispenses only a soda (no change) and returns to state q1.

But, despite the fact that this is a soda machine, dispensing a soda is not *always* the output of this machine, for example, if it is in state q1 and receives only a nickel as input. When the antecedent of one of these function-conditionals is met, then—if the machine is functioning properly in a congenial environment—the consequent will ensue. I will call such a function-conditional in which the antecedent is met an *activated function*. So, for example, if the machine is in state q3 and a nickel is put in, then this function-conditional is activated: *If* the machine is in state q3 and receives a nickel as input, *then* it dispenses only a soda (no change) and returns to state q1. If the machine is functioning properly in a congenial environment, a soda will be dispensed and the machine will return to state q1.

The notion of an *activated function* will be crucial to understand our AHOF account of the sexes, so I'll give one more example. Suppose I have a universal remote control, communicating with both my television and an auxiliary component, for example, a sound system. This remote has the function of turning on the television, and this function is activated—triggered, realized—when (and only when) the remote is in the right internal state, in television mode, and the "Power" button is pressed. That is, the system has this function-conditional: If the remote is in the television mode state, and the television is off, and the "Power" button is pressed, then—if the system is functioning properly in a congenial environment—the television will turn on. When the conditions of the antecedent are met, the conditional is an *activated conditional*, as I'm calling it. Now, if the remote is in auxiliary mode and I push the "Power" button, it is no malfunction of the remote that the television doesn't turn on. I simply fail to activate that function of the remote, since it's in the wrong state. So, to repeat, for a function-conditional to be activated, the machine must be in the correct internal state and receive the correct input.

Now, how does this apply to biological organisms? Nelson's sequential machines are so abstract that they allow us to describe not just human creations like soda machines, but also biological systems and sub-systems. One can fairly clearly imagine a complete machine table for a relatively simple biological sub-system like a voltage-gated sodium channel,[17] or molecular motors like kinesin walking along a microtubule.[18] Given certain inputs—microtubule binding, depolarization of the nearby cell membrane potential, etc.—and when in certain states, these systems move to a different internal state (realized by a different configuration, for example, when the activation gate of a sodium channel opens, or when the motor domain of kinesin changes shape), and/or produce some output (e.g. ADP release, or sodium ions inside the cell).

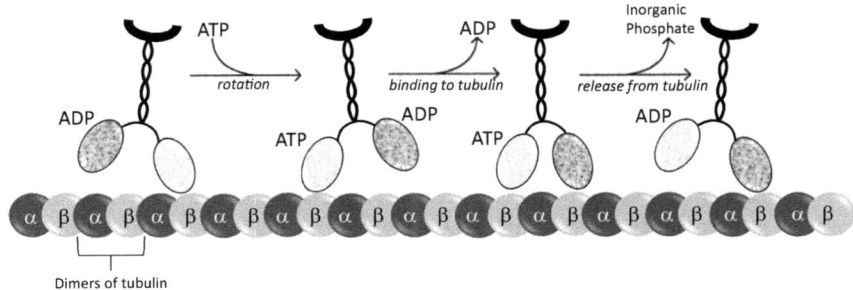

FIGURE 3.4   Movement of kinesin.

One can also see, through a glass darkly, the machine tables for things like organs, organ systems, whole organisms, and even bee hives or ant colonies. But the tools we use to describe sequential machines seem to apply in both cases: inputs, outputs, transition functions, output functions, internal states—and, most importantly, function-conditionals, and activated functions.

Next, a word about malfunction. In his seminal paper on functions, Robert Cummins (1975, 758) said that "to attribute a function to something is, in part, to attribute a disposition to it." This mousetrap has the function of capturing mice because it is disposed to, you might think, at least when it's set and ready to go. Surely there are connections between dispositions and functions, but Cummins' view rules out the possibility of malfunction. For there are cases in which something has a function, and yet it is *not* disposed to perform this function, due to some error in its *internal configuration*. Doubtless our soda machine has some internal mechanism that allows it to fulfill the function of dispensing sodas, a mechanism that actually presents the bottles of soda to the customer. Yet if that dispensing mechanism is stuck or broken, our soda machine will still have the function of dispensing a soda (in certain states, given certain inputs), while not at all being *disposed* to do so. The relevant function-conditional is still on the machine table. It can even become an activated function, if its antecedent is met. Yet the consequent will *not* ensue—no soda will be dispensed—due to this error of internal configuration.

There are also cases in which something has a function, but is not disposed to perform this function, due to a failure in the thing's *environment*. This is not properly called a malfunction. As Millikan (2013, 40) put it, "When a device does not perform some proper function only because the necessary background conditions are absent, we do not consider that to be a malfunction… Malfunction results only from abnormalities in the constitution of the device itself." If our soda machine is not disposed to dispense sodas because it's not plugged in to a power source, or because it's in a zero-gravity environment, then it is not performing its function, but this isn't a case of malfunction. It's rather a case of an *uncongenial environment*. The soda machine is missing some of the necessary, extrinsic background conditions required for it to realize its machine table. Malfunction is due to a failure of internal configuration, not merely an uncongenial environment. So, when a function-conditional is activated—when its antecedent is met—the consequent ensues, but only if the machine's internal configuration and environment cooperate. Only if, that is, there is proper function in a congenial environment.

Let's now understand a *higher-order* function. Instead of our simple soda machine, consider a factory that produces these soda machines as an output.

The factory floor would no doubt contain many workers operating machines for constructing and installing the various components of our soda machine, for example, its steel frame, its motherboard to run its machine table program, its coin-acceptor to receive inputs to return change, its motorized dispensing mechanism to deliver bottles of soda, and its refrigerated storage area. And we might represent the functions of this factory with a large, complicated machine table, with internal states (realized by component machines and workers) taking raw materials from the receiving department as well as stages of incomplete soda machines as input, and delivering more complete soda machines as output, until the final internal state, which would deliver a completed soda machine as an output (to the shipping department, say).

If the factory also produced in-house some of the *component* machines that it used to construct its final product—say, a sheet-metal machine to bend, cut, and punch the frame of the incipient soda machine—then the factory would have *the function of constructing a component that has a certain function*. (The factory would be, to a small degree, self-assembling.) I will call this a *higher-order* function, in this case, a *second-order* function. Interestingly, and importantly for our purposes, it seems right to say that one of the things *the factory* does is to bend, cut, and punch those frames— it does this *by* producing a *component* with this function. The factory also has the function of producing soda machines, which themselves have the function of dispensing bottles of soda. Yet it's inapt to describe the *factory* as having the function of dispensing sodas, even if we add that it does so by producing soda machines. And I believe this is the reason: the sheet-metal machine is a component of the factory, while the soda machine itself is merely a product of the factory. So, when a system has the function of producing a *component* with a function, that component's function can aptly be attributed to the system itself.

Probably, you see where I'm going with this. For our soda machine, the machine table was selected by a mind (or a group of minds), and then the machine was built (configured, programmed) so as to realize this machine table. There was a plan, in the minds of its fabricators, that was made manifest in the machine. And similarly with the machine table of the entire factory itself. So it goes with all the designs of men, and indeed with all functional artifacts.[19] But even with biological organisms, it is natural to speak, with Ernst Mayr, of an internal "program" (1985 [1974], 144), which he defines as "coded or prearranged information that controls a process (or behaviour) leading it toward a given end." These can be "closed programs," like DNA, or "open programs," that can be modified by "learning, conditioning, or through other experiences" (1985, 145). And Cummins (1975, 750) speaks of an organism's genetic "plan," which can "specify" certain components or sub-systems, very like the sequential machines we've been talking about.[20]

And just as we saw with the factory and the sheet-metal machine, when a self-assembling biological organism's internal machinery builds (configures, programs) a biological component (e.g. a liver), that component may have various functions; it may realize a machine table. Such a table will often be very complicated, and perhaps involve at best probabilistic conditionals, but the simple table we've discussed so far may still help us understand and speak about biological functions. For convenience, we can call the sheet-metal machine's machine table its *program*, and the machine table of the entire factory the *master program*. In a similar way, we can say that a biological component or sub-system (e.g. a liver) of an organism has a program, and the organism itself has a master program, a genetic plan which "[the organism] inherits and which, at a certain level of abstraction, is characteristic of [the organism's] species" (Cummins, 1975, 750).

But *which* functions are programmed? It's easy enough to know a thing's function in a case like the soda machine or a factory, where we simply stipulate the function or appeal to the intentions of the designer. This would answer any skeptic who wonders why the function of the factory is to produce soda machines, rather than to fill local landfills with cylindrical aluminum waste, say. It's more difficult in natural cases. Philosophers have had much to say about *which* machine table is programmed in a biological organism or component, if any—that is, what the function of a biological entity is, if it has one. To take a well-worn example from the literature, presumably it's the function of the heart to pump blood, but *not* to make its characteristic thump-*thump* sound—yet *why* is that? What is it that makes circulation of blood a function of the heart, but not its thumping sound?

Here, it's common for philosophers to cite the selection history of the system—as Rifkin and Garson (2023) do—or the benefit that the operation of this entity conferred on the larger system.[21] The literature is circuitous, vast, and ever-expanding. Fortunately for us, we can sidestep this sprawling labyrinth and note merely that, since there are functions in biology, there must be *some* fact about what functions are, some explanation of why pumping blood is a function of the heart but thump-*thump*ing isn't. And just as an epistemologist might propose a theory of knowledge that appeals to causation, without knowing the real definition of causation itself, or as a physicist might propose a theory that appeals to time, without also having at his fingertips a theory about the nature of time, so too might we propose a theory of the sexes of organisms that appeals to biological functions, without being able to articulate the nature—the real definition—of biological functions, whatever it is.[22] So long as causation, or time, or biological functions are real, then the epistemologist, or the physicist, or we ourselves are on firm footing. And it's hard to deny that such things are real.

One final bit of this preamble. I am about to propose a definition of the sexes, according to which organisms have (higher-order) functions. In this way, I depart from Rifkin and Garson, who focus on the functions of *parts or processes* of organisms. Some may be concerned that, while its component *sub*-systems might have functions, an individual organism cannot *itself* have a function the way that a factory can, precisely because, as Peter Godfrey-Smith (1994, 349) put it, the bearers of functions need to "reside within a larger biologically real system." And one might wonder what larger biological whole an individual organism might be part of. However, Godfrey-Smith notes that populations are arguably examples of these larger, biologically real systems.[23] If so, then an organism can indeed have biological functions, and plausibly second-order functions, just like our soda machine factory. And wouldn't it make perfect sense to appeal to the selection history of a *population*, or benefits conferred upon a *population*, when explaining why some members of that population are male and others are female? Sexual reproduction confers an important benefit on the population, after all—namely, propagation with genetic variation, in a changeable environment.

Let's sum up. Evidently, there are *functions* in nature. Herculean efforts have been made to naturalize function-talk in biology, but we will stay neutral on the nature of biological functions. Machine tables can help us speak about these functions, and they illuminate the notion of *function-conditionals* and of an *activated function*. Biological organisms have components with functions, encoded in programs, and entire organisms have genetic plans, master programs specifying the structure and organization of component systems: these are *higher-order functions*. Take an embryonic human, who comes packaged with a genetic plan, a function of which is to develop, organize, and maintain component organs like the liver, the lungs, and the heart. When a master program specifies the development and maintenance of a functional sub-system, and that sub-system has been developed and maintained, the functions of that sub-system can aptly be attributed to the entire organism itself as a higher-order function: the *human* breathes, the *human* produces bile, the *human* circulates blood, in virtue of having the function of developing and maintaining components with the functions in question. Malfunction results when the actual dispositions of a system diverge from the functions specified by the program, by the machine table, and this due to the internal (mis)configuration of the system, rather than an uncongenial environment. Let's now apply these lessons to the sexes.

Supporting the Activated Higher-Order Function (AHOF) Account

Put simply, a male is an organism with the function of producing sperm, and a female is an organism with the function of producing eggs. Put more carefully, the sexes are particular kinds of functions—activated higher-order functions—of entire organisms, coded in master programs specifying the development, organization, and maintenance of components themselves programmed to produce (and transport, etc.) some type of anisogamous gamete, for example, sperm or ova.[24] In the case of sperm, examples of such components include testes, stamen in flowering plants,[25] and antheridia in non-flowering plants. For ova, examples include ovaries, ovules (in flowering plants), and archegonia. In this way, sexed bodies are very much like the self-assembling soda-machine factories discussed above, operating according to a master program, which specifies the development, organization, and maintenance of components with various functions. And, just as with the soda-machine factory, second-order function ascriptions collapse: if an organism has the activated function of developing and maintaining a *component* with the function of producing sperm, then it is apt to say that the *organism* has the function of producing sperm. This is why we can say, more simply, that a male is an organism with the function of producing sperm, and a female is an organism with the function of producing ova. It seems to me that biologists further abbreviate this function-talk with present-tense locutions like *males produce sperm*, and *females produce eggs* (e.g. Lehtonen and Parker 2014, 1161–2).

In my view, our sex terms—at least, as used in gerund phrases like 'being male', and 'being female', and speaking of ways organisms can be—name types of activated higher-order functions. In this way, our sex terms are similar to 'vertebrate'. Biologists are happy to use 'vertebrate' to describe embryos, well prior to the development of the spinal cord.[26] The natural interpretation of this, it seems to me, is that 'being a vertebrate' picks out the property of having a certain activated higher-order function: the function of developing and maintaining a component (a spine) that has a certain function. *Mutatis mutandis* with biological sex.

To support this synthesized Gamete View of the sexes, we'll take it through a gauntlet of challenging cases and potential objections:

- *Drosophila bifurca*
- Isogamy
- Embryos and juveniles
- Disease, injury, and malfunction
- Environmental sex-determination
- Simultaneous hermaphrodites
- Sequential hermaphrodites
- Intersex conditions
- Postmenopausal females

Showing that this AHOF definition of the sexes accommodates the various ways biologists use sex terms is strong evidence that biologists are indeed referring to these activated higher-order functions with their uses of 'male' and 'female', and therefore that the AHOF account is correct.[27,28]

Let's start with fruit flies, and one species in particular: *Drosophila bifurca*. According to Roughgarden (2004, 25), the males of this species produce sperm that is 20 times as long as each male himself. Watkins and DiMarco (2025, 4) offer this as an objection to gamete-based views of the sexes:

> the gametic definition is susceptible to counterexamples. For example, it is not guaranteed that all gametes with sperm-like morphology are necessarily smaller than all gametes with egg-like morphology; *Drosophila bifurca*, for instance, have gametes otherwise homologous to sperm but which range up to 5.8 cm in length.

To frame this as a challenge to the AHOF account of the sexes, one might reason as follows: The AHOF account says that something is a male if and only if it has the function of producing sperm, which is to say, *small gametes*. But male *Drosophila bifurca* do not have the function of producing small gametes. They produce quite enormous gametes, relative to those produced by the females of that (and other) species, and yet are male all the same. So, this is a counterexample to the AHOF account of the sexes. So ends the objection.

In response, the AHOF account does not take a stand on the nature of sperm or of eggs. Specifically, the AHOF account does not say that to be male is to produce *small* gametes, and to be female is to produce *large* gametes. While many friends of gamete-based views of the sexes that I've quoted *do* put it that way, I ask the reader to notice my diligence with respect to stating the AHOF account only in terms of anisogamous gamete-types like sperm and eggs, and not in terms of small or large gametes. Evidently, all that's required for anisogamy is that gamete-types are *dissimilar* in the right way, either in size, or form, or function, or... It is a further philosophical puzzle what exactly distinguishes sperm from eggs (cf. Gorelick et al. 2017, Roughgarden 2004, 412 n. 6, and Lachance et al. 2024). But insofar as sperm and eggs *exist*, which I daresay they do, each must have some nature: there must be something it is to be a sperm, and something it is to be an egg. And insofar as sperm and eggs are *distinct*, which I again daresay they are, something must distinguish them. We may stay neutral on what exactly that is, and leave that question for future research projects. (Though perhaps Lachance et al. [2024] are correct to reject motility- and size-differences, and settle instead on this: "We see the direction of movement of nuclei as a clear and widely applicable means of identifying male and female sexes." The male's gamete is "that which donates its nucleus" in fertilization.

The female's is that which receives a nucleus.) In the meantime, my first response to this objection is simply this: to say that males have the function of producing sperm is *not* to say that they have the function of producing small gametes. Apparently, the gametes produced by this species of fruit fly are dissimilar in such a way as to earn the names 'sperm' and 'eggs' from biologists, despite the size of the sperm. So long as those male fruit flies have the function of producing *sperm*, which evidently they do, this is not a counterexample to the AHOF account.

But even if we thought that, for each species, sperm are necessarily smaller than eggs, *Drosophila bifurca* do not present us with a clear counterexample. And that's because, while these male fruit flies produce sperm of astonishing *length*, these sperm are still not as *massive* as the eggs produced by their females. As Franklin-Hall (2021, 190) put it, "since even the *Drosophila's* giant sperm remain smaller than eggs by mass–arguably the size comparison that matters most–this observation is hardly definitive." Yes, just so. She goes on to wonder (Franklin-Hall 2021, 191) what one should say about a "counterfactual scenario in which sperm evolved to be more massive than eggs." Perhaps one thing to say is that relative size is not the only consideration when distinguishing sperm from eggs, but also, as Watkins and DiMarco themselves recognize (2025, 3 fn. 4), motility and relative quantity. Due to their enormous tails, these fruit fly sperm score high on motility, at least, which is perhaps partly why biologists consider them to be sperm. Again, stating the exact natures of sperm and eggs will wait for another day; it's sufficient for our purposes to note only that these male fruit flies have the function of producing sperm, and are therefore not counterexamples to the AHOF account of the sexes.

Let's turn to the second challenge. Some organisms reproduce sexually, but isogamously, that is, via gametes that are morphologically virtually identical. And some biologists claim that such organisms also feature sexes. For example, Yoh Iwasa and Akira Sasaki (1987, 49) say:

> [A]mong ciliates in which mating occurs by the contact of two diploid cells and the subsequent exchange of haploid genomes, cells are grouped into several mating types (or sexes) so that mating occurs only between cells of different sexes (Sonneborn, 1939; Preer, 1969). *Stylonychia spp.* have as many as 48 sexes (*Ammermann, 1965; Nanney, 1980*).

According to the AHOF account of the sexes, the sexes are activated higher-order functions specifying the development, organization, and maintenance of components themselves programmed to produce (and transport, etc.) some type of *anisogamous* gamete. There are two such gametes—sperm and ova—and so there are two sexes, according to the AHOF account. But if there are sexes that produce *isogamous* gamete-types, then the AHOF account would require some light revision to allow for more than two sexes—'anisogamous' would have to be deleted from the definition. And given my insistence that biologists have a special authority vis-à-vis our inquiry into the nature of the sexes, it's especially awkward that some *biologists* seem to say there are many sexes in isogamous organisms.

In response, I admit it's possible that, when confronted with isogamous sexually reproducing organisms, biologists *could* have decided to track the more general functions to produce *any* gamete-type with the use of 'sex', and as a result, truly say there are many sexes. That's what Iwasa and Sasaki seem to be *trying* to do with their use of 'sex', and this pressures us to interpret their use of 'sex' as referring to those more general functions.[29] However, at the same time, they seem to intend to join and defer to the common linguistic practice of using 'sex', which pressures us to interpret their use of 'sex' as referring to whatever biologists on the whole use that word to refer to. And, as a matter of fact, it seems that biologists went in a different direction, reserving 'sex' for the functions we've described, to produce *anisogamous* gamete-types. For consider that while Iwasa and Sasaki try to support their claim that there are many sexes, they fail rather badly. They say there are sexes in ciliates, and they cite T.M. Sonneborn (1939) and John Preer (1969). But Sonneborn (1939, 390) says that individuals in the species he studied could produce asexually, producing "caryonides," and here's the crucial bit: "Two caryonides that...conjugate when brought together are said to be of diverse *mating types*." Only mating types are mentioned, *not* sexes. And Preer (1969) speaks almost exclusively of mating types throughout this lengthy work on protozoa, though there is one mention of two strains of the species *Eudorina*, consisting of two types, "each producing either ova or sperm" (Preer 1969, 137). These he calls sexes. But, if there are sperm and ova involved, this is no threat to the AHOF account of the sexes.

Iwasa and Sasaki also claim that species in the genus *Stylonychia*. have as many as 48 sexes, and they cite Dieter Ammermann (1965) and David Nanney (1980). But while "Paarungstyp" (mating type) appears multiple times in the German-language Ammermann article, "Geschlecht(s)" (sex[es]) appears not at all. And Ammermann (1982) seems to be well aware of the distinction between sexes and mating types, in his later article explicitly about mating types in *Stylonychia mytilus*. Most shockingly, Nanney (1980, 49) says this: "The term mating type [sic] is preferable to *sexes*, because sexes

[sic] suggests a differentiation of gametic function that is inapplicable in conjugation." Lachance et al. (2024, 1) diagnose the situation this way:

> the supposition that some fungi feature thousands of sexes…, that a cellular slime mould has three sexes…, or that *Tetrahymena thermophila* is a seven-sex species…, is in every case a patent misuse of 'sexes' as a synonym of mating types, perhaps motivated by the wish to enhance the allure of journal article titles.

So, it seems as though biologists have decided *not* to use 'sex' to refer to the more general function of producing any gamete-type—isogamous *or* anisogamous—but instead to refer to the more specific function described by the AHOF account of the sexes. And therefore, motivated by a desire to maximize relevance rather than truth in our interpretation, we ought to read Iwasa and Sasaki (and others like them) *not* as using the term 'sex' ambiguously, with some novel referent, but rather as using it with the ordinary referent, and saying something false about the sexes—namely, that there are more than two.

One more wrinkle about isogamy. *Spirogyra* is a genus of green algae, commonly known as water silk. These algae can reproduce sexually. One such method involves the formation of canals—"conjugation tubes"—connecting individual cells of each filament of green algae, forming a ladder-like structure. Once neighboring cells are connected via conjugation tubes, they form a structure that looks like the capital letter 'H'. The additional Hs stacked above and below them are what create the ladder-like appearance of this structure, with the conjugation tubes forming the rungs of the ladder. Once connected via conjugation tubes, the contents of each cell condense, and the condensed contents are considered to be gametes. Sometimes, the condensed contents of the cell both migrate, meeting in the middle of the conjugation canal. But it can also happen that one cell plays an active role in migrating its contents—including its nucleus—to the other cell across this canal. In that case, this other cell plays the passive role of a recipient. When this happens, the donor cell is commonly called "male," and the recipient cell is commonly called "female," and the result is a diploid zygote—*voilà*, fertilization. Lachance (2024, 2) says these are "clear cases of male-female polarity in isogamous organisms." If this were so, then it may seem as though the AHOF account of the sexes would need to be revised, specifically its requirement that the relevant gamete-types be *anisogamous*.

However, two things should be said in defense of the AHOF account as written. First, it may be that 'male' and 'female' are being used metaphorically to describe *Spirogyra* cells. When one cell donates its protoplasm to another cell, it is *as if* it were male. It is *reminiscent* of a male's role in copulation. But, one might think, the cell is not *literally* male. In this way, to call these cells male is like calling a pipe fitting male: either literally false but pragmatically conveying the truth that these cells are *like* males, or a case of genuine polysemy, like 'mouse' and 'mouse'. Either way, it's not a threat to the AHOF account as written. Second, though there is isogamy with respect to the *morphology* of these cells and their condensed contents, there is *physiological anisogamy*. Speaking of a similar reproductive strategy in diatoms, Lothar Geitler (1935, 154) says this:

> The gametes are entirely alike in both sexes or only slightly differentiated. In many species, however, they are distinctly different physiologically, since one gamete, the male, is motile and moves toward the other which is non-motile and female. There thus prevails a physiological anisogamy similar to that known in *Spirogyra*.

In other words, there is some flexibility in the terms 'isogamy' and 'anisogamy'; like most biological concepts, there is fuzziness at the boundaries. During the reproductive process described above, there is a relevant difference between the two gametes: one migrates, the other doesn't. This plausibly explains biologists' inclination to describe one cell as male and the other as female. Recall from above that all that's required for anisogamy is that gamete-types are *dissimilar* in the right way, either in size, or form, or function, or... If this physiological difference is enough to count as anisogamy, then the AHOF account of the sexes need not be revised. If this difference is *not* enough to count as anisogamy, then the AHOF account of sex would have to be revised, substituting for 'anisogamous' a good general expression for sperm and ova, and similarly for the AHOF definitions of 'male' and 'female'. Perhaps 'donor or recipient gametes' would capture the real distinction between sexed gametes, which, recall, Lachance et al. (2024, 2) say is the "direction of movement of nuclei."

Next, embryos and juveniles may seem to lack any *first-order* function of producing gametes, well prior to sexual maturity, as we saw above when considering Griffith's view. Yet such organisms can have sexes, according to our AHOF definition, so long as their genetic plan specifies the development and organization of components, of sub-systems, that produce either ova or sperm, and this function is activated: the organism is in the right state, according to its machine table, and has received all the required inputs in order to eventuate the development and maintenance of gonads, provided there's proper function in a congenial environment. And this is precisely the case, for species in which sex is genetically determined. Our factory above is rightly called a soda machine factory, and a factory that bends, cuts, and punches steel, even while it's being set up, while the various components are developed and organized (e.g. a sheet-metal machine), in virtue of the activated master program of that factory. In a similar way, an embryo is rightly called a male or a female, even while it's self-assembling, in virtue of the activated genetic master program of that organism.[30] And similarly with juveniles, prior to the production of gametes.

Speaking of embryos, some readers and auditors have raised concerns over the fact that, as we noted above with respect to the Developmental Pathway view, the male and female reproductive pathways in humans are said to overlap during very early development. At that time, in virtue of having an X chromosome, a human male embryo has all the genes that a human female embryo has, and even components that would, in a female, develop into ovaries. As MacLaughlin et al. (2001) put it, each human embryo develops an intermediate mesoderm, which becomes the urogenital ridge. Eventually, the urogenital ridge develops indifferent (bipotential) gonads in both male and female embryos. These indifferent gonads eventually differentiate, either into testes (in males) or ovaries (in females). Does it follow, then, on the AHOF account, that human males have the function of producing components (the indifferent gonads) that have the function of producing ovaries, and that therefore producing ovaries is part of the master program of a male embryo, making him female as well? That would be a bad result for the AHOF view. But evidently it's not the case. Despite having the genetic information required to produce ovaries, the human male embryo's SRY gene on his Y chromosome makes it the case that his master program includes the transformation of the indifferent gonads into testes, foreclosing the possibility of ovaries. So, while male embryos may have the function of producing components (indifferent gonads) that have the (unactivated) function of developing into ovaries, they do not have the function of developing any components with the function of producing ova. So, the presence of indifferent gonads in male embryos does not entail that these embryos are (also) female, on our AHOF account.

Disease, injury, and malfunction are no obstacle to our AHOF account of the sexes.[31] Our simple soda machine above is programmed to dispense bottles of soda (in certain states, given certain inputs). That is one of its functions, as displayed by its machine table. And this function may be activated—its antecedent may be met—even if the machine is not at all disposed to dispense bottles of soda, due to damage to its internal configuration, or to an uncongenial environment. For example, if we damaged or removed the mechanism by which it delivered bottles of soda to the user, or if we unplugged it, or if we pushed it to the bottom of the La Brea Tar Pits. And a soda machine factory is programmed to produce soda machines—that is one of its functions—even if we damage or remove some component or sub-system required for the production of these soda machines. For example, if we damaged or removed the sheet-metal machine responsible for producing the steel frames of the soda machines. In just the same way, an organism may have the higher-order function of developing and maintaining a component with the function of producing sperm and therefore be a male, and that function may be activated, even if we damage or remove some component or sub-system required for the production of sperm. For example, by orchiectomy, that is, the removal of the testes. And the same goes for the effects of disease or other varieties of malfunction.

Environmental sex-determination was described above, with the example of crocodiles, whose sex depends on the temperature at which the egg is incubated. One might worry that every crocodile has *both* the function of producing testes *and* also the function of producing ovaries, and is therefore both male and female at the same time. That would be a bad result. However, the crocodile's genetic plan merely *allows* for the development of either testes or ovaries; both of those functions are on every crocodile's machine table. But an environmental input is required in order to *activate* one of these functions, to satisfy the antecedent of the function-conditional. Recall my universal remote control, which turns on either the television or my auxiliary sound system, depending on which mode or state I put it in before pressing the "Power" button, that is, which function I activate. Similarly, the crocodile becomes a male or a female depending on which higher-order function is activated by its environment. So, only after that activation does the crocodile have a sex. Prior to having one of those higher-order functions activated via incubation temperature, each embryonic crocodile is neither male nor female. But that seems like the right result.

Simultaneous hermaphrodites can be explained briefly: some organisms are both male and female. One can find examples of biologists saying otherwise,[32] but the preponderance of evidence suggests this is a mistake and points in the direction of biologists using 'male' and 'female' in such a way that simultaneous hermaphrodites count as both.[33] And the AHOF definition presented here accounts for this usage. A male is an organism with the activated function of producing a component with the function of producing sperm, and similarly with females and ova. Clearly, it is possible for an organism to satisfy both of these definitions, to have both higher-order functions activated, and thereby be both male and female. It would be akin to a universal remote control with *two* power buttons, one for the television and one for the streaming device, and if both buttons were pressed simultaneously: Presto, two functions activated simultaneously. (The same can be said of bilateral gynandromorphism in butterflies, in which an insect has one male half and one female half.)

Sequential hermaphrodites can also be accounted for by our AHOF definition of the sexes. Return again to our universal remote control, with two modes or states: television mode and auxiliary mode. The "Power" button features in two function-conditionals of this remote control, depending on what mode (i.e. internal state) the remote control is in. Yet the functions cannot be activated simultaneously, but only sequentially, by toggling the mode or state of the remote control. When in television mode, pressing the "Power" button activates the function resulting in turning on the television. When in auxiliary mode, pressing that same button activates the function resulting in turning on the sound system. These functions cannot be activated simultaneously, but only sequentially.

Sequential hermaphroditism involves a similar sort of toggling. Unlike crocodiles, sequential hermaphrodites begin life with one activated higher-order function to produce anisogamous gametes, either sperm or eggs, determined genetically. But then, upon receiving a certain input from the environment, that higher-order function is deactivated, and the other is activated.[34] Most commonly, this involves the degeneration of the original gonadal tissue and the replacement or repurposing of that tissue with a functional gonad of the other sex. With serial bidirectional sequential hermaphrodites, as we saw above, the bisexual gonad (ovotestis) is permanent, but one tissue matures into a functional gonad and actively produces gametes, while the other is dormant, "unable to produce gametes," and "inactive," as Casas and Saborido-Rey put it (2021, 113). The proto-gonad does not have the function of producing gametes; it is no malfunction that it fails to do so.

Sex change in serial bidirectional sequential hermaphrodites consists in a shift of which proto-gonadal tissue is elevated to maturity, that is, to a functional gonad. A bidirectional sequential hermaphrodite changing from male to female goes from a condition with an activated function of developing and maintaining a component with the function of producing sperm—as evidenced by its functional male gonad and proto-ovarian gonadal tissue that lacks the function of producing ova—to a condition with an activated function of developing and maintaining a component with the function of producing ova, a condition in which a functional female gonad is formed, and the male gonad is demoted to dormant proto-gonadal tissue, tissue which lacks the function of producing sperm. In both types of sequential hermaphroditism, then, which higher-order function is activated can change, thereby changing the sex of the organism from male to female, or vice versa, according to our AHOF definition of the sexes. And this again accords with how biologists describe the phenomenon.

Next are intersex conditions, also known as differences or disorders of sexual development (DSDs). Some humans are born with XY chromosomes, for example, but have a genetic condition that causes them to be completely insensitive to masculinizing hormones—Complete Androgen Insensitivity Syndrome. These individuals develop bodies that are incompletely masculinized. They have internal testes and no ovaries, yet from the outside appear to be female, with genitals and secondary-sex characteristics that appear like those of a female. There are many other DSDs as well, many precluding the production of gametes, and some involving people with both ovarian and testicular tissue, though of questionable functionality.[35] Do cases like these pose problems for our higher-order function definition of the sexes, based as that definition is on anisogamy? Some think so. For example, Hane Maung (2023, 45) says, "the essentialist model based on anisogamy assumes a discrete binary classification based on relative gamete size, and so fails to account for people who do not produce gametes and people with both ovaries and testes."[36]

We've already considered cases in which people don't produce any gametes, above. And we have the conceptual resources available to understand that *any* intersex case poses no problem for the AHOF definition of the sexes, provided we also point out that it's compatible with that definition of the sexes that an organism have no sex at all. Some organisms are not anisogametic, after all, and therefore have neither activated higher-order function required to be either male or female. They are sexless. So, it is *compatible* with the AHOF definitions of the sexes that a human be neither male nor female. Of course, I hasten to add, I'm not saying that any human has ever been neither male nor female; I mean to point out only that it's a *logical possibility*, given the AHOF definitions. And we have already seen that our definitions of the sexes are *compatible* with an organism's being both male and female. So, *if*—and this is a big 'if'—*if* there were a human that had both the activated function of developing and maintaining components with the function of producing sperm, and also the activated function of developing and maintaining components with the function of producing ova, such a human would be both male and female.[37] This is not to say that any of the alleged cases of true simultaneous hermaphroditism in humans are genuine cases of an individual who is both male and also female. It is to say only that *if* such cases are genuine, they are not counterexamples to the AHOF definitions of the sexes, because such cases are possible, according to that definition. And, needless to say, an organism may be only male, or only female.

Now, in some cases, it may be *difficult to discern* whether an organism is only male, only female, both, or neither. Just as it may be hard to discern, of some newly discovered species, whether it is carnivorous or herbivorous, nocturnal or diurnal, or benthic or pelagic, a chordate or a nonchordate, a prokaryote or a eukaryote, etc. Simone de Beauvoir ([1949]

1956, 52) may overstate things when she says, "In nature, nothing is ever perfectly clear." But she's correct in spirit: nature is messy. But this much is clear: the only potential counterexamples to our AHOF definition of the sexes in the neighborhood here would be a DSD in which the individual clearly has the AHOF of producing some gamete-type, and yet clearly does not have the corresponding sex, or a DSD in which the individual clearly has a sex, and yet does not have the AHOF of producing the corresponding gamete-type. And there do not seem to be any such cases. Certainly not Complete Androgen Insensitivity Syndrome, to take one example. Such individuals do *superficially appear* to be female, but of course, some things look to be ways other than they actually are. Similarly, with cases of Swyer Syndrome, in which XY individuals have a Y chromosome that's either missing the SRY gene completely, or has a non-functional version of the gene. Such individuals superficially appear to be female, due to the reproductive development process halting when the SRY gene would usually initiate masculinization. But such individuals do not have ovaries or ova, but rather exhibit gonadal dysgenesis—they have non-functional "streak gonads." Given the presence of the Y chromosome and what it evolved to do, it's plausible to say that such individuals have the activated higher-order function of producing testes, but fail to do so due to this DSD. In that case, such individuals are male, according to the AHOF account. No doubt such individuals *appear* to be female, superficially, but again, superficially resembling a female does not guarantee that one actually is female. And none of this should be read as a prescription of public policy.

Let's take a brief tangent to consider this question: Is sex binary, according to our AHOF definition of the sexes? After all, there are four possible states of an organism with regard to sex—only male, only female, both, or neither—which may suggest that sex is not binary. It certainly means that there are more than two of *those* states, those *combinations* of the sexes. But consider binary computer code, which allows for very many combinations of its bits, and yet is called binary in virtue of the fact that there are only two values for each bit—0 or 1. DNA is called a quaternary code in virtue of its four bases—A, T, C, and G (e.g. Zhang et al. 2019, 2)—despite the fact that, of course, DNA consists of an enormous combination of base pairs. In a similar way, if there are exactly two sexes, it seems apt to describe the system of sexual reproduction as a binary system (e.g. see Fusco and Minelli 2019, 112), even if there are four ways of combining these two sexes.

Menopause is the last challenging case that we'll consider. Postmenopausal women are commonly called females by biologists, as a quick search on PubMed for 'postmenopausal female' reveals. And our AHOF account agrees, since these females also have the activated higher-order function of developing and maintaining a component with the function of producing ova. Indeed, menopause does not remove or degenerate the *ovaries* themselves. Rather, as Edwards and Li (2013, 178) put it, in the years leading up to menopause, "ovarian follicles undergo an accelerated rate of loss until eventually the supply of follicles is depleted." (Ovarian follicles are small, fluid-filled sacs inside the ovary. Each follicle has the potential to release a mature ovum.) Ideally, ovarian follicles secrete inhibin, which "exerts an important negative-feedback influence over follicle-stimulating hormone secretion by the pituitary gland" (Edwards and Li, 2013). But as the follicles become fewer, less inhibin is secreted, and more follicle-stimulating hormone is secreted by the pituitary gland, until eventually no follicles remain and menses ceases.

Now, two things may be going on here with menopause. First, menopause may be an adaptation (Takahashi et al. 2017, 4; Sear 2024). If so, then what's happening with a woman's ovaries during menopause is akin to what happens to a worker bee's ovaries in the presence of a queen bee's pheromones: programmed deactivation.[38] It would be as though, in our factory with the function of producing a sheet-metal machine with the function of bending metal, before leaving for vacation, we turned off the machine to save electricity, thereby deactivating the machine's function. Still, *the factory* would have that activated higher-order function of developing and maintaining a component—a sheet-metal machine—with the function of bending metal, even if *the sheet-metal machine's* function is deactivated. Similarly, if it is adaptive for the ovaries' function to be deactivated later in life, it is still true to say of a menopausal woman that *she* has the activated higher-order function of developing and maintaining a component—ovaries—with the function of producing eggs, even if the *ovaries'* function is deactivated. And, so, she's as female as ever, on the AHOF account of the sexes.[39]

Alternatively, menopause is the result of natural degeneration that accompanies aging, just as men's sperm quality diminishes with age. Though it is *statistically normal*, it is nevertheless a case of malfunction of the ovaries, just as human vision *typically* degenerates as we age, and yet still counts as a malfunction of the eyes. Here, menopause would be akin to our factory's sheet-metal machine wearing down over time until it can no longer realize its (activated) function. If this is the right way to describe menopause, then menopause may receive the same diagnosis as cases of malfunction described above: even if the *ovaries* are malfunctioning (due to age), it is still true to say of a menopausal woman that *she* has the activated higher-order function of developing and maintaining a component—ovaries—with the function of producing eggs. On this alternative, though the ovaries' function of producing eggs is activated, the output (eggs) does not ensue, due to malfunction. And yet, again, the woman retains the relevant AHOF, and therefore she is as female as ever, on the AHOF account of the sexes. Behold how the AHOF account again neatly handles a prima facie troubling case. Its ability to do so is evidence in its favor.

One final question, before we move to the next chapter. Could medical intervention—hormone administration, surgery, and the like—change an individual's sex, on the AHOF account of the sexes? Through human intervention and intention, could someone go from having the function of producing sperm to the function of producing eggs, or vice versa? Well, it's evident that human intervention and intention are sufficient to imbue *artifacts* with functions. We make tools, and these have functions. Hammers drive nails, toasters cook bread, and so on. And we can do this with biological entities, with artificial, synthetic, biological machines. Researchers have already created synthetic bacterial cells, and synthetic eukaryotic cells are in the works (cf. Venter et al., 2022). Biologists have also made great strides toward commandeering the machinery of natural cells and organisms in order to produce a variety of useful materials. For example, *Escherichia coli* bacteria have been transformed to produce amyloid proteins, which can be spun into a synthetic spider silk (cf. Li et al. 2021). We can reprogram a natural organism and harness its productive powers for our own ends. (What could go wrong?)

Now, in the event that we do this—if we transform some *E. coli* to fabricate spider-silk precursors—what is the function of those *E. coli*? If the transformation doesn't take and the *E. coli* fail to produce spider-silk precursors, but instead function as they would in the wild, in nature, are the *E. coli* malfunctioning? I'm sure the *researchers* would consider this a malfunction, a failure. But, of course, the *E. coli* are doing what they naturally do, realizing the functions of their genetic master program. So, is this a case of proper function or a case of malfunction? That's the puzzle. And it's a difficult one. But a few things are clear. First, merely *wishing* or even *intending* that the *E. coli* produce spider-silk precursors would not be enough on the part of the researchers to make it the case that the *E. coli* have the function of doing so, nor that they malfunction when not doing so.[40] And things aren't better if we suppose that the researchers take measures such as gently sloshing the bacteria about, while softly singing the 1967 Spiderman theme song. If Jingyao Li and his cohorts successfully bestowed the function of producing spider-silk precursors on their *E. coli*, it's because they did much more than wishing or softly singing (see Li et al. 2021). Evidently, then, in order for humans to give some biological entity a function, mere intention is not enough. What seems to be required is that humans undertake some strategy with a *sufficiently high objective probability of success*. To get a biological entity to have some function, humans must implement some strategy that has a sufficiently high objective probability of getting the entity to fulfill that function. Only then would we be at all tempted to say that, for example, the *E. coli* have the function of producing spider-silk precursors.

If we take a sober look at current medical technology, I think we have to admit that the medical interventions currently available to us to try to change a person's sex have virtually no hope of actually succeeding in that. To change a person's sex on the AHOF account of the sexes—to make a male into a female, say—we would have to bring it about that the person has a new (activated) function to produce a component with the function of producing ova. We would have to, that is, implement some strategy that has a sufficiently high objective probability of activating within that male person the function of producing ovaries; for this, it would not be enough for a male body merely to tolerate or even maintain *transplanted* ovaries. We would have to manipulate the male person's biology in such a way that, probably, this person's body would activate that function and, so, absent any malfunction or failure of the environment, come to include ovaries. And, for better or worse, that simply is not presently the case. While we've proven quite adept at manipulating people's hormone levels, and at producing simulated genitalia via plastic surgery, we are nowhere near any intervention that would—absent malfunction or failure of the environment—probably result in functional ovaries (for males who wish to be females) or testes (for females who wish to be males). Perhaps such a thing would be technologically feasible in the future. But, as things stand, it is not feasible now, with our current technology.[41]

Notes

1 Aatsha et al. 2023: "the absence of an active SRY gene in a chromosomal male will not result in ovarian differentiation but in variable gonadal dysgenesis."

2 Some readers may wonder whether Franklin-Hall means to endorse a *disjunctive* definition of the sexes. In the case of being male, something like this: An organism is male if and only if EITHER it has undergone a reproductive developmental process that is a variant of that at work in its earliest small-gamete-producing ancestor, OR it produces small gametes. The third problem I discuss below, having to do with sequential hermaphrodites, is a counterexample to this proposal. Also, this proposed disjunctive property is less natural than a rival that features only the second disjunct, which is evidence against the claim that biologists have been tracking it with their thought and language about the sexes, instead of tracking its simple gamete-based rival.

It's also unclear how this proposal enjoys the theoretical advantages that Franklin-Hall claims her proposal has over a simple gamete-based account. One alleged advantage is that her proposal "makes immediate sense of *diversity* in the current characteristics of kind- members–in this case, in male and female traits across the animal kingdom" (Franklin-Hall 2021, 189). The idea seems to be that because her view *entails* that contemporary males and females have an ancestry, it therefore "makes…sense of" or predicts "kind-members with radically different characteristics" (Franklin-Hall 2021) better than a simple gamete-based view, which doesn't entail that contemporary males and females have any ancestry at all. Because, I suppose, a significant ancestry is required to generate all that diversity. But, unfortunately, her view is merely a biconditional, a definition, and does *not* entail that there are males or females at all, let alone that they have a long ancestry that might allow for the evolution of a splendid diversity in their current characteristics. To issue that prediction, the view presumably tacks on some assumptions, namely that males and females *exist*, that their ancestry is quite *long*, and that there's been descent with modification, natural selection, etc. A simple gamete-based view can tack these on as well, in addition to the assumption that contemporary males and females *have an ancestry*. So, one must really squint to see any theoretical advantage for Franklin-Hall's view here, and any such advantage does not seem to outweigh the cost of proposing an unnatural, disjunctive definition as the referent of biologists' thought and language about the sexes. The same can be said with another alleged explanatory advantage she proposes (Franklin-Hall 2021), namely that her view explains "coarse-grained trends in sex differences–and in male and female traits–across the animal kingdom." She proposes to explain this via three theoretical add-ons to her definition, which the simple gamete-based view can readily accept in addition to the proposition that modern males and females have an ancestry. So, again, it's hard to see any theoretical advantage here.

She also says (Franklin-Hall 2021) that her proposal exhibits "openness to intra-species diversity in male traits, and in female traits," and gives the example of an individual who "might not produce sex-typical gametes." Her idea seems to be that, on her view, such an organism may be male or female (in virtue of its ancestry), yet will not be male or female at all on the rival simple gamete-based view. But on the contrary, as we'll see below, a function-based account of the sexes can accommodate the fact that not every male actively produces sperm (e.g. eunuchs, juvenile males, etc.). So, there is nothing to recommend Franklin-Hall's view over a simpler gamete-based rival here.

3   True, Franklin-Hall doesn't mean to be engaged in *conceptual analysis*. So, we can't dismiss her proposal solely on the grounds that *we cannot see that it's true* from the armchair. After all, water is H_2O, and gold is atomic number 79, even though we couldn't discern these truths from the armchair. Empirical investigation was needed. But there are limits to what science might discover about the natures of things; eschewing conceptual analysis does not immunize one against any counterintuitive consequence of one's view. If a chemist reported back to us that water is the number nine, I'd say we can rule this out from the armchair. In other words, the fact that *we cannot see from the armchair* that some phenomenon has some particular nature does not guarantee that it doesn't; some scientific discoveries are illuminating and surprising. Yet it might turn out that *we can see from the armchair* that some phenomenon *cannot* have some particular nature. And this is what I'm proposing is going on here with Franklin-Hall's proposal. We can see from the armchair that the sexes are not historical kinds. They do not depend on an organism's ancestry.

4   Watkins and DiMarco (2025, 5) present an objection to Franklin-Hall that is similar in spirit to this objection, namely that "Franklin-Hall's historical explanatory kinds account rules out analytically the possibility of a lineage evolving to have no sexes."

5 Cf. Parker (2011, 17), Fusco and Minelli (2019, 112), Bigelow (1904, 144), and the *Encyclopaedia Britannica* (1911, 746).
6 A genotype is the genetic constitution of an organism. A phenotype, by contrast, consists of the observable traits that result from the interaction of an organism's genotype and its environment. Your recessive genes, for example, are not expressed when only one copy is present, and, in that case, will be part of your genotype but not part of your phenotype. "Regions of phenotypic space" seems to refer to the range of possible phenotypes.
7 I hold dear the idea that the female to whom I'm married is *not* some life-history stage, whatever precisely that is, but rather a human being, the mother of my daughter. I suspect this may be Griffith's way of expressing his view through the lens of a process theory of biology, a lens to which he seems sympathetic (see Griffiths and Stotz 2018). But it remains counterintuitive. As with Franklin-Hall above, these sorts of observations are strikes against views, even if those views are not meant to provide conceptual analyses. It's true that both Franklin-Hall and Griffiths are trying to tell us what the sexes actually are–what natural kind terms like 'male' and 'female' actually refer to in the world. Whatever they refer to, you might think, it's probably going to be a bit complicated and not intuitive or commonsensical. I agree that it may not be *entirely* intuitive or commonsensical; there are no doubt facts about the natures of the sexes that we cannot see from the armchair. But it's too far to say that the true account of the nature of the sexes is going to be complicated and *not at all* intuitive or commonsensical. Given what we know about the sexes going into this investigation, for example, if a theorist proposed that every single organism is a simultaneous hermaphrodite, or that no organisms are sexed at all, that would certainly be so revisionary as to count against the proposal.
8 See also Griffiths and Spencer (2024): "Organisms can be male, female, both at the same time, male at one time and female at another, or have no clear and unambiguous sex."
9 A early predecessor of this Active Capacity View can be found in the *Encyclopaedia Britannica* (1911, 745–6), which says "An organism that contains the germinal tissue or mass of tissue known as the testis, and producing the sexual cells known as spermatozoa, is a male; an organism containing the tissue which produces ova is known as a female;…" Another is Horatio Hackett Newman ([1929] 1924, 448), who says: "Any individual, then, is sexual if it produces gametes—ova or spermatozoa, or their equivalents. Thus we would be justified in calling any individual that produces ova a female, and one that produces spermatozoa a male. One that produces both kinds of gametes is a male-female or, more technically, a HERMAPHRODITE."
10 Griffiths (2021) says that, although Byrne seeks to vindicate biological sex, he (Byrne) has "not defined it in the way biologists do." But see Byrne 2018 and 2023, note 124, and consider also the unconventional implications of Griffiths' view described below, implications that conflict with the ways in which biologists commonly talk and think about the sexes.
11 Even more so if we import contextual information back in: "Arthur the juvenile human and Brian the adult human are male." To my ears, the resulting sentence seems natural and felicitous. If that's right, this is strong evidence against Griffith's ambiguity hypothesis.
12 For one example of *very* many, see Reece et al. (2010, 405ff), where we're told that "DNA technology allows us to study the sequence, expression, and function of a gene." The National Library of Medicine (2023) provides many details

about fibroblast growth factor 9 (fgf9), including details explicitly about that gene's *function*.
13 At least, assuming there are no other parts or processes that would give the embryo a sex, on this view from Rifkin and Garson. But if there were such parts or processes, the worry that both male and female embryos would share them reemerges, with the threat that all such embryos are simultaneous hermaphrodites.
14 Though they purport to be arguing for anti-realism about sex, Watkins and DiMarco (2025, 18) offer this quotation from Roughgarden approvingly, saying "the sex concept needs to work across taxa." They are skeptical that this can be done for reasons we'll see below, but I hope to show otherwise.
15 A little less poetically, "Function statements are used throughout the biological disciplines" (Garson 2008, 525). And also, "Teleological language is frequently used in biology in order to make statements about the functions of organs, about physiological processes, and about the behavior and actions of species and individuals" (Mayr 1985 [1974], 133).
16 The Campbell text also speaks of malfunction, for example, of cell-surface receptor molecules (Reece et al., 2010, 210), protein phosphatases (Reece et al., 2010, 223), cell-signaling pathways (Reece et al., 2010, 243), cells (Reece et al., 2010, 394), the heart (Reece et al., 2010, 908), the kidneys (Reece et al., 2010, 946), cilia and sperm flagella (Reece et al., 2010, Appendix A-5). There are also very many instances of variations of 'defect', 'disorder', 'disease', and 'dysfunction'.
17 See, for example, Yu and Catterall (2003).
18 See, for example, Gennerich and Vale (2009).
19 Cf. Krohs and Kroes (2009).
20 To say that there are genetic programs or plans is *not* to endorse genetic determinism, the thesis that an organism's phenotype—let alone its behavior—is entailed by its genome. No, as Richard Prum (2023, 77–8) points out, an organism's phenotype and behavior are in part the result of the interaction of its genome and its *environment*. And yet nevertheless, as Prum (2023, 79) puts it, developmental biology is in the business of studying the "genetic and molecular mechanisms that regulate cell division, cell fate (i.e. self-renewal, differentiation, or death), morphogenesis (i.e. the creation of diversified anatomical parts), and pattern formation, which all give rise to the cell types; tissues; organs; and complex, modular but integrated parts of multicellular plants, fungi, and animals." These are the kinds of genetic mechanisms that I'm calling an organism's genetic "plan" or "program." And Prum adds later (2023, 80), "genes in the genome either specify the structure of stuff, or the molecular tools to manage and regulate the production of stuff." As Prum says, some of these mechanisms regulate the development of an organism's components—its cells, tissues, and organs—including those that have the function of producing gametes.
21 For theories in terms of selected effects, see Neander (1983, 1991, and 2017), Millikan (1984, 1993), Griffiths (1993), Kitcher (1993), Lennox (1993), Godfrey-Smith (1994), and Allen and Bekoff (1995). For theories in terms of the benefit or contribution that an entity makes, see Hempel (1965 [1959]), Nagel (1953, 1977), Canfield (1964), Ruse (1971), Cummins (1975), Boorse (1976), Bigelow and Pargetter (1987), and Walsh (1996). For an overview of these theories, see Garson (2008), and for a more recent contribution and synthesis, see Garson's (2019, 93) generalized selected effects theory, according to which "A function of a trait is an activity that led to its differential reproduction, or its differential retention, in a population."

22 On real definitions, see Kit Fine (1994).
23 Garson (2019, 155) reasons similarly, first saying "organisms, as wholes, don't have functions." But soon after, he qualifies that statement: "The only exception to this rule is when we think about organisms as parts of ecosystems; in that case, it makes perfect sense to say that organisms have functions."
24 I add 'anisogamous' because, evidently, biologists refer to the same-sized gametes of isogamous species as 'mating types', rather than 'sexes'. Watkins and DiMarco (2025, 9) complain that "there cannot be any taxa with more than two sexes, if sex is *defined* in such a way as only applies to organisms with two gamete types." But notice that the AHOF account does not claim that only organisms with two gamete-types have sexes. It's compatible with the AHOF account that there be more than two sexes. If there were a species of organisms with functions of producing components with functions of producing some third or fourth (or…) anisogamous gamete-type beyond sperm and ova, then these would be additional sexes, according to the AHOF account. And, as we'll see, there is good reason to believe that the AHOF theory is correct that this is the type that biologists refer to with their talk of "sex." So, we should accept the implication. This is orthogonal to the debate about whether sex is "binary," that is, whether there are only two sexes. Here in reality, there may be only two sexes, especially in humans, even if it's hypothetically, conceptually, philosophically *possible* for there to be more than two sexes. It's a virtue of the AHOF account that it allows for this possibility.
25 Stamen produce gametophytes, pollen grains, which mature to include sperm.
26 For examples, see Slack (2006, 3, 104, 106, 221, 307, 329, and 336).
27 There's a popular-level objection that we can dispatch quickly. It has also appeared in print. McLaughlin et al. (2023, 892) say that they "find several limitations to this gametic sex definition," a definition on which "gametes are the only meaningful sex categories." And one such limitation is that "gametes are rarely measured directly, with researchers instead relying on genetic and phenotypic proxies." The idea seems to be that, if being male is defined in terms of gamete production, then to know that someone is male, we would have to measure his gametes directly. But this, of course, does not follow. Being gold is defined in terms of atomic number—gold is atomic number 79—but it hardly follows that, to know that something is gold, we would have to measure its protons directly. People have managed to find and use gold for millennia before modern atomic theory, by relying on typical, superficial appearances of gold: luster, color, malleability, conductivity, etc. These indications are fallible, sure—hence, fool's gold—but knowledge does not require absolute certainty. Other examples abound. In a similar way, we might rely on typical, superficial appearances when classifying males and females, without the need to measure gametes directly.
28 Another objection can be dispatched quickly. Smiley et al. (2024, 2) rest their case against any version of the Gamete View on this single objection: such a view "is overly deterministic in that it assumes anisogamy is ultimately causal for variation and diversity in sex biology." In response, no, the AHOF account simply doesn't entail anything about whether anisogamy causes any variation of diversity in sex biology. One wonders why Smiley et al. think otherwise, but unfortunately, they don't say.
29 See Yan et al. (2024, 1) for an example that vacillates between 'sex' and 'mating-type': "Although most species have two sexes, multisexual (or multi-mating type) species are also widespread." See also Hurst (1996, 415): "…why do so many organisms have only two sexes/mating-types?".

30 It's no coincidence that this concords well with what the Department of Health and Human Services recently declared: "The sex of a human, female or male, is determined genetically at conception (fertilization)…" See this page from the Office on Women's Health: https://womenshealth.gov/article/sex-based-definitions.
31 This is a common, if flat-footed, objection to a functional account of the sexes. As Butler (2024, chapter 6) recently put it, "if reproductive capacity defines one's sex, then… one loses that sex, or never arrives at that sex, if one cannot or does not engage in sexual reproduction." See also Prum (2023, 38), and Franklin-Hall (2021, 189). The AHOF account easily handles such cases.
32 See, for example, Hine (2019), whose definition of 'male' is: "an individual whose reproductive organs produce only male gametes." Notice the "only" there. He defines 'female' in a similar way. Surprisingly, though, he defines 'hermaphrodite' as being "bisexual," and like so: "An animal, such as the earthworm, that has both male and female reproductive organs." Hine's view is confused since, if males produce only sperm and females only eggs, it's hard to see how a simultaneous hermaphrodite could be *bisexual*. It would have been more consistent had he said that hermaphrodites, rather than being bisexual, are a distinct sex, as Riddle et al. (1997, ch. 9 sec. II) say of nematodes: "*C. elegans* has two natural sexes, XO males and XX hermaphrodites." Though, confusingly, those authors go on to say that the hermaphrodites are "simply self-fertile females" with the "male character" of producing sperm. Smiley et al. (2024, 3) include "hermaphrodite" on their list of sexes (along with "intersex"!). But their definition of a sex—"a group of traits that are often, but not always, associated with reproduction"—entails that there are far too many sexes, one for each group of traits often but not always associated with reproduction, for example, being pregnant, being a eunuch, and having testicular cancer. Those conditions, I suggest, are simply not sexes. This confusion has made its way into gender studies; see, for example, Shannon Dea (2016, 61), who says, "Papaya trees come in three sexes—male, female, and hermaphroditic." And yet, in the glossary (Dea 2016, 179), Dea defines a hermaphroditic species as one in which individuals may "possess both sexes of sexual organs…" *Both* sexes, i.e. two. Neither sex nor gender is defined in Dea's glossary, even ostensively, nor anywhere else in this book, which by the way is titled, *Thinking about Sex and Gender*. The same goes with male, female, man, and woman. The closest we get are some proposed necessary conditions (Dea 2016, 18).
33 As we saw above in footnote 26, Fusco and Minelli (2019, 112) characterize hermaphrodites as both male and female, as does Parker (2011, 17), the 9th edition of Campbell Biology (Reece et al., 2010, 996), and Rifkin and Garson (2023, 8). Griffiths (2020) along with Griffiths and Spencer (2024) do as well. And long ago, Bigelow (1904, 144) said the same: "In most of the higher plans and in a few of the lower animals both sexes are included in a single individual, which is then said to be *hermaphrodite*." The *Encyclopaedia Britannica* (1911, 746) says males produce sperm and females produce ova, and then says that "[an organism] producing both ova and spermatozoa is a true hermaphrodite." Newman ([1929] 1924, 448) says that any organism "that produces both kinds of gametes is a male-female or, more technically, a HERMAPHRODITE."
34 Casas and Saborido-Rey (2021, 109) describe these inputs like so: "Environmental cues triggering sex change differ among species but are typically either size (and/or age) dependent or due to changes in social structure."
35 See, for example, Parvin (1982), Özdemir et al. (2019), and Li et al. (2020).

36 Watkins and DiMarco (2025, 4) may have a similar thought in mind when they offer this as an objection to the Gamete View: "the biological world is 'messy' and not amenable to categorization using anything as strict as necessary and sufficient conditions." They seem to assume that necessary and sufficient conditions must be "strict," that is, not allow for borderline cases in a "messy" biological world. But this is a mistake. If the sexes exist, they have some nature, some real definition. Something must make an organism male, and something must make an organism female. It may be extremely difficult to *articulate* this real definition, these necessary and sufficient conditions, but if we succeed, we should expect the definiens to be vague in the same ways in which the definiendum is vague. (Supposing roosters are adult male chickens, we should expect borderline cases of roosters to be borderline cases of adult male chickens, and vice versa.) The conditions in a real definition need not be "strict," that is, not vague, and neither should we expect them to be when it comes to biological sexes. Watkins and DiMarco (2025) also object to the Gamete View on the grounds that "gametic sexes are not able to explain non-gametic sex differences, or trait variations between gametic 'males' and 'females'..." They attribute this argument to John Dupré (1986). However, this too is a misunderstanding on their part. Recall that Dupré himself subscribes to the Gamete View, saying (Dupré 1986, 446) that the sexes have to do with "producing relatively large, or small, gametes." So it would be very surprising indeed if Dupré endorses an argument against his own view, as Watkins and DiMarco seem to suggest. Instead, what Dupré actually concludes Dupré 1986, 447) is that "sex is a very significant property that may be appealed to in the analysis of innumerable different taxonomic groupings but that, nevertheless, it is not a property that is sufficient to define any significant kind." I myself am content to claim merely that sex is a very significant property while remaining agnostic about whether it defines any "significant" or natural kind, so nothing Dupré says here threatens that. And yet Dupré concedes even more, saying (Dupré 1986), "Alternatively, if one wishes to insist that males and females do form natural kinds, then there are natural kinds with little or no explanatory power." So, even someone who thinks the sexes are *natural kinds* need not be threatened by Dupré's argument here. So, even if Watkins and DiMarco are correct that "gametic sexes" cannot explain non-gametic sex differences, or trait variations between males and females, it hardly follows that "gametic sex" does not exist, or that it's not a natural kind, or that it's not sex simpliciter.

37 See Parvin (1982) for a description of an alleged case of true hermaphroditism in a human. Though, on the AHOF account, I'd think that this individual counts as male and not (also) female.

38 On bees, see Hoover et al. (2003).

39 If the ovaries *degenerated* to a proto-gonadal tissue during menopause, tissue which *lacked* the relevant function, then the case would look more like sequential hermaphroditism in that respect, with a loss of being female. But that's not what actually happens.

40 This follows from a more general principle about the function of artifacts. Merely wishing that an object—such as the nearest tortilla chip—would drive nails is not enough to make it a hammer. Nor would it be enough to attempt to give it this function with a hopeless strategy—drawing pictures of hammers on the tortilla chip, for example, or trying to manifest a chip-hammer through positive thinking, or even cutting the chip into a shape reminiscent of a hammer. The same goes if instead of the chip I choose a biological entity, such as this floppy houseplant to my left. Drawing hammers on his leaves would not a

hammer make, nor would pruning his leaves into a shape reminiscent of hammers.
41 The prospects look even worse if the goal of so-called "gender affirming" medical treatment is not merely to make someone who is male also to be female (at the same time), but instead to become *only* female and no longer male. This would require not only adding a new function, but somehow deactivating the higher-order function that makes someone male, that is, the AHOF of producing testes. As we saw above in the discussion about disease, injury, and malfunction, not even removing the testes would deactivate the AHOF of producing testes. At most, it would introduce malfunction while the activated function persists. This is highly speculative, but it seems to me that one would have to, somehow, change the person's master program, so that the production and maintenance of testes is no longer a function of the person's machine table.

References

Aatsha, P. A., Tafline Arbor, and Kewal Krishan (2023). "Embryology, Sexual Development," in *StatPearls* (Treasure Island, FL: StatPearls Publishing). Available from: https://www.ncbi.nlm.nih.gov/books/NBK557601/

Allen, Colin, and Mark Bekoff (1995). "Biological Function, Adaptation, and Natural Design," *Philosophy of Science* 62 (4): 609–22.

Ammermann, Dieter (1965). "Cytologische und genetische Untersuchungen an den Ciliaten *Stylonychia mytilus* Ehrenberg," *Archiv für Protistenkunde* 108: 109–52.

Ammermann, Dieter (1982). "Mating Types in Stylonychia mytilus EHRBG," *Archiv für Protistenkunde* 126 (4): 373–81.

Bigelow, John, and Robert Pargetter (1987). "Functions," *Journal of Philosophy* 84: 181–96.

Bigelow, Robert Payne (1904). "Sex," in *A Reference Handbook of the Medical Sciences Embracing the Entire Range of Scientific and Practical Medicine and Allied Science*, Vol. 7, Alfred H. Buck (ed.) (New York: William Wood and Company), 144–7.

Boorse, Christopher (1976). "Wright on Functions," *Philosophical Review* 85: 70–86.

Butler, Judith (2024). *Who's Afraid of Gender?* (New York: Farrar, Straus, and Giroux).

Byrne, Alex (2018). "Is Sex Binary?" *Arc Digital*. https://medium.com/arc-digital/is-sex-binary-16bec97d161e

Byrne, Alex (2023). *Trouble with Gender* (Cambridge, UK: Polity Press).

Canfield, John (1964). "Teleological Explanations in Biology," *British Journal for the Philosophy of Science* 14: 285–95.

Casas, L., and F. Saborido-Rey (2021). "Environmental Cues and Mechanisms Underpinning Sex Change in Fish," *Sexual Development* 15 (1–3): 108–21.

Cummins, Robert (1975). "Functional Analysis," *Journal of Philosophy* 72 (20): 741–65.

Currah, Paisely (2022). *Sex Is as Sex Does: Governing Transgender Identity* (New York: New York University Press).

Dea, Shannon (2016). *Beyond the Binary: Thinking about Sex and Gender*(Peterborough, Canada: Broadview Press).

de Beauvoir, Simone [1949] (1956). *The Second Sex*, translated by H. M. Parshley (New York: Vintage Books).

Dupré, John (1986). "Sex, Gender, and Essence," *Midwest Studies in Philosophy* 11 (1): 441–57.

Edwards, Beatrice, and Jin Li (2013). "Endocrinology of Menopause," *Periodontology 2000* 61: 177–94.
Encyclopaedia Britannica (1911). Volume 14, EleventhEdition (Cambridge: Cambridge University Press).
Fine, Kit (1994). "Essence and Modality," *Philosophical Perspectives* 8: 1–16.
Franklin-Hall, Laura (2021). "The Animal Sexes as Historical Explanatory Kinds," in *Current Controversies in Philosophy of Science*, S. Dasgupta, R. Dotan, and B. Weslake (eds.) (New York: Routledge) 177–97.
Fusco, Giuseppe, and Alessandro Minelli (2019). *The Biology of Reproduction* (New York: Cambridge University Press).
Garson, Justin (2008). "Functions and Teleology," in *A Companion to the Philosophy of Biology*, Sahotra Sarkar and Anya Plutynski (eds.) (Malden, MA: Blackwell Publishing).
Garson, Justin (2019). *What Biological Functions Are and Why They Matter* (New York: Cambridge University Press).
Geitler, Lothar (1935). "Reproduction and Life History in Diatoms," *Botanical Review* 1 (5): 149–61.
Gennerich, A., and R. D. Vale (2009). "Walking the Walk: How Kinesin and Dynein Coordinate their Steps," *Current Opinion in Cell Biology* 21 (1): 59–67.
Godfrey-Smith, Peter (1994). "A Modern History Theory of Functions," *Noûs* 28 (3): 344–62.
Gorelick, Root, Jessica Carpinone, and Lindsay Jackson Derraugh (2017). "No Universal Differences Between Female and Male Eukaryotes: Anisogamy and Asymmetrical Female Meiosis," *Biological Journal of the Linnean Society* 120: 1–21
Griffiths, Paul and Hamish Spencer (2024). "To Explain Biological Sex, Look to Evolution," *Nature* 631 (8020): 275–5.
Griffiths, Paul, and Karola Stotz (2018). "Developmental Systems Theory as a Process Theory," in *Everything Flows: Towards a Processual Philosophy of Biology*, Daniel Nicholson and John Dupré (eds.) (Oxford: Oxford University Press), 225–45.
Griffiths, Paul (1993). "Functional Analysis and Proper Function," *British Journal for the Philosophy of Science*, 44: 409–22.
Griffiths, Paul (2020). "Sex is Real," *Aeon*. https://aeon.co/essays/the-existence-of-biological-sex-is-no-constraint-on-human-diversity, accessed May 23, 2023.
Griffiths, Paul (2021). "What are Biological Sexes?" *PhilSci Archive*. http://philsci-archive.pitt.edu/19906/, accessed May 25, 2023.
Hempel, Carl (1965[1959]). "The Logic of Functional Analysis," in *Aspects of Scientific Explanation*, C. G. Hempel (ed.) (New York: Free Press), 297–330.
Hine, Robert (2019). *A Dictionary of Biology*, EighthEdition (Oxford, UK: Oxford University Press).
Hoover, S. E. R., C. I. Keeling, M. L. Winston, and K. N. Slessor (2003). "The Effect of Queen Pheromones on Worker Honey Bee Ovary Development," *Naturwissenschaften* 90: 477–80.
Hurst, L. D. (1996). "Why are There Only Two Sexes?" *Proceedings of the Royal Society of London Series B: Biological Sciences* 263 (1369): 415–22.
Iwasa, Yoh and Akira Sasaki (1987). "Evolution of the Number of Sexes," *Evolution* 41 (1): 49–65.
Kitcher, Philip (1993). "Function and Design," *Midwest Studies in Philosophy* 18: 379–97.
Krohs, Ulrich, and Peter Kroes (eds.) (2009). *Functions in Biological and Artificial Worlds* (Cambridge, MA: MIT Press).
Lachance, Marc-André, Christopher Burke, Karen Nygard, Marc Courchesne, and Alexander Timoshenko (2024). "Yeast Sexes: Mating Types do not Determine the Sexes in *Metschnikowia* Species," *FEMS Yeast Research* 24: foae014.

Lehtonen, Jussi, and Geoff Parker (2014). "Gamete Competition, Gamete Limitation, and the Evolution of the Two Sexes," *Molecular Human Reproduction* 20 (12): 1161–8.

Lennox, James G. (1993). "Darwin *was* a Teleologist," *Biology and Philosophy* 8: 409–21.

Li, Jingyao, Yaguang Zhu, Han Yu, Bin Dai, Young-Shin Jun, and Fuzhong Zhang (2021). "Microbially Synthesized Polymeric Amyloid Fiber Promotes β-Nanocrystal Formation and Displays Gigapascal Tensile Strength," *ACS Nano* 15: 11843–53.

Li, Z., J. Liu, Y. Peng, R. Chen, P. Ge, and J. Wang (2020). "46, XX Ovotesticular Disorder of Sex Development (True Hermaphroditism) with Seminoma: A Case Report," *Medicine* 99 (40).

MacLaughlin, David T., Jose Teixeira, and Patricia K. Donahoe (2001). "Perspective: Reproductive Tract Development—New Discoveries and Future Directions," *Endocrinology* 142 (6): 2167–72.

Maung, Hane Htut (2023). "Classifying Sexes," *DiGeSt: Journal of Diversity and Gender Studies* 10 (1): 36–52.

Mayr, Ernst (1985[1974]). "Teleological and Teleonomic: A New Analysis," reprinted in *A Portrait of Twenty-Five Years: Boston Studies in the Philosophy of Science*, Robert Cohen and Marx Wartofsky (eds.) (Hingham, MA: Kluwer Academic Publishers), 133–59.

McLaughlin, J. F., Kinsey M. Brock, Isabella Gates, Anisha Pethkar, Marcus Piattoni, Alexis Rossi, and Sara E. Lipshutz (2023). "Multivariate Models of Animal Sex: Breaking Binaries Leads to a Better Understanding of Ecology and Evolution," *Integrative and Comparative Biology* 63 (4): 891–906.

Millikan, Ruth (1984). *Language, Thought, and Other Biological Categories* (Cambridge, MA: MIT Press).

Millikan, Ruth (1993). *White Queen Psychology and Other Essays for Alice* (Cambridge, MA: MIT Press).

Millikan, Ruth (2013). "Reply to Neander," in *Millikan and Her Critics*, D. Ryder, J. Kingsbury, and K. Williford (eds.) (Malden, MA: Wiley-Blackwell), 37–40.

Moutos, Christopher P., William G. Kearns, Sarah E. Farmer, Jon P. Richards, Antonio F. Saad, and John R. Crochet (2021). "Embryo Quality, Ploidy, and Transfer Outcomes in Male Versus Female Blastocysts," *Journal of Assisted Reproduction and Genetics* 38 (9): 2363–70.

Nagel, Ernst (1953). "Teleological Explanation and Teleological Systems," in *Vision and Action*, S. Ratner (ed.) (New Brunswick, NJ: Rutgers University Press), 537–58.

Nagel, Ernst (1977). "Teleology Revisited: Goal-Directed Processes in Biology and Functional Explanation in Biology," *Journal of Philosophy* 74: 261–301.

Nanney, David Ledbetter (1980). *Experimental Ciliatology: An Introduction to Genetic and Developmental Analysis in Ciliates* (New York: Wiley).

National Library of Medicine (2023). "FGF9," https://www.ncbi.nlm.nih.gov/gene/?term=2254

Neander, Karen (1983). *Abnormal Psychobiology*. Dissertation, La Trobe University, Bundoora, Australia.

Neander, Karen (1991). "Functions as Selected Effects: The Conceptual Analyst's Defense," *Philosophy of Science* 58 (2): 168–84.

Neander, Karen (2017). *A Mark of the Mental: In Defense of Informational Teleosemantics* (Cambridge, MA: MIT Press).

Nelson, R. J. (1975). "Behaviorism, Finite Automata, and Stimulus Response Theory," *Theory and Decision* 6: 249–67.

Newman, Horatio Hackett ([1929] 1924). *Outlines of General Zoölogy*, Second Edition (New York: The Macmillan Company).

Özdemir, M., R. P. Kavak, I. Yalcinkaya, and K. Guresci (2019). "Ovotesticular Disorder of Sex Development: An Unusual Presentation," *Journal of Clinical Imaging Science* 12 (9): 34.

Parker, Geoff A. (2011). "The Origin and Maintenance of Two Sexes (Anisogamy), and their Gamete Sizes by Gamete Competition," in *The Evolution of Anisogamy: A Fundamental Phenomenon Underlying Sexual Selection*, Tatsuya Togashi and Paul A. Cox (eds.) (Cambridge, UK: Cambridge University Press), 17–74.

Parvin, Simon (1982). "Ovulation in a Cytogenetically Proved Phenotypically Male Fertile Hermaphrodite," *British Journal of Surgery* 69 (5): 279–80.

Preer, John (1969). "Genetics of the Protozoa," in *Research in Proto-zoology*, Vol. 3, Tze-Tuan Chen (ed.) (Oxford: Pergamon), 130–278.

Prum, Richard (2023). *Performance All the Way Down* (Chicago: University of Chicago Press).

Reece, Jane, Lisa Urry, Michael Cain, Steven Wasserman, Peter Minorsky, and Robert Jackson (2010). *Campbell Biology*, Ninth Edition (San Francisco, CA: Benjamin Cummings).

Riddle, D. L., T. Blumenthal, B. J. Meyer, et al. (eds.) (1997). *C. elegans II*, SecondEdition (Cold Spring Harbor, NY: Cold Spring Harbor Laboratory Press). Accessed via: https://www.ncbi.nlm.nih.gov/books/NBK20094/

Rifkin, Maximiliana, and Justin Garson. (2023). "Sex by Design," *Biology and Philosophy* 38 (13): 1–17.

Roughgarden, Joan (2004). *Evolution's Rainbow* (Berkeley, CA: University of California Press).

Ruse, Michael (1971). "Functional Statements in Biology," *Philosophy of Science* 38: 87–95.

Sadler, T. W. (2004). *Langman's Medical Embryology*, Ninth Edition (Philadelphia, PA: Lippincott Williams and Wilkins).

Sear, Rebecca (2024). "Whale Clues to Why Menopause Evolved," *Nature* 627: 496–497.

Slack, Jonathan (2006). *Essential Developmental Biology* (Malden, MA: Blackwell Publishing).

Smiley, Kristina O., Kathleen M. Munley, Krisha Aghi, Sara E. Lipshutz, Tessa M. Patton, Devaleena S. Pradhan, Tessa K. Solomon-Lane, and Simón(e) D. Sun (2024). "Sex Diversity in the 21st Century: Concepts, Frameworks, and Approaches for the Future of Neuroendocrinology," *Hormones and Behavior* 157: 105445.

Sonneborn, T. M. (1939). "Paramecium Aurelia: Mating Types and Groups; Lethal Interactions; Determination and Inheritance," *The American Naturalist* 73 (748): 390–413.

Takahashi, M., R. S. Singh, and J. Stone (2017). "A Theory for the Origin of Human Menopause," *Frontiers in Genetics* 7: 1–12.

Venter, J. Craig, John I. Glass, Clyde A. Hutchison III, and Sanjay Vashee (2022). "Synthetic Chromosomes, Genomes, Viruses, and Cells," *Cell* 185: 2708–24.

Walsh, Denis (1996). "Fitness and Function," *British Journal for the Philosophy of Science* 47: 553–74.

Watkins, Aja and Marina DiMarco (2025). "Sex Eliminativism," *Biology and Philosophy* 40 (2): 1–30.

Yan, G., Y. Ma, Y. Wang, J. Zhang, H. Cheng, F. Tan, S. Wang, D. Zhang, J. Xiong, P. Yin, and W. Miao (2024). "A Seven-Sex Species Recognizes Self and Non-Self Mating-Type via A Novel Protein Complex," *Elife* 13: RP93770.

Yu, F. H., and W. A. Catterall (2003). "Overview of the Voltage-Gated Sodium Channel Family," *Genome Biology* 4 (3): 207.

Zhang, S., B. Huang, X. Song, T. Zhang, H. Wang, and Y. Liu (2019). "A High Storage Density Strategy for Digital Information Based on Synthetic DNA," *Biotech* 9 (9): 342.

4
GENDER IS DEFINED IN TERMS OF THE SEXES

I'd like now to connect our investigation to broader issues in the field, including conversations about what gender is. Sex and gender are distinct, we're often told. But are they distinct in such a way that our investigation into the nature of the sexes has no implications for discussions about gender? Or is gender in some important way connected to sex, or dependent on sex, so that our conclusions on the nature of the sexes bear on conversations about gender? My answer is that gender is indeed dependent on sex in such a way that the activated higher-order function (AHOF) account of the sexes has significant implications for conversations about gender, and I'll explain why. In the following chapter, I will defend the methodology of previous chapters, specifically the special authority I propose giving to biologists when attempting to figure out the natures of the sexes, the referents of 'sex', 'male', and 'female'. I will also consider the suggestion that, instead of thinking merely about what sex *is*, we ought to think about what it *should* be, what we want it to be, what sense of our sex terms would best suit our purposes and aspirations. I will consider, that is, the prospects of what philosophers have come to call "conceptual engineering" with regard to our sex terms.

First, let's talk about gender. This book has defended the Gamete View of the sexes, and in particular the thesis that sexes are activated higher-order functions to produce (anisogamous) types of gametes. Given the many social controversies surrounding sex and gender, along with the tendency to conflate or misunderstand sex and gender, the reader may reasonably wonder what implications, if any, the AHOF account of the sexes has on social controversies surrounding gender. For example, as I write this on

January 20, 2025, President Donald Trump has just declared, in his inaugural address, that "As of today, it will henceforth be the official policy of the United States government that there are only two genders: male and female."[1] Is our investigation into the nature of the sexes particularly relevant to this claim about gender? In order to answer that question, we first have to get clear on what gender is supposed to be. And to do that, we have to talk about the word 'gender' and its many meanings.

Kathleen Stock (2021, ch. 1) and Alex Byrne (2023a, ch. 2) have catalogued many candidate senses of the word 'gender', beginning with its use as a polite synonym for biological sex. As Sally Haslanger (2000, 31) put it, "outside a rather narrow segment of the academic world, the term 'gender' has come to function as a polite way to talk about the sexes." Indeed, that's correct.[2] As just one example, consider a page from the website for the Natural History Museum, in South Kensington, London.[3] Speaking of bilateral gynandromorphism in butterflies, the museum says, "A handful of creatures are born divided down the middle, one half male and the other female, two sexes in one body." This is notable, since "it's rare to see even one dual-sex insect," we're told. So far, so good. And yet the title of the article is, "Beauty of the dual-gender butterfly," and the article goes on to say that "All three insects had two equal-sized, perfectly formed halves—one of each gender." There are two *sexes* in each body, that is, one of each *gender*. Clearly, the article uses 'gender' as a synonym for sex.

Further evidence for this linguistic claim is found in surprising places, and this evidence is less well known. For example, Robert Stoller (1964, 220) was at least partly[4] responsible for coining the term 'gender identity', and defined it like so: "Gender identity is the sense of knowing to which sex one belongs, that is, the awareness 'I am a male' or 'I am a female'."[5] Stoller might as well have called this sense "sex identity," as it is the sense of one's own sex, and in fact did originally call it "sexual identity" (cf. Byrne 2023c). Stoller seems, therefore, to be using 'gender' as a synonym for sex, and, for him, gender identity is defined partly in terms of sex. Perhaps surprisingly, the American Civil Liberties Union (2025, 6) very recently defined 'gender identity' in the same way as Stoller originally did: "'Gender identity' refers to a person's core, internal sense of belonging to a particular sex."

Stoller also seems to have used the word 'gender' in a second way. A few years later ([1984] 1968, 9), he wrote that "Gender is the amount of masculinity or femininity found in a person." But what are masculinity and femininity? Stoller ([1984] 1968, 29) says that the two sexes have two "resultant" genders, masculinity and femininity, so he seems to think there's *some* connection between masculinity and being male, and between femininity and being female. Later ([1984] 1968, 40), he seems to equate being manly with being masculine, and he speaks of the period of development in which a child "has learned how his parents expect him to express masculinity; that is, to behave as they feel males should." So, for Stoller, it appears that to be masculine is to behave as one's parents—and plausibly one's society more broadly—feels males *should* behave. In that case, this use of the word 'gender' names the genus of masculinity and femininity, and these seem to be the norms or expectations that some individual or group has *of males* and *of females* in humans,[6] respectively.[7] So, for Stoller, 'gender' is (also) evidently used as shorthand for what we now might call gender norms, but which we might more precisely call *sex* norms, since they are the norms and expectations of the sexes. In speaking of 'gender norms' as we ourselves do, then, we seem to be using 'gender' as a synonym for the sexes. And Stoller, who used 'gender' to name the sex *norms*, is using the word in such a way that it is partly defined in terms of the sexes: something is a gender if and only if it is a set of norms that an individual or group has for a *sex*. Clearly, then, the nature of the sexes will be highly relevant to conversations about gender, using 'gender' as Stoller did: either as a synonym for sex, or to name social norms about the sexes.

And the same can be said if we extend these sex norms and expectations to include social roles more broadly, including occupations.[8] Here, too, to call these 'gender roles' is to use 'gender' as a synonym for sex, since these roles are sex-typed social roles, roles typically occupied by—or expected to be occupied by—*the sexes* (cf. Byrne 2023a, ch. 2). As the word 'gender' is used in these ways, then, our AHOF account of the sexes has clear implications for gender. Knowing what the sexes are should inform our understanding of what it is to have a gender identity (in Stoller's sense), what masculinity and femininity are, what gender norms are (and who they apply to), and what gender roles are.[9] Knowing what the sexes are should even help us make progress on interesting questions such as whether there are any *true* norms about the human sexes, that is, any way that human males should be, *qua* human males, and any way human females should be, *qua* human females. Whether, in particular, there are any ways to be an excellent man, or an excellent woman, that are unique and more particular than ways in which one may be an excellent *human*. Many seem to reflexively assume that the answer is 'no', and that our species' sex norms are purely conventional, "socially constructed," corresponding to no mind-independent truths. But the reasons typically provided wouldn't pass muster in an introductory course about moral relativism—for example, "witness the *diversity* of sex norms across time and culture," one might hear—and it does seem as though there would at least be different ways to be a *healthy* human female compared to *healthy* human male, given the biological differences between these groups. And just as the tallest person in a grocery store may take on certain *pro tanto* moral duties regarding reaching items on the top shelf in virtue of his height, it might be that biological differences between the sexes generate differing *pro tanto* moral duties. Perhaps. But further investigation of that question will have to wait for another occasion.

Now we sail into murkier waters. Consider some examples of another use of the word 'gender'. First, an example from Ann Oakley ([1985] 1972, 158):

> 'Sex' is a biological term: 'gender' a psychological and cultural one. Common sense suggests that they are merely two ways of looking at the same division and that someone who belongs to, say, the female sex will automatically belong to the corresponding (feminine) gender. In reality this is not so. To be a man or a woman, a boy or a girl, is as much a function of dress, gesture, occupation, social network and personality, as it is of possessing a particular set of genitals.

More recently, Susan Stryker (2008, 11) says, "The words 'man' and 'woman' refer to gender."[10] And Mari Mikkola (2016, 23) puts it this way:

> [M]any [feminists] have historically endorsed a sex/gender distinction. Its standard formulation holds that 'sex' denotes human females and males, and depends on biological features… Then again, 'gender' denotes women and men and depends on social factors
> *(social roles, positions, behavior, self-ascription)*.

But these statements are imprecise. Does Oakley really mean to say that, in order to be a woman, one must not only be (an adult human) female but also one must *dress* and *behave* in ways typical of (adult human) females, and occupy social roles and occupations typical of (adult human) females? Do we really want to say, with Stryker, that 'man' and 'woman' refer to *the same thing*, namely gender? And is Mikkola really correct that many feminists say 'gender' denotes women and men, so that if I wonder how many women and men were at the concert, I may just as well ask how many *gender* [sic] were at the concert? These interpretations are no doubt overly literal. The authors must intend some other, non-literal interpretation.

I'd like to venture a guess about what's going on here with these thinkers. I believe they may well be confusing sense and reference. Like Stoller and others, these thinkers seem to take 'gender' to name the genus of masculinity and femininity, that is, those norms and expectations of the sexes. And then they mistake *the ways in which we commonly identify men and women*—namely, finding masculine and feminine people—for *what it is* to be a man or a woman. That is, they mistake the procedure we use to find the men and women—the typical masculine modes of presentation of men and feminine modes of presentation of women, the *contingent marks* by which we identify men and women—for the *natures* of men and women. Here's another way to put it: these thinkers reflect on our concept of men and our concept of women, and mistake our *conceptions* of men and women—the features we typically associate with men and with women—for the *referents* of these concepts.

Let me give some examples. If you imagine yourself in the *Superman* stories, it's easy to suppose that you would have one way of thinking about Superman and a distinct way of thinking about Clark Kent. There would be one procedure you'd use to apply the name 'Superman', and a distinct procedure for applying 'Clark Kent', one set of contingent marks by which you identify Superman, and another set of contingent marks by which you identify Clark Kent. These names have distinct senses; the concepts are associated with distinct conceptions. To find Superman, you'd likely look for a man in a cape, flying around, performing feats of strength, defending peace, justice, and the American way, etc. To find Clark Kent, you'd likely look for a mild-mannered reporter for the *Daily Planet*, who wears glasses, and so on. And some may be tempted to think that this is just *what it is* to be Superman, or to be Clark Kent, to have those typical features, to have those contingent marks, to match our conceptions. But that's a mistake. Each of these names refers to an individual, and it could be—and *is*, according to the story—that *one* individual answers to *both* names. And it could be that one man fails to match either of the descriptions we associate with 'Superman' and 'Clark Kent'. He could quit his job at the *Daily Planet*, surrender his superpowers to a kryptonite necklace, stop fighting crime, etc., and yet continue to be Superman, continue to be Clark Kent (cf. Kripke ([1980], 1972).

Think also about water. We have various conceptions of water, various procedures we follow when we apply the word, various contingent marks we look for to find the water in our vicinity, a description we use to fix the reference of the term, something like: the odorless, colorless stuff that falls from the sky, comes out of our taps, fills lakes and rivers, etc. But 'water' refers to a particular kind of stuff that *happens to* but *does not necessarily* fit that description. We know that some water is frozen, for example, and some has been colored or tinted, etc. And we know that a *different* kind of stuff could perfectly match our conception of water, the description we associate with the term 'water'. Some other kind of stuff could come to be the colorless, odorless stuff that falls from the sky, fills lakes and rivers, comes out of our taps, etc. That *could* happen, and if it did, that stuff would *still* not be water. It would be *water-y*, water-*ish*, water-*like*. But it would not be *water*. (Just as an impostor of Clark Kent would be Clark-Kent-*like*, but he would not be *Clark Kent*.)

Now, in a similar way, we have a formula or procedure we follow when we apply the words 'man' and 'woman'. Often, we look for *masculine* people when applying the word 'man', and *feminine* people when applying the word 'woman'. We look, that is, for people abiding by norms and expectations our society has of males when we use the word 'man', and similarly for norms and expectations our society has of females when we use the word 'woman'. Commonly. Most of the time. Of course, we also know there could be exceptions, just as we recognize there could be water that isn't water-y, or something other than water that is water-y, and just as we recognize that Superman need not appear in typical Superman fashion, and an impostor could appear in typical Superman fashion.

The mistake I suggest these thinkers are making is this: they confuse the senses of the words 'man' and 'woman'—those formulas or procedures that we use when applying the words, the descriptions we use to fix the reference of the term—with what those words actually refer to. First, as I've said, they use 'gender' to pick out the genus of masculinity and femininity. Then, they mistakenly think 'man' picks out anyone who is masculine and 'woman' picks out anyone who is feminine. And they conclude, as Stryker said, that the words 'man' and 'woman' refer to gender, or as Mikkola put it, that 'gender' denotes women and men and depends on social factors. They are victims, that is, of a proposition confusion.[11] One might incorrectly think that the sentence 'Clark Kent is in the office' expresses the proposition that the mild-mannered reporter for the *Daily Planet* is in the office, when in actuality it expresses the proposition that *that actual guy* is in the office. This is a mistake, because the name 'Clark Kent' is not short for, and is not equivalent to, the description 'the mild-mannered reporter for the *Daily Planet*'. Clark Kent is not *defined* by the contingent marks we commonly use to *identify* him. In a similar way, one might also incorrectly think that the sentence 'One is not born but rather becomes a woman' expresses the proposition that one is not born but rather becomes a *feminine* person, when in actuality it expresses the proposition that one is not born but rather becomes an adult human female. (Probably it *pragmatically conveys* the proposition that one is not born but rather becomes a feminine person. But even Simone de Beauvoir was under no misapprehensions about what a woman actually is.[12]) This is a mistake, because the kind-term 'woman' is not short for, and is not equivalent to, the description 'a feminine person', or 'a person who abides by norms and expectations that our society has of females', or anything of the like. Womanhood is not defined by the contingent marks we commonly use to identify women. And likewise with manhood. So, I don't believe that Stryker, Mikkola, and others are correct that this is an additional sense of the word 'gender'. While Stoller and many others may use 'gender' to name the genus of masculinity and femininity, only by misunderstanding the semantics of 'man' and 'woman' could we draw the conclusion that 'gender' denotes women and men.

That's my diagnosis of the mistake these thinkers are making. But *even if* they were correct that 'gender' denotes women and men because it denotes the genus of masculinity and femininity, still, 'gender' would be defined ultimately in terms of the sexes. And, therefore, our inquiry into the nature of the sexes would still be relevant for discussions of gender using this alleged sense of 'gender'. We can see that by considering this question: if 'man' and 'woman' name genders, and are therefore gender terms, how many gender terms are there, and how many genders are there? Presumably, 'hombre' and 'mujer' are novel gender *terms*, on this view, yet they do not name new *genders*.[13] But what about 'boy' and 'girl'? Do these novel gender terms also name new *genders*, genders that are distinct from those named by 'man' and 'woman'? And what of other terms in the neighborhood, for example, 'widow', 'eunuch', 'bachelor', 'tomboy', 'concubine', 'matriarch', 'father', 'mother', and so on? And what about words similar to 'man' and 'woman' but for other species, for example, 'rooster', 'hen', 'mare', 'stallion', 'buck', 'doe', and the like? Presumably, none of these name genders; none of these is a gender term. But... why not?

I propose that the answer has to do with the idea—again, the *mistaken* idea, in my view—that 'man' and 'woman' are defined in terms of masculinity and femininity, in terms, that is, of the social norms and expectations *of the sexes*. There may be social norms and expectations of widows, eunuchs, bachelors, tomboys, concubines, matriarchs, mothers, fathers, and so on, yet these are not themselves sexes. Even though eunuchs, bachelors, and fathers are all by definition male, the norms and expectations a society might have of eunuchs, bachelors, and fathers are not norms and expectations of (human) males simpliciter. Because, of course, many (human) males are not eunuchs, nor bachelors, nor fathers. And likewise with the other items on our list. So, it seems that, even on this mistaken view that 'gender' denotes men and women, the number of genders is limited to the number of sexes, because 'gender' denotes sets of social norms and expectations of the sexes.[14] And therefore, as I said, our investigation into the nature of the sexes will be relevant even to this (mistaken) idea of what 'gender' refers to, both in defining what a gender is, and in explaining how many there are.

Finally, we sail into the murkiest waters of 'gender' semantics, and here there be dragons. Or at least, here there be "trannydyke genderqueer wombat fantasticas," according to Florence Ashley (2021, 38). I'm speaking, of course, of the term 'gender identity', used in a way far removed from Stoller's original definition. It's notoriously unclear what 'gender identity' refers to, as used by contemporary trans activists. Often, by way of definition, we're given an incomplete list of so-called 'genders'. As Advocates for Trans Equality puts it, "Gender identity is your internal knowledge of your gender—for example, your knowledge that you're a man, a woman, or another gender."[15] And when the time comes to define 'gender' there, sometimes no definition is given—as is the case with Advocates for Trans Equality—or an unilluminating definition is offered, as one finds from the World Professional Association for Transgender Health's most recent Standards of Care (Coleman et al. 2022, S252).[16] They define 'gender identity' like so:

GENDER IDENTITY refers to a person's deeply felt, internal, intrinsic sense of their own gender.

And they offer this definition of 'gender':

GENDER: Depending on the context, gender may reference gender identity, gender expression, and/or social gender role, including understandings and expectations culturally tied to people who were assigned male or female at birth. Gender identities other than those of men and women (who can be either cisgender or transgender) include transgender, nonbinary, genderqueer, gender neutral, agender, gender fluid, and "third" gender, among others; many other genders are recognized around the world.

Unfortunately, we're not told which sense of 'gender' is used in the context of that definition of 'gender identity'. But each of the given options is puzzling. Presumably, gender identity is not one's deeply felt internal sense of his own gender identity, otherwise, we've gone in a circle, an ouroboros twisting through a house of mirrors. Nor does it seem right to say that gender identity is one's deeply felt internal sense of his own gender expression, or social gender role, even setting aside the repeated use of 'gender' in what's meant to be a definition of 'gender'.[17] And that's because, I should think, trans activists would say, it's possible for one's gender identity to be distinct from his sense of how he expresses himself, or what his social role is. Someone may identify as a woman—and therefore have that gender identity—and yet not present as a woman, and not be read or treated as a woman, socially. This person may know that her gender expression and gender role are masculine, and yet have a gender identity that activists would call a woman gender identity. In light of all this, one may well wish to join Katharine Jenkins (2018, 713) as she laments: "Although the concept of gender identity plays a prominent role in campaigns for trans rights, it is not well understood, and common definitions suffer from a problematic circularity."

However, I think philosophers have shed some little light on this question, and here together we can shed a little more. In a recent book, R.A. Briggs and B.R. George (2023, 23) say, "we propose framing things in terms of gender *feels*: attitudes about one's relationships to various non-subjective aspects of our shared material and social reality, which we'll refer to collectively as *gendered traits*." When one looks up what a gendered trait is, he's told (Briggs and George 2023, 52, n. 9): "we are adopting 'gendered trait' as a convenient umbrella term for the various stuff about which individuals have gender feels and about which societies have gender norms." It would be clearly circular to define gender feels in terms of gendered traits, and then gendered traits in terms of gender feels, so we can be grateful that they added that last bit about gender norms. And yet, unfortunately, when they later tell us what a gender norm is (Briggs and George 2023, 65), they define gender norms in terms of gendered traits: "A gender norm is *a social expectation linking two or more gendered traits, which is considered generally applicable or binding.*" So, while we don't have *one* simple viciously circular definition, these three definitions do seem to have some interlinking loops. Gender feels are defined in terms of gendered traits. Gendered traits are defined partly in terms of gender feels (one loop), but partly in terms of gender norms. And gender norms are defined in terms of gendered traits (a second loop). In the end, these interlocking loops render the definitions viciously circular.

But I think we can start to untangle what Briggs and George seem to have in mind, if we take 'gender norms' to have the same meaning that we explored above: norms or expectations that an individual or group has about *the sexes*. On this understanding, gender feels are attitudes about gendered traits, and gendered traits are those traits that feature in our social norms and expectations of *the sexes*. They give examples (Briggs and George 2023, 32), such as "having a Y chromosome, wearing dresses, or being a man," as well as (Briggs and George 2023, 39) traits expressed by the predicates "*operating power tools* or *being in the process of dyeing one's hair blue.*" The idea is that, because our society has a widely shared belief to the effect that men (i.e. adult human males) should be adept at operating power tools, properties like being a man and operating power tools are "gendered traits." And, importantly, one can have various feelings or attitudes about these traits—including about one's own sex—and about the norms generally.

I think that's on the right track. I propose that what activists mean by 'gender identity' is a person's attitude(s) toward the sexes, including his own, and toward his society's norms about the sexes. When one introspects and takes note of these attitudes, he may self-describe using various labels that he takes to best fit these attitudes, for example, 'man', 'woman', 'boy', 'girl', 'genderfluid', 'agender', 'feminazgûl', 'tenderqueer' [sic], etc. (cf. Ashley 2021, note 1). As Elizabeth Barnes (2018, 587–8) puts it, "For the most part, when philosophers talk about gender identity, they mean your internally felt sense of your relationship to the gender norms and categories that are common within our society." *Gender* norms and [*gender*] categories; yes, I think that's right, so long as we take 'gender' to be a polite synonym for sex there. And in a recent paper about the psychology of gender identity, transfeminine jurist and bioethicist Florence Ashley (2023, 1059) writes that "The totality of our gendered experiences is gender subjectivity and forms the basic substrate of gender identity." Ashley proposes that a person's gender identity is his interpretation of his gendered experiences, as an interpreter makes meaning from a text (Ashley 2023, 1061): "we could imagine the process as the psyche asking: 'Which gender category would make the most sense out of my feels?'" And in an even more recent paper, Rach Cosker-Rowland (2024, 2723) defends a "subjective fit" account of gender identity, on which, for instance,

> a trans woman's desire to have female sex characteristics or judgment that she ought not have male sex characteristics can be an important part of her gender identity because it is the reason why she takes the gender category *woman* to fit her.

Cosker-Rowland, unfortunately, has nothing illuminating to say about what a gender is, providing only an incomplete list of alleged genders (2024, 2702): woman, man, genderqueer, or *another gender*. Yet I believe there's some truth here: one notices features of the sexes—including his own—and norms about the sexes in one's society, and judges that a certain category best "fits" the attitudes that he has about the sexes (including his own) and the norms about the sexes. This category, activists would say, names the person's "gender identity."[18]

One such attitude that a person might have toward the sexes, including his own, or toward the norms our society holds about the sexes, is one of by-and-large acceptance. One might accept that he's a male, and that he's a man, and on the whole accept our society's norms of masculinity (the good ones, anyway). That's basically me, for example: your average masculinity-acceptor. Such a person would count as having the gender identity of man, and/or male, according to these thinkers. Another attitude one might have toward the sexes, including his own, and toward the norms our society holds about the sexes, is one of *rejection* or defiance. Such a person might take the label 'non-binary' to "make the most sense out of [his] feels," as Ashley might put it, and follow Robin Dembroff (2018b), who considers "nonbinary identity to be an unabashedly political identity. It is for anyone who wishes to wield self-understanding in service of dismantling a mandatory, self-reproducing gender system that strictly controls what we can do and be." Another attitude one might take is *ambivalence*, or vacillation, toward the sexes, including his own, and toward his society's sex norms, and interpret this attitude as fitting the name 'genderfluid'. Perhaps such a person sometimes has a pro-attitude toward masculinity, being neutral with respect to femininity, while at other times these attitudes flip. Ashley (2023, 1066) lists "thrashgender" as a possible gender identity, and suggests that someone may arrive at that label due to "the inability of common labels to capture the nuances of their gender subjectivity." So, whatever attitude this person has toward the sexes and toward sex norms, 'thrashgender' is meant to communicate that attitude.[19]

If this is indeed the nature of gender identity, one can see why Dembroff (2018a) would believe that "the scope of gender identities outside of male and female is vast and effectively unlimited": because the scope of *attitudes* that one might take toward the sexes and toward his society's sex norms is vast and effectively unlimited, as are the terms that might describe these attitudes. And—importantly—it would also explain why being a bachelor is not a gender identity, nor is having mixed feelings about being a bachelor or about the norms of bachelorhood: because 'bachelor' does not name a sex, nor does it name an attitude one might have about the sexes, or about the social norms or expectations of the sexes. This account would help make sense of activists' use of 'gender' in this area: when they say that gender identity is the internal sense of one's own *gender*, the latter use of 'gender' is short-hand for biological sex itself, and for a society's norms, roles, expectations, and stereotypes about the sexes.

Note well: none of this is to *condone* the appropriation of the words 'male', 'female', 'man', and 'woman' to try to name gender identities, as, for example, Advocates for Trans Equality explicitly do.[20] As I've argued elsewhere, no good reasons have been given for thinking that women are not adult human females and men are not adult human males (Bogardus 2020), and there are reasons to think that intentionally revising the meanings of these words will not accomplish the revisionists' own goals (Bogardus 2019, 2022). In the next chapter, I will argue that the same goes for our sex terms. And it's hard to see how, for example, one could *correctly* judge that 'female' best describes him, given his attitudes toward the sexes and his society's sex norms, if he himself is not in fact female. It seems the most a male could correctly say is that he has attitudes (about the sexes, including his own, and about sex norms) that are *typically had by* females. But, of course, it wouldn't follow from this that he himself is female, and it would be misleading to say so. At least, while using 'female' with its ordinary meaning.

Rather, here I mean only to offer a suggestion about what type of psychological state trans activists have in mind when they talk about gender identities. This suggestion also makes sense of why trans activists claim to have—or claim that they *should be treated* as having—a special sort of first-person authority over, or privileged access to, their gender identities (cf. Bettcher 2009, 99–103): because humans generally have—or should be treated as having—that sort of authority over their mental attitudes, even if we recognize that this privileged access is not *infallible*. As I said above with respect to being a bachelor, this suggestion about the nature of gender identity also explains why gender identities are so closely related to the sexes and to sex norms, and why other (very important) aspects of one's identity do *not* count as gender identities, for example, being a brother, or a father, or a Californian, or a philosopher.

Summing up: often, 'gender' is used as a synonym for sex. This is true even when people talk about gender roles and gender norms. Gender roles are typical social roles of *the sexes*. Gender norms are norms and expectations about *the sexes*. So, in this usage of 'gender', there simply is no distinction between sex and gender, and therefore our investigation into the nature of the sexes was simultaneously an investigation into the nature of the genders, and whatever is true of one is true of the other. But there are other uses of 'gender', for example, Robert Stoller's use of 'gender' to refer to the genus of masculinity and femininity, where these are norms, expectations, and stereotypes about the sexes. On this use of 'gender', gender is indeed distinct from sex, but, in the end, gender is defined *partly* in terms of sex. So, our investigation into the nature of the sexes will have implications for this sense of 'gender' as well; in order to understand what Stoller and others mean by 'gender', one must understand masculinity and femininity, and in order to understand those, one must understand the sexes.

Next, there's the claim that 'gender' refers to men and women. I argued that, suitably clarified, this claim rests on a mistake about how the terms 'man' and 'woman' work. These terms are not short for 'the masculine people' and 'the feminine people', respectively. Really, the person making this claim likely means to use 'gender' as Stoller did, to name the genus of masculinity and femininity. Finally, there's a use of 'gender' to refer to a psychological state, namely gender identity. I proposed that gender identity is a person's internal sense of his own attitudes toward the sexes, or toward his society's norms about the sexes (or both), and which label best fits, best describes, best captures those attitudes. As before, if this is correct, then again sex is distinct from gender, but, in the end, gender is defined partly in terms of sex. So, our investigation into the nature of the sexes will have implications for this use of 'gender' as well. To understand what gender identity is, one must understand what a gender is, and to understand that, one must understand the sexes. To the degree that we have disclosed the nature of the sexes, we have helped to shed some light on what gender identity is meant to be.

Like Stock (2021, ch. 1) and Byrne (2023a, ch. 2), I think much of what's happening with our society's use of 'gender' these days is confused and obscure. I hope this chapter has offered some degree of clarity. Like Stock, but unlike Byrne, this confusion and obscurity lead me to conclude that we shouldn't hold onto the word 'gender' at all, and not even for a polite synonym for the sexes. An alternative has emerged in recent years: 'biological sex'. This phrase avoids any conflation with copulation, and therefore is polite and modest in the way we'd like. And if we wish to talk about the genus of masculinity and femininity—the norms or roles typically associated with the biological sexes—we certainly can, perhaps by using the phrase 'norms of the sexes' or 'roles of the sexes'. And if we wish to talk about men and women, we certainly can, without any need to speak of a genus for these, beyond being human. Or, if need be, we might talk about the *adult sexes* in humans (men and women), and the *juvenile sexes* in humans (boys and girls). Unlike Stock, I think we could get by even without 'gender identity', and jettisoning that phrase would likely clarify the conversation. If we wish to talk about gender identities, we can say more exactly what we mean, without using the word 'gender'. Perhaps we might revert to a previous candidate from Robert Stoller: 'sexual identity'. While this might initially be confused with 'sexual orientation', I believe that latter phrase has become so common that such confusion would be unlikely, especially with repeated, regular use of 'sexual identity'. Alternatively, if we like, we might use 'attitudes about the sexes' to more accurately name what now swirls under the heading of 'gender identity'. The perplexity produced by the proliferative uses of 'gender' is well worth avoiding. So, the benefits of using these sex-based alternatives to 'gender' are apparent. As for the costs, well, personally, I see none. So, I'd recommend that, for the sake of clarity and ease of communication, we should all shift toward using sex-based alternatives to 'gender' and similar constructions. 'Gender' has caused far more trouble than it's worth.

Notes

1 https://www.c-span.org/classroom/document/?23985. In a corresponding Executive Order, titled 'Defending women from gender ideology extremism and restoring biological truth to the federal government', Trump writes that "It is the policy of the United States to recognize two sexes, male and female." It seems that President Trump is among those who use 'gender' as a polite synonym for 'sex', as we'll soon discuss. https://www.whitehouse.gov/presidential-

actions/2025/01/defending-women-from-gender-ideology-extremism-and-restoring-biological-truth-to-the-federal-government/.
2 See also Mari Mikkola (2016, 23), who says "Speakers ordinarily seem to think that 'gender' and 'sex' are coextensive." And see a nice statement on 'gender' from W.V.O. Quine's "intermittently philosophical dictionary," quoted in Byrne (2023a, 35):

> The latter-day upheaval in sexual mores has increased the frequency of occasions for referring politely to copulation, and has thus created a demand for a short but equally polite word for the practice. The word *sex* has been pressed into that service, and thus rendered less convenient as a means of referring to the sexes. The resulting need has been met in turn by calling the sexes *genders*.

Quine sets this use aside and goes on to discuss *grammatical* gender (at length).
3 https://www.nhm.ac.uk/discover/beauty-dual-gender-butterfly.html.
4 See also Ralph Greenson (1964). According to Byrne (2023b, 2709), coining 'gender identity' was a "joint endeavor" between Stoller and Greenson. Like Stoller, Greenson (1964, 217) defines it in terms of sex: "*Gender identity* refers to one's sense of being a member of a particular sex …".
5 See Byrne 2023b and 2023c on the origin of 'gender identity'.
6 I will omit the "in humans" qualifier in what follows.
7 See Holly Lawford-Smith (2023, chapter 2) for a useful discussion of what accounts for femininity, and "what phenomenon accounts for sex-differentiated behaviour and treatment."
8 See John Money (1955, 254), who defines 'gender role' very broadly so as to include "all those things that a person says or does to disclose himself or herself as having the status of boy or man, girl or woman, respectively. It includes, but is not restricted to sexuality in the sense of eroticism." For inclusion of occupations, see Ann Oakley ([1985] 1972). See also Dupré (1986, 449): "The term 'gender', as it has been developed in contemporary feminist theory, refers to the sexually specific roles that are occupied by men and women in various societies."
9 This will also be the case for other, more idiosyncratic uses of 'gender'. For example, here is Roughgarden (2004, 27) on the genders: "gender is appearance plus action, how an organism uses morphology, including color and shape, plus behavior to carry out a sexual role." So, for Roughgarden, peacocks have a gender, a typical way in which they use their morphology plus behavior to carry out their sexual role. And so do male nematodes, and many plants, presumably. And, generally, anything with a sexual role, which uses its shape and behavior to fulfill that sexual role, will thereby exemplify a gender according to Roughgarden. But why not just speak instead about ways in which the *sexes* reproduce, the body-shapes and behaviors that allow males and females to reproduce? What not, that is, express ourselves using sex terms, rather than multiply the ambiguity of the term 'gender'? Either way, what the sexes are will clearly have a bearing on what the genders are, since gender is defined in terms of the sexes, for Roughgarden.
10 In the second edition, Stryker ([2017] 2008b, chapter 1) moderates this claim a bit, saying "It's usually a safe bet to use the words *man* and *woman* to refer to gender," and yet later says, "[The] set of cultural beliefs and practices about what biological sex means can be called 'gender'." Together, and taken literally, these claims seem to imply that it's usually a safe bet that 'man' refers to a set of cultural beliefs and practices about what it means to be male. But surely, the

fact that I am a man does not make it a safe bet that I am a set of cultural beliefs and practices. And that's a fairly paradigmatic use of the word 'man'. Stryker must intend some other, non-literal interpretation.
11 See Saul Kripke's ([1980] 1972, 102–5) diagnosis of a similar confusion concerning the sentence 'Hesperus is Phosphorus' in *Naming and Necessity*.
12 As late as 1976, de Beauvoir endorsed the traditional definition of woman, saying in an interview, "A positive definition of 'woman'? Woman is a human being with a certain physiology…" (Brison 2003, 192). If that's surprising to you, perhaps that's because, as Sara Heinämaa (1997) argues, de Beauvoir's more famous dictum that "one is not born, but rather becomes, a woman" is commonly misread metaphysically, as a statement about the nature of women, when really de Beauvoir is interested only in a phenomenological description of women's situation. See also Kate Kirkpatrick (2019), who nicely traces the lineage of de Beauvoir's famous saying back to philosophical debates in the 1920s, specifically to similar constructions by Maurice Blondel (Kirkpatrick 2019, 79) and especially Alfred Fouillée's "One isn't born, but rather becomes, free" (Kirkpatrick 2019, 255), a play on Rousseau's famous line, "Man is born free, and everywhere he is in chains." In that light, Kirkpatrick interprets de Beauvoir's dictum as a claim about the socialization and oppression of women (i.e. adult human females), rather than a revisionary claim about the metaphysics of womanhood.
13 If you want to say that 'hombre' refers to a gender distinct from that named by 'man', because the norms and expectations of males in Spain, say, are at least a little different from the norms and expectations of males in the United States, say, then some strange things follow. One implication is that there are no men in Spain, or at least far fewer than one might have originally thought, and they're mostly tourists. Another implication is that there haven't *always* been men in the United States, since the norms and expectations of males in the United States have changed over time.
14 Or, at least, the number of genders *for a society* will be limited to the number of sexes, if you hold the view described in the previous note. But see that note for a couple implausible implications of that view.
15 https://transequality.org/trans-101/about-transgender-people. See also the Human Rights Campaign: https://www.hrc.org/resources/sexual-orientation-and-gender-identity-terminology-and-definitions. See also the US Centers for Disease Control and Prevention: https://www.cdc.gov/healthy-youth/lgbtq-youth/terminology.html. See also the American Psychological Association: https://www.apa.org/topics/lgbtq/transgender-people-gender-identity-gender-expression. See also Stonewall: https://www.stonewall.org.uk/resources/list-lgbtq-terms.
16 Briggs and George (2023, 1) open chapter 1 with this stunning admission: "despite the title *What Even Is Gender?*, we're not going to tell you what 'gender' is…" Of course, it's no mystery what 'gender' is—an English word of six letters. But they intend, I take it, to say they also won't tell us what gender is. They later offer (Briggs and George, 2023, 139–40) an incomplete list of gender categories, including the hypothetical ad hoc self-descriptive category *cactus*. If Cass declares his gender category is *cactus*, we're told, then we should designate him accordingly.
17 For another viciously circular definition of 'gender', see this page from the American Psychological Association: https://dictionary.apa.org/gender. The APA then defines 'gender identity' in terms of this viciously circular definition

of 'gender', here: https://dictionary.apa.org/gender-identity. The definition: "a person's psychological sense of self in relation to their gender."
18 Kathleen Stock (2021, ch. 4) advances an "identification model" of gender identity, according to which "to have a misaligned female gender identity is to identify strongly, in this psychological sense, either with a particular female or with femaleness as a general object or ideal." That's certainly in the same ballpark as what I'm suggesting here, though I would define gender identity more generally to mean one's attitude(s) toward the sexes, including one's own, and toward his society's norms about the sexes.
19 Maybe what one means to communicate by using that label is that his attitude toward his sex and to his society's sex norms is akin to the feeling one typically has while listening to thrash metal, a fast, aggressive version of heavy metal, influenced by gritty early punk music: perhaps intense anger or even angst. Maybe. I can only speculate.
20 They say, "Note: A4TE uses both the adjectives 'male' and 'female' and the nouns 'man' and 'woman' to refer to a person's gender identity." https://transequality.org/trans-101/about-transgender-people. So does the CDC, that is, the US Centers for Disease Control and Prevention, apparently, when they say that gender identity is a person's "inner sense of being a boy/man/male, girl/woman/female, another gender, or no gender." Notice that 'male' allegedly names a gender, there. https://www.cdc.gov/healthy-youth/lgbtq-youth/terminology.html. Jenkins (2018, 714 n. 3) uses 'male' and 'female' to describe gender identities, and explicitly says she is not "using 'male/female' as sex terms rather than gender terms." And Cosker-Rowland (2024, 2701) does the same:

> To be trans is to have a gender identity that is different from the gender you were assigned at birth: for instance, trans women were assigned male at birth but have a female gender identity; trans men were assigned female at birth but have a male gender identity.

Question 32 of a New York Times/Ipsos public poll, conducted in January of 2025, asks respondents about "transgender female athletes—meaning athletes who were male at birth but who currently identify as female." Notice the use of 'female' to describe these athletes who identify as female. https://static01.nyt.com/newsgraphics/documenttools/f548560f100205ef/e656ddda-full.pdf. And Dea (2016, 21) does the same, saying "If I think of myself as female, that is my gender identity".

References

American Civil Liberties Union (2025). Orr v. Trump, "Class Action Complaint for Declaratory and Injunctive Relief." https://www.aclu.org/cases/orr-v-trump

Ashley, Florence (2021). "'X' Why? Gender Markers and Non-binary Transgender People," in *Trans Rights and Wrongs: A Comparative Study of Legal Reform Concerning Trans Persons*, Isabel C. Jaramillo, and Laura Carlson (eds.) (Cham, Switzerland: Springer).

Ashley, Florence (2023). "What is it Like to Have a Gender Identity?" *Mind* 132: 1053–73.

Barnes, Elizabeth (2018). "The Metaphysics of Gender," in *The Norton Introduction to Philosophy*, G. Rosen, A. Byrne, J. Cohen, E. Harman, and S. Shiffrin (eds.) (New York: Norton), 581–9.

Bettcher, Talia Mae (2009). "Trans Identities and First-Person Authority," in *You've Changed: Sex Reassignment and Personal Identity*, Laurie Shrage (ed.) (New York: Oxford University Press), 98–120.
Bogardus, Tomas (2019). "Some Internal Problems for Revisionary Gender Concepts," *Philosophia* 48: 55–75.
Bogardus, Tomas (2020). "Evaluating Arguments for the Sex/Gender Distinction," *Philosophia* 48: 873–92.
Bogardus, Tomas (2022). "Why the Trans Inclusion Problem cannot be Solved," *Philosophia* 50: 1639–64.
Briggs, R. A., and B. R. George (2023). *What Even is Gender?* (New York: Routledge).
Brison, Susan J. (2003). "Beauvoir and Feminism: Interview and Reflections," in *The Cambridge Companion to Simone de Beauvoir*, C. Card (ed.) (Cambridge: Cambridge University Press).
Byrne, Alex (2023a). *Trouble with Gender* (Cambridge, UK: Polity Press).
Byrne, Alex (2023b). "The Origin of 'Gender Identity'," *Archives of Sexual Behavior* 52: 2709–11.
Byrne, Alex (2023c). "More on 'Gender Identity'," *Archives of Sexual Behavior* 52: 2719–21.
Coleman, E., A. E. Radix, W. P. Bouman, G. R. Brown, A. L. C. de Vries, M. B. Deutsch, ... J. Arcelus (2022). "Standards of Care for the Health of Transgender and Gender Diverse People, Version 8," *International Journal of Transgender Health* 23 (sup1): S1–259.
Cosker-Rowland, Rach (2024). "Gender Identity: The Subjective Fit Account," *Philosophical Studies* 181: 2701–36.
Dea, Shannon (2016). *Beyond the Binary: Thinking about Sex and Gender* (Peterborough, Canada: Broadview Press).
Dembroff, Robin (2018a). "The Non-Binary Gender Trap," *New York Review of Books*, January 30th, 2018. https://www.nybooks.com/online/2018/01/30/the-nonbinary-gender-trap
Dembroff, Robin (2018b). "Why be Nonbinary?," *Aeon Magazine*, October 30th, 2018. https://aeon.co/essays/nonbinary-identity-is-a-radical-stance-against-gender-segregation
Dupré, John (1986). "Sex, Gender, and Essence," *Midwest Studies in Philosophy* 11 (1): 441–57.
Greenson, Ralph R. (1964). "On Homosexuality and Gender Identity," *International Journal of Psycho-Analysis* 45: 217–9.
Haslanger, Sally (2000). "Gender and Race: (What) are They? (What) do We Want Them to be?," *Noûs* 34 (1): 31–55.
Heinämaa, Sara (1997). "What is a Woman?," *Hypatia* 12 (1): 20–39.
Jenkins, Katarine (2018). "Toward an Account of Gender Identity," *Ergo* 5 (27): 713–44.
Kirkpatrick, Kate (2019). *Becoming Beauvoir: A Life* (New York: Bloomsbury Academic).
Kripke, Saul ([1980], 1972). *Naming and Necessity* (Cambridge, MA: Harvard University Press).
Lawford-Smith, Holly (2023). *Sex Matters: Essays in Gender-Critical Philosophy* (Oxford: Oxford University Press).
Mikkola, Mari (2016). *The Wrong of Injustice: Dehumanization and its Role in Feminist Philosophy* (New York: Oxford University Press).

Money, John (1955). "Hermaphroditism, Gender and Precocity in Hyperadrenocorticism: Psychologic Findings," *Bulletin of the Johns Hopkins Hospital* 96: 253–64.
Oakley, Ann ([1985] 1972). *Sex, Gender, and Society* (Aldershot, UK: Gower Publishing Company Ltd.).
Roughgarden, Joan (2004). *Evolution's Rainbow* (Berkeley: University of California Press).
Stock, Kathleen (2021). *Material Girls* (London: Fleet).
Stoller, Robert (1964). "A Contribution to the Study of Gender Identity," *International Journal of Psychoanalysis* 45: 220–6.
Stoller, Robert ([1984] 1968). *Sex and Gender: On the Development of Masculinity and Femininity* (London: Karnac Books, Ltd.).
Stryker, Susan (2008). *Transgender History* (Berkeley, CA: Seal Press).
Stryker, Susan ([2017] 2008). *Transgender History*, Second Edition (Berkeley, CA: Seal Press).

5
WHEN BIOLOGY MEETS POLITICS

Introduction

As I said in the introduction, I believe Rifkin and Garson (2023, 2) are correct when they suggest that biology has special authority to shape our ontology of sex: the way that biologists talk and think about sex should inform our understanding of what sex is. In this chapter, I will argue for that claim and respond to some recent objections against it. After that, I will consider the suggestion that, whatever 'male' and 'female' currently refer to, we should endeavor to change that through a process philosophers call "conceptual engineering," for the sake of social justice. I will describe some problems and limitations of that sort of revisionary project.

Why Defer to Biologists?

Many thinkers and writers in this area agree that, when we investigate the nature of the sexes—when we attempt to figure out exactly what 'male' and 'female' are referring to—we are joining a *long-standing* conversation about the sexes, about males and females. They don't mean to change the subject, to simply borrow the words 'sex', 'male', and 'female', and use these words to express novel concepts, and to speak, rather misleadingly, of new topics. This long-standing conversation goes back at least to Aristotle. Very early in *Generation of Animals* ([1943], 5. I.i.715a18–20), Aristotle makes it clear that the subject of his study will include θηλεος and αρρενος. What are these two things, one wonders? When one reads the context, there is no great mystery:

> some animals are formed as a result of the copulation of θηλεος and αρρενος, namely, animals belonging to those groups in which there exist both θηλεος and αρρενος, for we must remember that not all groups have both θηλεος and αρρενος (NB: substitution of the Greek terms for their English translations is due to me).

As one reads through this text, it is clear that Aristotle is talking about males and females, the same males and females we've been thinking about in this book. This conversation about males and females has persisted through the centuries. It's hard to doubt that our early human ancestors noted the distinction between males and females while hunting, domesticating plants and animals, mating, etc.

Now, it's quite plausible that, in joining this long-standing conversation, we are *deferring* to an established linguistic practice. As Mark Sainsbury and Michael Tye put it (2012, 42), deference occurs when

> we aim to conform in our usage to our previous usage, and to the usage of those in our conceptual community... The deference takes the form of intending to use the concept as it has been used by oneself or others on previous occasions...

That is, many of those working in this area demonstrate, as Sainsbury and Tye later put it (2012, 70), "the recognition that others already use a concept, together with the desire to use the very concept they use, with the very reference it has in their uses." So, as I say, many of those working in this area intend to conform to the usage of those in our conceptual community, and particularly to the experts, if there be any.

Let me quickly forestall one possible misunderstanding. To say that many working in the field desire to use a *concept* already in circulation, with the same *reference*, is decidedly *not* to say that these folks desire to use the same *conception* already in circulation. As an example of this distinction, consider that both proponents and opponents of President Donald Trump use the same *concept* when thinking and speaking *about him*, the same mental representation of Trump, something like a word in the language of thought. And yet at the same time, of course, the groups have very different *conceptions* of the man, different ideas, beliefs, attitudes, and so on. They use different *contingent marks* to identify Trump, to fix the reference of the name 'Trump'. One group has a positive conception of Trump, the other has a negative conception of Trump, but both of these are conceptions *of Trump*. Each group certainly doesn't defer to the other's *conception* of Trump. But each group manifests the intention to speak of *that guy*, to speak to (and contradict) each other, by using the same concept with the same reference (i.e. Trump). In a similar way, what I mean to say is that many people working in this area intend to think and speak of the same *phenomenon* that, for example, Aristotle was thinking and speaking about, though of course our conceptions surrounding that phenomenon are different—and better match reality—than Aristotle's conceptions.[1]

Beans Velocci (2024) recently illustrated the importance of this distinction, albeit by conflating it. On the one hand, Velocci says (2024, 1343), "Sex has been a topic of inquiry since at least antiquity…" Yes, just so, as I've said. Velocci then catalogs different theories about what the sexes are, different "definitions and ways of identifying sex" (Velocci 2024, 1344). There is the conflation between, on the one hand, *definitions* of sex—theories about what the sexes are, theories about what exactly it is that our sex terms refer to—and, on the other hand, "ways of identifying sex," that is, the marks by which we fix the reference of our sex terms. Velocci then mistakenly concludes that "sex is neither static nor unitary in its meaning," and that "scientists have used multiple meanings of sex for a long time" (Velocci 2024, 1345).[2] Multiple *meanings*. But here too, the conflation manifests itself; this claim trades on an ambiguity in the word 'meaning'. What Velocci says is true if we take the meaning of 'sex' to be *in the head*, as it were, to be one's conception of sex, one's ideas or theories, or ways of identifying the sexes. But what Velocci says is false if we take the meaning of 'sex' to be sex, that is, the *referent* of the word out there in the world, what the word is picking out. And that's because, again, as Velocci seems to admit, sex—that phenomenon—has been a topic of inquiry since at least antiquity. We may join that ongoing conversation about a particular phenomenon out there in the world, while at the same time correcting mistaken ideas people have had in their heads about that phenomenon, as we might join long-standing conversations about light, or the Sun, or rainbows, or water, or blood, or the brain, or disease, etc., while correcting mistaken ideas that people in the past have had of these phenomena.[3]

Take, for example, Anne Fausto-Sterling (2012, 3), who proposes to "start with a traditional framework, fill in some of the things we currently know about the biology of sex development, and then loop back to offer some interesting tidbits that complicate the basic story just a bit." Evidently, Fausto-Sterling intends to join an ongoing conversation about the biology of sex development. She intends to talk about the same things that biologists have long been talking about, though she promises to say new things about that old topic. And consider Sarah Richardson (2022, 2), who says she aims to "analyze 'sex' in biomedicine as a similarly context-dependent construct, tracing its uses and meanings within the pragmatics of biomedical research." And even Sari van Anders (2024, 473), in a section titled "What is sex?" appears to be talking about the very same phenomenon that Aristotle was talking about, though of course she aspires to correct various misconceptions about it.[4] Here, too, we have thinkers who wish to join a conversation about sex in biological research, a conversation with a long history. So, there are quite a few people working in this area who don't wish to originate new concepts, and then borrow old *words* 'male' and 'female' to express those new concepts, the way that one repurposes an old name ("Joan," say) at a baptism ceremony, in order to originate a new concept to refer to the new baby.

But if that's right, then if we wish to know what these concepts *refer* to, what the paradigmatic cases of males and females are, we should look to those engaged in this ongoing conversation, and especially to the experts, if there be any. We should look, that is, to those most familiar with the phenomenon we're interested in, those most acquainted and knowledgeable about the phenomenon. This is not a novel methodology. One finds it expressed by thinkers working on the neighboring issue of discerning what the word 'woman' means. Jennifer Saul (2012, 200) recommends that we appeal to a "collection of ordinary usage data" when theorizing about the ordinary meaning of 'woman'. Nick Laskowski (2020) says that our theorizing should satisfy a "usage constraint": our theories should account for the available data about patterns of usage. This is the methodology that I recommend in this book: consider how our sex terms are used, especially by experts, if there be any, when homing in on the phenomenon that we'd like to define.

The phenomenon that I, Fausto-Sterling, Richardson, van Anders, and many others are interested in is, frankly, using Aristotle's words, *reproduction*: animals formed as a result of copulation. And, specifically, reproduction accomplished by species that seem to have two types, two forms. What we *call* these forms isn't so very important—θηλεος and αρρενος, мужской and женский, *männlich* and *weiblich*, *mannelijk* and *vrouwelijk*, *mâle* and *femelle*, male and female. The point is simply this: if we are indeed interested in sexual reproduction across the plant and animal kingdoms, then we ought to look toward those most familiar with the phenomenon, those most acquainted and knowledgeable about the phenomenon, when regulating our use of the words. If we intend to join an ongoing linguistic practice, and to use the concepts used by that practice, without shifting the reference of those concepts, then we should look to how the concept is being used in this practice, and especially to those who use the concepts most competently, that is, the experts. If someone thinks a certain seahorse is female because it's incubating its young, and yet biologists tell him that, nevertheless, it's a *male* seahorse, he should accept this correction, at least defeasibly. If someone is under the impression that nematodes couldn't possibly have sexes because they're too primitive, and then biologists tell him these nematodes come in male and hermaphroditic varieties, he should accept this correction, at least defeasibly. What I'm suggesting is that the experts on our phenomenon are the biologists, and, therefore, that biology has special authority to shape our ontology of sex. The ways in which they apply 'male' and 'female' should regulate our own use of these words. Of course, like any red-blooded American, a child of revolution, I say this authority is not *absolute*. It may be defeated, but the defeating considerations should be especially strong.[5]

In a recent essay, Watkins and DiMarco (2025) argue for the elimination of sex. Or, more accurately—and less provocatively—what they argue for is that "'sex', [sic] at least as currently conceived by biologists, is not biologically real" (Watkins and DiMarco 2025, 18).[6] So, they mean to show at least that our current *conceptions* of the sexes are mistaken. They also argue for "eliminativism about the concept of biological sex" (Watkins and DiMarco 2025, 1), just as Velocci (2024, 1346) argues that we should "let go" of the category of sex.[7] And yet even these authors acknowledge the following point (Watkins and DiMarco 2025, 22): "An account of biological sex should be accountable to the best of our biological knowledge, so evidence about birds, bees, and other systems of incredible sexual diversity can count as evidence against, e.g., phenotypic, chromosomal, or gametic accounts." Yes, that's exactly right. Any account of biological sex should be accountable to the best of our biological knowledge. As I've said, biology has special authority to shape our ontology of sex. If someone offers a naïve account of the sexes on which to be male is to have XY chromosomes, it is strong contrary evidence that, according to biologists, there are birds without XY chromosomes who are nevertheless male. (In birds, males have two identical sex chromosomes, ZZ, while females have one Z and one W chromosome.)

So, the methodology of this book has been simply this: to notice how members of our linguistic community—but *especially* the biologists—regularly use the terms 'male' and 'female', and to engage in an interpretive exercise, to try to discern what the natures of the sexes are, in a way that makes the best sense of how we—but *especially* biologists—use those sex terms across the natural world. That's the main constraint on the project. In this, I agree with Watkins and DiMarco (2025, 18), when they endorse this statement we've seen before from Roughgarden (2004, 23): "'Male' and 'female' are biological categories, and the criteria for classifying an organism as male or female have to work with worms to whales, with red seaweed to redwood trees." Understanding what the methodology of this book has been will help us respond to a few objections, below.

Objections to Deferring to Biologists

In this section, I'll respond to two recent objections to the methodology of this book, which I described and defended in the last section. One alleged problem is conceptual, the other is epistemic, but they both rest on the same misunderstanding. Then, I'll respond to an objection from Sally Haslanger.

The first two objections come from Watkins and DiMarco (2025). Their first objection, which I say is fairly called a conceptual problem, goes like this (Watkins and DiMarco 2025, 9):

> [Monist realist accounts of sex] carve out a subset of the natural world to which their proposed sex concept applies, in such a way that precludes the possibility that we might find empirical evidence that their concept doesn't apply... The problem is that when the reference class is circumscribed to be exactly those organisms to which the concept applies well, the concept itself cannot be tested for empirical adequacy...

They elaborate on the following page (Watkins and DiMarco 2025, 10):

> Another way to phrase our worry: why should the concept of sex apply to anisogamous-organisms-with-two-gamete-types, rather than anisogamous-organisms, or rather than sexually-reproducing-organisms (some of which are isogamous)? Why should we think that the concept of *sex* [sic] applies to anisogamous-organisms-with-two-gamete-types, while other concepts, like 'mating types' apply to all other sexually reproducing organisms?

Again (Watkins and DiMarco 2025, 9), they say "we should be able to be wrong about what [our sex terms] mean or what they reference." And, finally, they summarize the objection like so (Watkins and DiMarco 2025, 11): "the gametic sex concept precludes the possibility of disconfirming evidence for the hypothesis that there are really two sexes."

Let's make sure we understand the worry. Watkins and DiMarco seem concerned about any gamete-based definition of the sexes, including the AHOF account of the sexes we developed in Chapter 3. And the concern seems to be that there is something illegitimate about accepting this definition, something arbitrary, something not quite above board. It's *cheating*, you might say. By adopting a gamete-based definition of the sexes, they suggest, one precludes, from the start, the possibility of more than two sexes. One rules that possibility out, by fiat, rather than by a careful consideration of the evidence. And this gets things the wrong way around, methodologically. Instead, as they say (Watkins and DiMarco

2025, 22), "An account of biological sex should be accountable to the best of our biological knowledge." And, therefore, the proper way to approach the question is to survey the best of our biological knowledge and come up with a theory of the sexes that works across the natural world. We should form a theory in light of the data, rather than interpreting data in light of a theory we have already adopted arbitrarily. The concern is that—somehow—a gamete-based definition of the sexes gets the methodology wrong in exactly that way. It puts the cart before the horse, the theory before the data.

In response, I admit that an advocate of a gamete-based view *may* make that mistake, the mistake of starting with the theory, adopted arbitrarily, and interpreting the data in light of that theory. An advocate of a gamete-based view may well, that is, simply *stipulate* that the sexes are defined in terms of anisogamy—different gamete-types, for example, sperm and eggs—and then declare that isogametic species have only mating types rather than genuine sexes, because they don't have sperm or eggs.[8] Yes, an advocate of a gamete-based view *could* make that mistake. But... they also *might not* make that mistake. In fact, it's fairly easy to avoid. And an advocate of any other theory of the sexes could also make that same methodological mistake, including advocates of the view that we should eliminate the concept of the sexes, for example, Watkins and DiMarco. The more important question is: why think that all advocates of gamete-based theories of the sexes *are* in fact making that mistake?

For there's an obvious alternative explanation of how one might arrive at a gamete-based account of the sexes, or any other theory of the sexes, for that matter. One might, as I described in the last section, notice how members of our linguistic community—but *especially* the biologists—regularly use the terms 'male' and 'female', and to engage in an interpretive exercise, to try to discern what the natures of the sexes are, in a way that makes the best sense of how we—but *especially* biologists—use those sex terms across the natural world. And it may well be that the best such interpretation of our uses of our sex terms—the best theory about what exactly they refer to—is an (anisogamous) gamete-based account. Indeed, I've argued in Chapter 3 that this is the fact of the matter, and that our sex terms—when used as adjectives to describe organisms—are picking out activated higher-order functions to produce (anisogamous) gamete-types.

This approach does not illicitly beg any questions, or presume its truth from the outset, or illegitimately rule out additional sexes, or declare *by fiat* that isogamous organisms have only mating types, but no sexes. The theory is formed and justified in light of our best biological evidence. Additional sexes are *not* ruled out, even by a completed version of this theory. If there were additional anisogamous gamete-types, then there could be additional activated higher-order functions to produce them, and therefore additional sexes. And, as we've seen, the fact that biologists call some organisms 'male' and others 'female' does not entail that every organism is one or the other, nor does it entail that no organism is both (think hermaphrodites), nor does it entail that there could not be some new organism requiring a third name for an additional sex. So, I conclude that this objection is without merit.

A second objection to my deference to biologists also comes from Watkins and DiMarco. They say (2025, 10):

> We are not convinced that deference to biological practice is justified in this case... Biologists can be wrong, and part of the role of philosophers in relation to science is to provide guidance to scientists, including about whether the concepts that they are using are adequate... In the case of sex, one obvious reason to not defer to biologists is that there is disagreement among biologists themselves about what sex is and what role it should play in investigation...

But I hope that, by this point, the response is obvious. Biologists certainly differ in their *conceptions* of the sexes; they disagree over the nature of the referents of our sex terms. Aristotle said that an organism is female in virtue of its inability to effect the concoction of semen, and of the coldness of its bloodlike nourishment. What he said about the sexes was incorrect, but what he said was *about the sexes*. As we saw above, some say that our sex terms are ambiguous and are used to refer to a variety of things. I've argued that they're mistaken. Others say, with Griffiths, that sexes are regions of phenotypic space, and still others say that the sexes have something to do with developmental pathways. Some say the sexes are activated higher-order functions to produce anisogamous gamete-types. And so on. There is indeed widespread disagreement over proposed *analyses* of the sexes, but these analyses are proposed to be real definitions *of the sexes*. And, crucially, I should hope that everyone engaged in this project holds themselves accountable to how our linguistic community—and especially the biologists—employ these sex terms. These are the rules of the game, as it were, and we all abide by them. While we may have incompatible conceptions or theories about the natures of the sexes, we all hold ourselves accountable to the ways in which biologists apply these terms to various organisms. While we disagree over *theories* about what sex is, we agree on the *data* that these theories answer to: namely, the organisms that the relevant experts call 'male' and those they call 'female'. Just as epistemologists might disagree about *theories* of knowledge, and yet agree that these theories are answerable to certain *data*, in this case, to applications of the term 'knowledge' by competent speakers. So, this second objection seems no more successful than the first.

Finally, let's consider a third objection, this one from Sally Haslanger (2016, 139). She begins by noting that "there is considerable controversy over how to understand the kinds *males* and *females*." She then considers the suggestion that "the case should simply be settled 'by science', since the distinction is a biological one." But, she says, "that begs the question about the purposes of the distinction." To answer questions like "What is a male?" and "What is a female?" her recommendation is that first we "consider carefully the question we are asking, the purposes we have in asking the question, and evidence before us" (Haslanger 2016, 140). So, again, we have here an objection to the methodology I've employed in this book, namely that we should notice how members of our linguistic community—but *especially* the biologists—regularly use the terms 'male' and 'female', and to engage in an interpretive exercise, to try to discern what exactly they're referring to, that is, to try to discern the natures of the sexes.

In response, I believe that Haslanger's suggestion gets things the wrong way around. Before we can think about what purposes we'd like to put the male/female distinction to, we first must understand what the distinction *is* and what the words mean. Suppose I ask you, "What is the بیرغ / میرا distinction?" Would you really begin by reflecting on what purpose you'd like to put the distinction to? *Could* you even do that? Wouldn't you rather first figure out what the words mean, what they refer to, what the distinction *is*? And, no doubt, you'd give special authority to the relevant experts, which in that case would be the Urdu speakers. This is what I propose to do with our sex terms 'male' and 'female': figure out what the words refer to, giving special authority to the relevant experts on biological sex, namely biologists. But, of course, it's one thing to say that this is what our sex terms *do* refer to, and another thing to say that they *should*. And it's to that latter question we now turn.

Should We Revise What Our Sex Terms Refer To?

There is a great deal of political interest in the answer to the question of what a sex is. As Sarah Richardson (2022, 1) put it, "the biological construct of 'sex' is a site of power and politics." For example, shortly after the inauguration of his second term, President Donald Trump issued an Executive Order declaring that "It is the policy of the United States to recognize two sexes, male and female," and section 3 of that order requires the Secretary of Health and Human Services to "expand[] on the sex-based definitions set forth in this order," as well as requiring every federal agency to use gamete-based definitions of the sexes "when interpreting or applying statutes, regulations, or guidance and in all other official agency business, documents, and communications."[9] Power and politics indeed, and at the highest level. Zachary DuBois and Heather Shattuck-Heidorn (2021, 2) say that there are

> renewed debates regarding the boundaries of human sex, where lines of genetics, 'sex hormones', and secondary sex characteristics are drawn to defend a strict biologically based sex binary, with attendant implications for the acceptability and limits of gender identity and expression for all people. Whether regulating testosterone levels and bodies of women and girls in sports, legislating the use of gender-specific bathrooms, or enacting broad-sweeping federal definitions of sex, bodily 'norms' are being weaponized as a means to discriminate.

So, there is no doubt that any proposed definition of the sexes is pregnant with political implications. What sex is— that is, what our sex terms refer to—matters a great deal. But, one might think, isn't it up to *us* what our sex terms refer to? Aren't words our servants, and we their masters? And, therefore, shouldn't we consider the aforementioned political implications when deciding what those terms refer to? Even if we defer to biologists to figure out what our sex terms *actually* refer to, shouldn't we also reflect on what our sex terms *ought* to refer to, in order to achieve our scientific, moral, or political ends? And shouldn't one of those ends be respecting everyone's self-identification? As Jenkins (2016, 396) puts it with regard to *gender* concepts,

> an important desideratum of a feminist analysis of gender concepts is that it respect these identifications by including trans people within the gender categories with which they identify and not including them within any categories with which they do not identify.

But, since trans-identifying individuals also identify themselves using *sex* terms,[10] and these identifications are just as "conceptually linked to forms of transphobic oppression and even violence" (Jenkins 2016, 396) as are identifications as a man or as a woman, a trans activist may just as well think that it's important to respect those self-identifications as well, identifications as male, female, both, neither, or something else. Indeed, Jenkins (2018, 714, n. 3) herself uses 'male' and 'female' to name the sort of "gender identity" categories that she strongly feels must be regulated by a criterion of self-identification.

Among philosophers, this project of intentionally revising our concepts has come to be known as ameliorative inquiry, conceptual ethics, or conceptual engineering.[11] I'll call it conceptual engineering. As I understand it, the procedure involves two stages: a Preparation Stage and a Revisionary Stage.[12] In the Preparation Stage, we identify the current meanings associated with the terms that we wish to reengineer, in this case 'male' and 'female'. This would involve identifying what Sally Haslanger (2012, 375–6) calls the "manifest" concepts—what we *believe* the sexes to be, that is, our *conceptions* of the sexes—as well as the "operative" concepts—the natures of the *referents* of our sex terms, out there in the world. The goal of Chapter 2 of this book was to correct some misconceptions about the sexes, and the goal of Chapter 3 was to identify the actual referents of our sex terms. In slogan form: *females* have the function of producing ova, and *males* have the function of producing sperm, and a *sex* is a function of producing an (anisogamous) gamete-type. This is the subject of our engineering project, the concepts which are to be repaired or enhanced. And then, in the Revisionary Stage, the goal is to modify these concepts via conceptual engineering, and thereby arrive at acceptable "target" concepts of maleness and femaleness, the definitions of which draw just the right boundaries. Concepts that draw the boundaries, that is, where we think they *should* be, to achieve some worthwhile goal(s) of ours.

Chapters 2 and 3 of this text have, in my estimation, completed the Preparation Stage of this two-part process. Now we know what it *actually* is to be male and what it is to be female. "But what *should* the sexes be?" the conceptual engineer asks. If we were inclined to think that's an interesting philosophical question, and thereby motivated to conceptually engineer our sex terms, we would now proceed to the Revisionary Stage of the project. In this stage, we're meant to modify, enhance, or perhaps simply replace the ordinary concepts we identified in the Preparation Stage, and come out the other side with our improved target concepts to express with the words 'male' and 'female', concepts which draw boundaries we find satisfactory. The Preparation Stage took some real effort, and has befuddled many thinkers up to now. However, it's the Revisionary Stage of conceptual engineering that is the *truly* tricky part; that's where the deep difficulties are. There are three challenges associated with this stage of conceptual engineering.

First and foremost, we must *provide acceptably inclusive target concepts*. This is challenging if, from the conceptual engineer's perspective, the goal is to craft a concept to express with the word 'male' that refers to all and only those individuals who identify as male, and similarly with a concept to express with the word 'female'. This is because it's difficult to see, *from the trans activist's perspective*, what all and only (self-identifying) males have in common, and similarly for (self-identifying) females. As the word 'female' is *ordinarily* used, many trans-identifying individuals are female, and yet identify as male. Others, like Buck Angel, are female and also identify as such. Self-identifying males and females, whether they also identify as trans or not, have a wide diversity of sex-linked traits, and a wide diversity of so-called "gender identities," that is, attitudes toward the sexes, including their own, and to their society's norms about the sexes. So, if the trans activists' target extension of 'female' includes individuals from all across each dimension of biological sex, social role, "lived experience," performativity, sexual orientation, attitudes about the sexes, etc., then it will be very difficult to specify a target concept that draws the boundaries in a satisfying way.[13] And we cannot successfully draw these boundaries if we attempt to specify a target concept in a viciously circular way, as seems to be the case with "sincere self-identification" approaches (e.g. Bettcher 2017, 396). We cannot, that is, say that 'male' shall refer to all and only those people who identify as *male*, in the same sense to be defined. No concept is successfully specified by a viciously circular proposal.

The problem is, it sure looks like any other criteria will not be necessarily co-extensive with people's self-identifications: no matter which criteria we choose when designing a target concept, whether someone meets those criteria seems to have no necessary connection with him *identifying* as a female or as a male, in the senses of 'female' and 'male' to be cashed out by those criteria. In that case, there will always be a failure to respect self-identification, and so the project of conceptually engineering our sex terms so as to respect everyone's self-identification is bound to fail. Here's another way to put the worry. Suppose someone new enters a trans-inclusive or queer community, where the meanings of sex terms have (allegedly) already been revised. There should be something that determines whether or not this person is a male. What would this be? The answer is the meaning of the predicate 'is a male' in these communities—the property expressed by that predicate—and the answer must be a set of necessary and sufficient conditions, even if these conditions are vague (like very many definitions in nature), or ineffable due to our conceptual poverty. Maybe we cannot *articulate* what it is to be male, in these communities, but there must be something it *is* to be male.

Suppose we're given this answer: our newcomer is a male if and only if he identifies as a male. The problem is that we seem to be getting *two* answers to our question, which is one too many. This person would have to identify *as* a male, in order to *be* a male. What would he be identifying as? A male, evidently. That's one sense of 'male' that this answer presupposes: the sense that gives the content of the intentional state of *identifying as*. Yet we're also told that to be a male just is to *have* that intentional state: *identifying in that way* is what makes this person a male. This is a *second*, distinct sense of 'male' that the answer proposes. This is the source of my confusion.

Consider this biconditional:

S is a male if and only if S identifies as a male.

If I'm told that the occurrence of 'male' in each bijunct of the proposed biconditional expresses the same concept, the same sense, then the biconditional looks necessarily false. For how could it be, for any feature at all, that to have this feature is to identify as having it? It seems that, in the case at hand at least, each bijunct could be true while the other is false.[14] Indeed, it looks as though it *must* fail to solve this challenge; that challenge looks to be broadly logically insurmountable. And, if so, then the project of conceptually engineering our sex concepts so as to respect everyone's self-identification looks to be impossible.

But imagine we abandon that project, and endeavor instead to revise the meanings of our sex terms in a way that may not respect everyone's self-identification, but which at least will accomplish some other worthwhile scientific, moral, or political end. Now we've traded an insurmountable conceptual or logical problem of the Revisionary Stage for a thorny, obscure, empirical, and political problem. We'd have to suss out the real-world impact of revising our sex concepts on every interested group. We'd have to check not only how this revision would affect trans-identifying individuals, but also males and females more broadly, as those terms 'male' and 'female' are ordinarily used. What costs would be imposed on females, for example, by no longer using 'female' to refer to them? And by interpreting our laws so that laws mentioning 'females' are no longer about females, as the term is ordinarily used? We'd have to weigh a large number of competing, *prima facie* incommensurable interests. This is an enormous task, currently being undertaken by societies across the world, in the cauldron of democracy. Until it's completed in a satisfactory, comprehensive way, it's hard to see how we could complete the Revisionary Stage of conceptual engineering; that process is on hold until we evaluate the proposed target concepts in this arduous, byzantine process. And the stakes are sky high.

Even setting that problem aside, the conceptual engineer will face two additional challenges. The second challenge facing the Revisionary Stage is this: *don't change the subject*. That is, those engaged in conceptual engineering intend to continue a long-standing conversation about sex, males, females, etc. They don't mean to simply borrow the words 'sex', 'male', and 'female', and use them to express novel concepts, and to speak, rather misleadingly, of new topics. (It would be a hollow victory to admit that one's theory of what is to be male is not really about being *male*, but rather about being male*, in some novel, stipulative sense of the word. What's more, it would be difficult to explain why laws intended for males and females should be reinterpreted in an anachronistic way, as really being about males* and females*, rather than replaced with new laws about males* and females*, laws passed via legitimate democratic processes.) This is challenging because it's quite plausible that, like words, concepts are individuated by their origins, and originating uses of concepts—that is, mental acts that instantiate new concepts, rather than existing concepts— are marked by *an intentional lack of deference to established practice.* As Mark Sainsbury and Michael Tye put it (2012, 42), deference occurs when

> we aim to conform in our usage to our previous usage, and to the usage of those in our conceptual community… This is typical of non-originating uses. The deference takes the form of intending to use the concept as it has been used by oneself or others on previous occasions… One characteristic of originating uses is the absence of any such conformist requirement.[15]

Since it is a self-aware project of *revision*, conceptual engineering evidently lacks any intention to conform to the usage of those in our conceptual community. That is, those engaged in conceptual engineering lack, as Sainsbury and Tye say (2012, 70), "the recognition that others already use a concept, together with the desire to use the very concept they use, with the very reference it has in their uses." Conceptual engineers certainly recognize how others already use the relevant concept—in the case of 'male' and 'female', it's pretty clear that a trans-identifying individual may be paradigmatically male and yet identify as female—but they have no desire to use the concept with the very reference it has in common uses. So, the worry is that the Revisionary Stage of conceptual engineering necessarily originates a new concept, appropriates an existing word to express this new concept, and therefore equivocates, changing the subject.[16] And, so, it looks as though the output of conceptual engineering is a *new* concept, not a modified old concept. In which case, we've changed the subject and introduced ambiguity.[17]

The third and final challenge for the Revisionary Stage of Ameliorative Inquiry is that of *using a comprehensive, non-circular methodology.* During the Revisionary Stage, we're meant to engineer a target concept with an eye toward advancing some scientific, moral, or political cause. One potential pitfall during this stage of conceptual engineering is that, in order to understand these causes, and to weigh the pros and the cons, we will have to use some concept of sex, and of males, and of females. But which sex concepts shall we use when evaluating how well these proposed, engineered target concepts advance our various causes? We can't use the novel target concepts themselves at this stage of conceptual engineering, because we're still not sure whether those are good concepts to use; they are the concepts we're evaluating, not yet employing. But if we use the ordinary, biological concepts of sex, of males, and of females in this evaluation process, then (to repeat a point I made above) the challenge is for our methodology to be *comprehensive*, to consider the benefits and costs to all involved. We will have to explain how the revisionary target concept advances our scientific, moral, and political causes in a way that's worth the trade-off to males and females, as those words are ordinarily used. Will science really be better off if we ignore this distinction in nature, a distinction so obvious and widespread that humans have been noticing it, speaking about it, utilizing it in hunting, agriculture, etc., for millennia? Will science really be better served by eliminating the current concept of sex, as Velocci (2024) and Watkins and DiMarco (2025) suggest, and expressing a new concept with the word 'sex'? And as for our moral and political goals, will females, for example, be well served by either ceasing to refer to them as 'females', and reinterpreting laws protecting 'females' so as to no longer be about females?

It's difficult to see how any of this would be other than a serious cost. To my knowledge, nobody engaged in conceptual engineering has tried to spell out exactly how the benefits would outweigh these costs. And at the very least, building that case should be a prerequisite before we rush headlong into an experimental project of conceptual (and social) engineering, just as knowing why a fence was built should be a prerequisite to removing the fence, as G.K. Chesterton famously said.

These, then, are some of the challenges facing the conceptual engineer. Personally, I believe that the status quo with regard to the meanings of our sex terms is morally acceptable, or at least not clearly morally unacceptable, and that whatever moral, political, and scientific goals we have with regard to the sexes could be accomplished using our current conceptual repertoire. We have made great progress, after all, in combating unjust discrimination based on race, age, immigration status, religion, and the like, without reengineering the relevant concepts. So, I'm cautiously optimistic that we could do the same with regard to the concepts we use when thinking and speaking about the sexes. But other parts of our language also seem connected to our ordinary understanding of the sexes, namely, third-person singular pronouns. In our final chapter, we'll turn our attention to these pronouns, whether they do in fact communicate information about the sexes and, if they do, whether we should undertake a project of conceptual engineering in order to change this.

Notes

1 For vivid examples of Aristotle's differing conceptions of the sexes, see especially Book IV, chapter 1 of *Generation of Animals*, where he discusses several different theories about the formation of males and females. Later in that same chapter, he gives this definition of the sexes ([1943], 385–7):

> [T]he male and the female are distinguished by a certain ability and inability. Male is that which is able to concoct, to take shape, and to discharge, semen possessing the 'principle' of the 'form'... Female is that which receives the semen, but is unable to cause semen to take shape or to discharge it. And... all concoction works by means of heat...

Later (Aristotle 1943, 395), he says an organism "is female in virtue of its inability to effect concoction, and of the coldness of its bloodlike nourishment." Though he says some false things here, he says false things *about the sexes*. He is talking about the same phenomena that we are talking about, though his ideas about these phenomena are different from our own.

2 As I said above, though Velocci appears to *use* the word 'sex' rather than *mention* it, I believe the charitable interpretation of this talk of "multiple meanings of sex" is that the *word* 'sex' has multiple meanings.

3 Velocci's ultimate recommendation seems to be that we should "let go of a category [i.e. the category of sex] that hundreds of years of history demonstrates to be more useful for maintaining social hierarchies than for generating scientific knowledge" (Velocci, 2024, 1346). But "letting go" of sex will not cause it to cease to exist, any more than "letting go" of an oncoming asteroid would save humanity from the impact. Even if we "let go" of our *concept* of sex, or of the word 'sex', and simply stop thinking and speaking about the sexes, nevertheless, the sexes will keep right on existing. Reality is very stubborn in that way.

4 She says (van Anders 2024, 473), for example, that "sex can be understood as biological/evolved, biomaterial, and/or bodily/physical aspects of organisms, individuals, or characteristics that can be classified as female, male, and/or sex diverse." When she says that *sex* can be understood in this way, what is she saying can be understood, if not the same phenomenon humans have been talking and thinking about for millennia? If an Aristotelian were to say that the sexes have to do with the heat of the body, wouldn't van Anders draw upon her work to contradict and correct Aristotle? But, if so, it seems that they're talking about *the same phenomenon*.

5 Paul Griffiths (2021, 10):

> This approach to the evolution of sexes is very widely accepted in contemporary biology. That does not mean that it is the final word, but it does mean that a philosopher who wants to dismiss it as a mass of error had better have some powerful arguments.

6 I'm not sure why Watkins and DiMarco put 'sex' in quotation marks. Are they merely mentioning the word, rather than using it? But if we're merely mentioning the word, surely we can all agree that the *word* 'sex' exists, even as currently conceived by biologists.

7 On the same page, they say that we should "eliminat[e] biological sex [sic] from large swaths of biological theory and practice." This must be a use/mention mistake, since surely Watkins and DiMarco do not wish to eliminate biological sex itself. If it doesn't exist, as they may well think, there is nothing to

eliminate. And if it does exist, eliminating it would stain our hands and our consciences. Presumably, they mean here that they'd like to eliminate the concept of biological sex, or the phrase 'biological sex', etc.

8 Watkins and DiMarco seem to suggest that the problem is that their opponents think the job of a theory of the sexes is to give 'male' and 'female' stipulative definitions, when really the job of a theory of the sexes is to figure out the natures of whatever 'male' and 'female' refer to. They say (Watkins and DiMarco 2025, 9):

> Of course, if 'male' and 'female' have merely stipulative definitions like 'bachelor' then this is not an issue. Our contention here is that perhaps at least some scientific concepts shouldn't be like this; we should be able to be wrong about what they mean or what they reference.

But I agree; at least some scientific concepts should not be like this. And the methodology I've recommended in this book does not require otherwise.

9 https://www.whitehouse.gov/presidential-actions/2025/01/defending-women-from-gender-ideology-extremism-and-restoring-biological-truth-to-the-federal-government/.

10 Recall trans-identifying philosopher Veronica Ivy, then going by the name "Rachel McKinnon" (2019), who appealed to sex in order to justify racing in the women's division: "The rules require me to race in the women's category. That's exactly where I belong: I am a woman, after all. I am female as well... Trans women are women. We are female." And Cosker-Rowland (2024, 2701) also appropriates sex terms to describe trans-identifying individuals:

> To be trans is to have a gender identity that is different from the gender you were assigned at birth: for instance, trans women were assigned male at birth but have a female gender identity; trans men were assigned female at birth but have a male gender identity.

Dea (2016, 21) also appropriates sex terms to describe a psychological state, saying, "If I think of myself as female, that is my gender identity."

11 The literature has exploded, but for some central texts, see Haslanger (2000, 2006), Burgess and Plunkett (2013a, 2013b), and Herman Cappelen (2018).

12 See Esa Díaz-León (2025, 4) description of conceptual engineering—sometimes called an "ameliorative project" in this part of the literature, following Haslanger (2006)—with regard to gender terms:

> ...the ultimate goal of an ameliorative approach is to examine which gender concepts we *should* use (or what we should mean by gender terms), but in order to ascertain this, it is useful also to figure out, to the extent that we can, what gender concepts we *actually* use (that is, what concepts our gender terms actually express)....

13 Or, if you prefer to think in terms of intensions—functions from contexts of utterance to referents—it will be very difficult to specify what this function is, that is, how it works, what characteristics determine the application of the term. Note: not what sort of heuristics or clues we happen to use, psychologically, to apply (or perhaps *mis*apply) the concept in thought. But, rather, what characteristics determine the *proper* application of the concept, that is, what characteristics are necessary and sufficient for genuine kind membership.

14 There might be recherché features like that of *identifying in some way*, such that if one identifies as having that feature, then necessarily one has that feature. But

surely the other direction of the biconditional will be false: it will be possible to have this feature without identifying as having this feature. Also, notice that the concern is not that, as David Lewis (1986, 26) put it, the predicate picks out a property, but the property makes for an "unduly miscellaneous class of things." Rather, it's that the alleged predicate fails to pick out any property at all, due to vicious circularity. It specifies no extension. It's not a genuine predicate. Or, if "is a woman" does specify a predicate, the biconditional "S is a woman if and only if S identifies as a woman" will be necessarily false.

15 As to why this view is plausible, confer Sainsbury and Tye (2012) to see how it offers elegant solutions to seven traditional puzzles of thought and language, including the puzzle of Hesperus and Phosphorus, the puzzle of Paderewski cases, and the puzzle of empty thoughts.

16 This is a well-known concern about conceptual engineering in general. See, for example, Part III of Cappelen 2018.

17 Herman Cappelen (2018) takes seriously the concern that conceptual engineering necessarily changes the subject, and proposes that there are cases in which two subjects can be truly said to be saying the same thing, even though they use a context-sensitive expression that has a different extension in each of the contexts (and therefore, he says, different intensions as well). His example (Cappelen 2018, 110) is light on details, but the idea focuses on the context-sensitive term "smart," and seems to be that subject A might truly utter, in one context, "Serena is really smart," and subject B might utter, in a different context, "Serena is really smart," and we can truly say, in some contexts, "A and B said the same thing about Serena." And then Cappelen concludes, "These descriptions of them as samesayers are true even if it turns out that A's and B's respective contexts fix somewhat different extensions and intensions for 'smart'." So, two people can say the same thing—and therefore speak to the same topic—even if the relevant term differs in extension and intension, Cappelen reasons. By way of reply, we might first point out that, even if A's and B's uses of 'smart' have different extensions in these contexts, this is not enough to prove that they have different *intensions*, since intensions are functions from *contexts of utterance* to extensions, and A and B are in different contexts. And the claim that A and B are samesayers is plausible only when we assume sameness of intension. But if they are in fact using the words (to express concepts) with *different* intensions, it's not at all clear that they really are saying the same thing, *pace* Cappelen. Second, as Mark Schroeder (2020) put it, "In general, appeals to semantic context-dependence are illuminating when they appeal to a common core meaning." Think of the relevant common core meanings revealed by Kaplan's treatment of the "character" of indexicals, Kratzer's treatment of modal verbs like 'must', DeRose's theory of 'knows', etc. In a similar way, any illuminating treatment of context-sensitive expressions like 'smart' will reveal a *commonality* between A's utterance and B's utterance. Cappelen prefers not to speak of concepts (he's non-committal on their existence), but this seems like a grand opportunity to appeal to them: A and B are expressing the same concept with 'smart'. If they do succeed in saying the same thing, sameness of concept will help explain why. But, in that case, we won't have an example here that could help us see how conceptual engineers might originate a *new* concept (with a new intension and extension), and yet manage to stay on the same topic, because, in Cappelen's example, A and B *are* using the same concept. Neither A nor B originates a new concept, while nevertheless staying on topic.

References

Aristotle (1943). *Generation of Animals*, translated by A. L. Peck, Loeb Classical Library 366 (Cambridge, MA: Harvard University Press).

Bettcher, Talia Mae (2017). "Through the Looking Glass," in *Routledge Companion to Feminist Philosophy*, Ann Garry, Serene Khader, and Alison Stone (eds.) (New York, NY: Routledge).

Burgess, Alexis, and David Plunkett (2013a). "Conceptual Ethics I," *Philosophy Compass* 8 (12): 1091–101.

Burgess, Alexis, and David Plunkett (2013b). "Conceptual Ethics II," *Philosophy Compass* 8 (12): 1102– 10.

Cappelen, Herman (2018). *Fixing Language: An Essay on Conceptual Engineering* (Oxford: Oxford University Press).

Cosker-Rowland, Rach (2024). "Gender Identity: The Subjective Fit Account," *Philosophical Studies* 181: 2701–36.

Dea, Shannon (2016). *Beyond the Binary: Thinking about Sex and Gender* (Peterborough, Canada: Broadview Press).

Díaz-León, Esa (2025). *The Metaphysics of Gender. Cambridge Elements in Metaphysics*, Tuomas E. Tahko (ed.) (Cambridge: Cambridge University Press).

DuBois, Zachary, and Heather Shattuck-Heidorn (2021). "Challenging the Binary: Gender/Sex and the Bio-Logics of Normalcy," *American Journal of Human Biology* 33: e23623.

Fausto-Sterling, Anne (2012). *Sex/Gender: Biology in a Social World* (New York: Routledge).

Griffiths, Paul (2021). "What are Biological Sexes?" *PhilSci Archive*, http://philsci-archive.pitt.edu/19906/, accessed May 25, 2023.

Haslanger, Sally (2000). "Gender and Race: (What) are They? (What) do We Want Them to be?" *Noûs* 34 (1): 31–55.

Haslanger, Sally (2006). "What Good are Our Intuitions? Philosophical Analysis and Social Kinds," *Proceedings of the Aristotelian Society* 80 (1): 89–118.

Haslanger, Sally (2012). *Resisting Reality* (New York: Oxford University Press).

Haslanger, Sally (2016). "Theorizing with a Purpose: The Many Kinds of Sex," in *Natural Kinds and Classification in Scientific Practice*, Catherine Kendig (ed.) (New York: Routledge), 129–44.

Jenkins, Katharine (2016). "Amelioration and Inclusion: Gender Identity and the Concept of *Woman*," *Ethics* 126: 394–421.

Jenkins, Katarine (2018). "Toward an Account of Gender Identity," *Ergo* 5 (27): 713–44.

Laskowski, Nick (2020). "Moral Constraints on Gender Concepts," *Ethical Theory and Moral Practice* 23 (1): 39–51.

Lewis, David (1986). "Against Structural Universals," *Australasian Journal of Philosophy* 64 (1): 25–46.

McKinnon, Rachel (2019, December 5). "I Won a World Championship. Some People Aren't Happy," *The New York Times*. https://www.nytimes.com/2019/12/05/opinion/i-won-a-world-championship-some-people-arent-happy.html

Richardson, Sarah (2022). "Sex Contextualism," *Philosophy, Theory, and Practice in Biology* 14 (2): 1–17.

Rifkin, Maximiliana, and Justin Garson (2023). "Sex by Design," *Biology and Philosophy* 38 (13): 1–17.

Roughgarden, Joan (2004). *Evolution's Rainbow* (Berkeley, CA: University of California Press).

Sainsbury, Richard M., and Michael Tye (2012). *Seven Puzzles of Thought and How to Solve Them: An Originalist Theory of Concepts* (Oxford: Oxford University Press).

Saul, Jennifer (2012). "Politically Significant Terms and Philosophy of Language: Methodolog Issues," in *Analytic Feminist Contributions to Traditional Philosophy*, Anita Superson and Sharon Crasnow (eds.) (Oxford University Press).

Schroeder, M. (2020). "Review of Semantics for Reasons," in *Notre Dame Philosophical Reviews*, B. R. Weaver, and K. Scharp (eds.), accessed May 10, 2023. https://ndpr.nd.edu/reviews/semantics-for-reasons/

van Anders, Sari (2024). "Gender/Sex/ual Diversity and Biobehavioral Research," *Psychology of Sexual Orientation and Gender Diversity* 11 (3): 471–87.

Velocci, Beans (2024). "The History of Sex Research: Is 'sex' a Useful Category?" *Cell* 187: 1343–6.

Watkins, Aja, and Marina DiMarco (2025). "Sex Eliminativism," *Biology and Philosophy* 40 (2): 1–30.

6
A DEFENSE OF THE SEX-TRACKING VIEW OF PRONOUNS

How *Do* We Use Third-Person Singular Pronouns in English? The Sex-Tracking View

It's one thing to ask how we *do* use third-person singular pronouns, and another to ask how we *should* use them. Take, for example, Robin Dembroff and Daniel Wodak (2021, 363), who argue that we *should* use 'they' universally as a gender-neutral third-person singular pronoun. Yet, in doing so, they concede that "our actual use of *he* and *she* mark male and female." That's how we actually *do* use these pronouns, according to them. Though again, they think we should revise our use. Sudo (2012, 19) agrees, saying that "A simple sentence containing a feminine *she* like ["She is drinking coffee"] necessarily implies that its referent, whoever that is, is female."[1]

What does it mean for our use of pronouns to "mark male and female"? Pronouns don't *refer* to the sexes; they refer to particular entities, for example, most commonly people and animals. But they do this by means of a formula, or a recipe, or a procedure. If you want to know what 'he' or 'him' refers to in a conversation, you do something like this: look back to find the most recent, or most salient, entity referred to in the conversation taken to be male.[2] (If there isn't any, then it's unclear to whom the pronoun refers. And, sometimes, pronouns get their referents from something *later* in the conversation. For example: "If he is willing, John will take you to the store.") That individual is the *content* of the pronoun; the *character* of the pronoun is the procedure for locating the content. When we use a third-person singular English pronoun in the traditional way, this procedure—this character of the pronoun—when spelled out, makes reference to biological sex. There are implications about sex, owing either to presupposition or to conventional implicature.[3] That, I take it, is what Dembroff and Wodak meant when they said our use of 'he' and 'she' "mark male and female." These pronouns track biological sex. I'll call this the Sex-Tracking View. Why think that it's true?

Reasons for the Sex-Tracking View

First, there is linguistic evidence. In a recent paper on pronouns and gender, Michael Glanzberg and Cameron Kirk-Giannini (2024) notice "the felicity of using gendered pronouns to refer to beings which possess sex but not gender, such as the higher nonhuman vertebrates." Consider the Wikipedia page for Shamu, the killer whale. As of the time of writing, in that Wikipedia entry, we're told that "She was sold to SeaWorld San Diego…" and "was the fourth orca ever captured, and the second female." We can read about when "she" bit the legs and hips of a trainer, what happened after "her" death, and so on. The entry is just about 300 words, but 'she' and 'her' are each used four times. There's nothing unusual in this entry, or in using third-person singular pronouns to refer to animals. Indeed, it's not uncommon to correct people's use of pronouns—from *she/her/hers/herself* to *he/him/his/himself* or vice versa—when it comes to animals, especially pets. Assuming that such creatures have no gender, and no gender identity, this is strong evidence against a view that third-person singular pronouns in English track gender or gender identity, whatever precisely we take those to be.

As I'll mention again below, it's not surprising that English evolved to track biological sex in this way. After all, given that biological males exhibit much higher rates of violence than do females, groups of humans do well to keep tabs on males, especially in order to help ensure the safety of sex-segregated spaces. Pronouns are one way of doing this. Also, humans have an interest in reproduction, at least historically. That's another reason English might have evolved to track sex with these pronouns, in order to facilitate finding a suitable partner for sexual reproduction.

This constitutes a prima facie case for the Sex-Tracking View. It's certainly possible, as Glanzberg and Kirk-Giannini put it, for a language to prioritize tracking gender over tracking sex, that is, to track gender if the referent has a gender, and otherwise to track sex. They take this Gender-First View to be the sober truth about how our third-person singular pronouns work in English. However, compared to the Sex-First View, such a theory is unclear, unmotivated, and complex. Regarding clarity: What exactly is a gender? Glanzberg and Kirk-Giannini say only that they use "'man', 'woman', 'boy', and 'girl' to pick out personal gender categories, without taking any further stand on what those categories are," and that they "are not interested here in the semantics of e.g. 'female' or 'woman' in English." I understand the desire to sidestep the controversial semantics of these gender terms. But, given that controversy, there are several salient incompatible interpretations of the proposal that our pronouns track gender, and it's unclear which one Glanzberg and Kirk-Giannini are proposing. One should like to know a little more exactly what the theory says our pronouns are tracking, when they're said to be tracking "gender."

As for the motivation: If genders are not defined in terms of sex, one wonders why a language would evolve to track genders, as opposed to, say, class, religion, age, nationality, or race. What's so important about genders, whatever exactly Glanzberg and Kirk-Giannini take them to be? These are genuine questions that should be answered in order to motivate the theory that the very character of these English pronouns evolved to track gender. By contrast, as I said above, it's fairly obvious why a language might evolve to track sex with its pronouns.

Finally, regarding complexity, the Gender-First (sex-second) theory proposed by Glanzberg and Kirk-Giannini is more complex than the Sex-Tracking View. On the Gender-First proposal, two distinct genders—girls and women—are referred to using the same *she/her/hers/herself* pronoun series, with no explanation for this coincidence. Similarly with boys, men, and *he/him/his/himself* pronouns. The Sex-Tracking View offers a simple explanation of why this is so—girls and women are the same sex, as boys and men are the same sex. Plus, the Sex-Tracking View accomplishes this without positing Gender-First's complex prioritizing conventions, namely: use the *she/her/hers/herself* pronoun series if the referent is a girl or a woman, and *he/him/his/himself* if the referent is a boy or a man, and, if the referent has no gender, then use the former series for females, and the latter series for males. Of course, natural languages can evolve complex conventions, but unless there are quite serious objections to a simple, motivated theory like the Sex-Tracking View, this complexity looks superfluous.

Worse, this complexity doesn't even buy us a view that respects everyone's self-identification. On Glanzberg's and Kirk-Giannini's proposal, "when nonbinary individuals do not identify with any gender category," then allegedly they have no gender, and therefore third-person singular pronouns should track their sexes according to the Gender-First View, even if that use is contrary to these individuals' preferences and self-identification. That would be the linguistic fact of the matter, and an implication of the Gender-First View that Glanzberg and Kirk-Giannini would not welcome. In response, the authors say, at least sometimes, "the relevant nonbinary individuals have explicitly permitted the use of semantically inappropriate pronouns to refer to them." But if the authors are willing to accept that implication in this case, why not adopt the clear, simple, and motivated Sex-Tracking View, adding that there are non-linguistic reasons to use semantically inappropriate pronouns on occasion? They do give reasons against the Sex-Tracking View, which we'll discuss next, but I do not believe these reasons stand up to scrutiny.

Objections to the Sex-Tracking View

In this section, I will consider and respond to several objections to the Sex-Tracking View of how pronouns *actually* work. In the following section, we'll consider how pronouns *ought* to be used.

Objection 1

Glanzberg and Kirk-Giannini say that the Sex-Tracking View "fails to predict that it is linguistically correct to refer to binary trans individuals using their preferred pronouns, and thus that there is anything mistaken about misgendering uses of gendered pronouns." They seem to be reasoning this way:

1 If the Sex-Tracking View is true, then there may be nothing linguistically incorrect about "misgendering" uses of third-person singular pronouns, for example, using 'she' to refer to a male who believes he is a woman.
2 But there certainly is something linguistically incorrect about "misgendering" uses of third-person singular pronouns.
3 So, the Sex-Tracking View is false.

Response 1

However, Glanzberg and Kirk-Giannini have an undercutting defeater for premise (2) of the above argument, their judgment here that it is linguistically correct to refer to binary trans-identifying individuals using their preferred pronouns, and "mistaken" to use *he/him/his/himself* pronouns for males who believe that they're not men or boys, or *she/her/hers/herself* pronouns to refer to females who believe they're not women or girls. The defeater is this: Glanzberg and Kirk-Giannini may well be confusing *social unacceptability* or *a lack of courtesy* for *linguistic error*, so that what seems true to them is not that such uses of pronouns are *linguistically incorrect*, but rather that such uses are *socially unacceptable* (in their social circles, at least).

To illustrate this distinction, consider that it would be rude for an undergraduate student to refer to his Ph.D.-holding professor as "Miss

Robinson," or to call her "buddy." It's presumptuous, too familiar, uncourteous, etc. But supposing Dr. Robinson is unmarried, and that the undergraduate fully grasps the concept of a buddy, it's not a *linguistic* error; it's not *semantically* infelicitous. Our judgment that he should use the title 'Dr.' and that he should address her in more professional terms would be judgments of social propriety, not a judgment that he's mistaken about the meanings of these words or the syntax of his constructions.

This is not a remote possibility of error, too remote to constitute a defeater. It is a pressing, nearby possibility of error for Glanzberg and Kirk-Giannini, since they themselves admit that, "In cases where conventions for usage are in flux and communities face complex issues about how to establish stable uses, acceptability judgements can reflect more than just semantic or syntactic well-formedness." And, in case that was unclear, they say also that, "we believe our linguistic judgments are sensitive to whether a given example sentence is linguistically well-formed in addition to whether it is acceptable in a social setting."

Yes, I believe them. Glanzberg and Kirk-Giannini seem to be members of such communities where acceptability judgments reflect more than just semantic or syntactic well-formedness. So, when they judge it to be "linguistically correct" to refer to males who believe they are women with *she/her/hers/herself* pronouns, it is by their own admission possible that they judge this merely to be *socially* acceptable or even obligatory. But, insofar as our question is one of linguistics, such a judgment of social propriety is irrelevant at best, and a troubling bias at worst. The salience and relevance of this possible confusion for Glanzberg and Kirk-Giannini undercuts their judgment that premise (2) in the above argument is true. Instead of taking a cool, dispassionate look at the linguistic appropriateness of pronoun use, these authors' judgments here may well be contaminated by facts about *social propriety* in their particular cultural context. Given the plausibility of this undercutting defeater, the authors' judgment here does not constitute strong evidence against the Sex-Tracking View.

Objection 2

Glanzberg and Kirk-Giannini consider the following two sentences as a second objection to the Sex-Tracking View (I preserve the numbering from their paper):

(13)

  a If Jonah is a transgender man, he is the first transgender man at his company.

b   *If Jonah is a transgender man, she is the first transgender man at her company.

They then say, "Our judgment is that (13b) is a linguistically incorrect use of [*she/her/hers/herself*] pronouns (not simply, for example, a discourteous one). [The Sex-Tracking View] cannot accommodate this intuition."

Response 2

In response, I report that my own judgment is that (13b) is *linguistically* correct, and (13a) is *linguistically* incorrect. There remains in force the undercutting defeater discussed in the last section, which Glanzberg and Kirk-Giannini are, by their own admission, subject to. But even if we accept that these authors have successfully reported purely linguistic judgments, as opposed to judgments of social propriety, I believe that the word 'man' may be confusing their linguistic judgments here, along with the name 'Jonah'. One may well hear 'man' and 'Jonah' as conveying that this person is male, and therefore judge 'she' to be linguistically incorrect. So, we have here an additional undercutting defeater for the authors' judgment that (13b) is linguistically incorrect.[4]

Here is some evidence that they may well be making this mistake: if we remove those sources of confusion, the judgment is clearer, and not what Glanzberg and Kirk-Giannini would predict. Consider this sentence:

(13)

c   If **Jane** is a trans-identifying **female**, then she is the first trans-identifying **female** at her company.

On the Glanzberg and Kirk-Giannini Gender-First View, (13c) is linguistically *incorrect*. And yet (13c) sounds pretty good to my ears; it seems linguistically correct. Insofar as you agree, you'll probably chalk up the difference between (13b) and (13c) to the fact that, in the latter, we describe this individual as female and use a female-coded name, 'Jane'. I believe this is partly why parties to this debate disagree over whether, for example, males who believe that they're women or girls should be called "trans women" or "trans girls" as opposed to "trans-identifying males." The former label is apt to produce judgments of the kind that Glanzberg and Kirk-Giannini form. The latter is apt to produce in us judgments in line with the Sex-Tracking View of third-person singular pronouns. An important question, then, is which label corresponds more closely with the *truth* of the matter, both with regard to the sex of such individuals and with regard to how third-person singular pronouns function in English. More importantly, we can see how Glanzberg's and Kirk-Giannini's judgments here are compatible with the Sex-Tracking View, and—given the plausibility of this undercutting defeater—do not constitute strong evidence against that view.

Objection 3

Glanzberg and Kirk-Giannini say this:

> it often seems that we can be ignorant about an individual's sex without being ignorant about which gendered pronouns are the linguistically correct ones to use to refer to that individual. The possession of a Y chromosome is, at least ceteris paribus, associated with male sex.

But, they say that they "judge the choices of gendered pronouns in the following examples felicitous because correct." Here are the examples:

(14)

a I don't know how many Y chromosomes Joan has because she hasn't told me.
b I don't know whether Joan is trans; it would be rude to ask her out of the blue.

They say that the Sex-Tracking View cannot predict these judgments.

Response 3

As before, it is plausible that these authors confuse linguistic error with social impropriety. But, also, that (14a) and (14b) are linguistically correct is compatible with the Sex-Tracking View. So, Glanzberg and Kirk-Giannini are mistaken when they say that the Sex-Tracking View cannot predict these judgments.

We can see that as follows. First, without additional context, it's unclear what the Sex-Tracking View would even predict about this case. Namely, we'd need to know whether, in the conversational context, Joan is taken to be female. The name 'Joan' is female-coded, and the authors judge that these sentences are felicitous, so presumably we're meant to assume that, in the conversational context, Joan is *taken* to be female, *presumed* to be female. In that case, the Sex-Tracking View would predict that *she/her/hers/herself* pronouns would be linguistically appropriate for her. So far, so good.

But with regard to (14a), it is possible that Joan be *presumed* in the conversational context to be female, while the possibility of strong (but inconclusive) evidence against this presumption is considered in the conversation. Considering the possibility of such contrary evidence would not rationally require canceling the presumption that Joan is female. Having a Y chromosome is very unusual for a human female, and therefore strong evidence that a human is male, but it *is* possible for a human female to have a Y chromosome. (Clear cases involve mosaicism, where some small number of female's cells have a Y chromosome. Here, the AHOF account entails the individual is female. The cells with the Y chromosome are not part of the female's genetic plan; they are biological stowaways, so to speak.) So, noting that that Joan may have a Y chromosome in the conversational context doesn't rationally require canceling the presumption that Joan is female, any more than noting that John may lack a penis (due to injury, say) rationally requires canceling the presumption that he's male. In that case, in (14a), 'she' is still linguistically correct, just as the Sex-Tracking View predicts. So, Glanzberg's and Kirk-Giannini's judgment that (14a) is felicitous is consistent with the Sex-Tracking View. Indeed, their judgment is evidence in favor of that view, suitably understood.

With regard to (14b), again, a presumption may not be *certain*. Presumptions are "not at issue," as linguists say, but that doesn't mean they're entailed by our evidence. One may consider a hypothesis entailing that a presumption is false, without being rationally required to cancel that presumption. In particular, pointing out that Joan may not be female doesn't rationally require canceling the presumption that she's female, any more than pointing out she may be a figment of my imagination (and therefore may not really exist) requires canceling that presumption:

(14)

    c I suppose it's possible that Joan is a figment of my imagination, but I'll continue to act as though she isn't.

Suppose Joan is a boxer, presumed to be female. Speaking with the International Boxing Association about whether Joan is actually a male with 5-alpha-reductase deficiency syndrome, I may utter, "I'm not sure whether Joan is a male with 5-ARD; but she should probably get tested just to be sure." The character of the pronoun seems to pick out Joan so long as she's presumed to be female, even if we're considering a hypothesis that's inconsistent with that presumption. Again, Glanzberg's and Kirk-Giannini's judgment that (14b) is felicitous is consistent with the

138 The Nature of the Sexes

Sex-Tracking View. Indeed, their judgment is evidence in favor of that view, suitably understood.

Objection 4

Glanzberg and Kirk-Giannini report the following concerning what they call "H-series pronouns" (i.e. *he/him/his/himself*) and "S-series pronouns" (i.e. *she/her/hers/herself*):

> It is also possible to use gendered pronouns to refer to individuals with no sex. It is easiest to find example of this in fiction, but we note that the fictional cases show no linguistic resistance. We naturally refer to fictional humanoid androids like C-3PO of the *Star Wars* franchise and Marvin the Paranoid Android from Douglas Adams's *The Hitchhiker's Guide to the Galaxy* using H-series pronouns. Though these things do not exist, we find no *linguistic* problems with the fictions. A similar point can be made about inanimate objects: it is acceptable to refer to watercraft using S-series pronouns, for example.

They conclude that these observations are difficult to reconcile with the Sex-Tracking View.

Response 4

I don't think these observations are difficult to reconcile with the Sex-Tracking View. True, we use 'she' to refer to the Statue of Liberty, and even call her 'Lady Liberty'. It is common to refer to C-3PO using 'he'. Many religious believers commonly use 'He' to refer to God. Reportedly, those neck-deep in maritime cultures occasionally refer to ships with 'she'. And this happens even when those users of the pronouns know full well that the Statue of Liberty, C-3PO, God, and ships have no biological sex at all. So what gives?

One of two things, I'd say. The first possibility involves *pretense* and amends our understanding of the character associated with these pronouns. I said above that, if you want to know what 'he' refers to in a conversation, you look back to find the most recent, or most salient, entity referred to in the conversation taken to be male. On this first possibility, "taken to be" should be understood broadly enough to include a kind of pretense.

We know full well that the Statue of Liberty is not female, but we *pretend* that she is, in conversation, due to her resemblance to adult human females. The resemblance is less obvious in the case of God, C-3PO, and ships, but perhaps the same thing goes: because ships are taken to have important characteristics stereotypical of females, and because God is taken to have important characteristics stereotypical of males, users of the pronouns call ships 'she' and God 'He'. Consider also our inclination to use *she/her/hers/herself* pronouns for Mrs. Doubtfire while watching the movie, knowing full well that the character, Daniel Harris, along with the actor, Robin Williams, is not a woman, does not sincerely identify as one, and is merely pretending to be one. Perhaps we join Harris (and Williams) in this pretense, and use *she/her/hers/herself* pronouns while we suspend our disbelief. That's one possibility. And it is consistent with the Sex-Tracking View, so long as "taken to be" male or female is understood in a suitably capacious way, to include pretense.

A second possibility is that we are witnessing a *pragmatic* phenomenon here, not a *semantic* phenomenon. As we discussed in Chapter 2, it's fairly standard to distinguish between what a speaker literally says and what he actually conveys. And, sometimes, as François Recanati (2005, 177) puts it, a pragmatic process "takes place in order to make sense of the communicative act performed by the speaker," modulating what a speaker literally says into the intuitive content of the utterance. For example, what a waiter literally says with the sentence, "The ham sandwich left without paying," is absurd. But, through a pragmatic process Recanati calls "transfer," the sentence may convey information to his audience about *the customer* who ordered the sandwich. That's what the audience may come to understand, even though it's not what the waiter literally said.

Consider also that the literal interpretation of the noun-phrase 'a stone lion' is a lion made of stone. In almost all cases, this is not what a speaker intends to convey. In those cases, a pragmatic process delivers the correct interpretation to the hearers: *(a representation of a lion) that is made of stone* (Recanati 2005, 179). Importantly, we don't need to posit any semantic ambiguity in these cases. 'Ham sandwich' continues to mean ham sandwich; it is just that a pragmatic process modulates literal content about a ham sandwich to conveyed content about a customer. 'Lion' continues to mean lion; it is just that a pragmatic process modulates literal content about a lion (made of stone) to conveyed content about a stone statue (of a lion).

In a similar way, the character of third-person singular pronouns in English might refer to biological sex, requiring us to find the most recent, or most salient, entity referred to in the conversation taken to be male or female. And yet, in cases involving C-3PO, God, ships, Lady Liberty, and the like, it may be that a pragmatic process modulates what the speaker literally says into the intuitive content of the utterance. To take an example, when I say "C-3PO has been dismantled, and now his head is near his own feet," what I say is true only if C-3PO is biologically male. He isn't, and so what I've said is literally false. But something that is *pragmatically conveyed* is that C-3PO has characteristics typical of males, a high number of sufficient importance.[5] What's conveyed is something like: this robot, which resembles a male in ways of sufficient number and importance, has been dismantled so that its head is near its feet. This proposition is what is understood by the hearer, and this proposition is true. This second alternative is, like the first, compatible with the Sex-Tracking View.

It is plausible that pretense and pragmatics are in play in our public language. And these views help explain why, for example, we switch to *she/her/hers/herself* pronouns when Robin Williams is in character as Daniel Harris in character as Mrs. Doubtfire, even though neither Williams nor Harris has literally become a woman, on contemporary theories of what a woman is, if only because neither one sincerely believes he's a woman. Also, these pretense and pragmatic views help explain why we switch third-person singular pronouns when speaking of, for example, Amazon's Alexa, when this bit of artificial intelligence switches from using a voice typical of human females to using a voice typical of human males. The phenomena of pretense and pragmatics help us see how these data about language use are not incompatible with the Sex-Tracking View of how pronouns are actually used in English.

We have seen, then, that there are no insurmountable objections to the Sex-Tracking View. Combined with the plausible explanations of why our language would evolve to track sex, and the view's simplicity compared to its rival Gender-First View, we have here a compelling case that the Sex-Tracking View accurately describes how we actually use third-person singular pronouns in English. But let's turn now to thinking about how we *should* use these pronouns.

How Should We Use These Pronouns?

We have seen that, from a linguistic perspective, there are strong reasons to think that the Sex-Tracking View is true, and no powerful objections to it. It seems that we *do, in fact,* use third-person singular pronouns to track biological sex in English. And even if that weren't the case, we certainly *could* use pronouns in that way. But, to paraphrase Dr. Ian Malcom during his visit to Jurassic Park, let's not be so preoccupied with whether we *could*, that we don't stop to think if we *should*.

To illustrate this distinction, consider a hypothetical language described by Dembroff and Wodak (2021), who borrow from Hofstadter (1985). This language tracks race in a way similar to how English tracks sex: there are race-specific pronouns (*whe* and *ble*, akin to our *he* and *she*), honorifics

(*Master* and *Niss*, akin to our *Mister; Miss*), suffixes (*-oon*, akin to our *-ess*), and generic terms (e.g. *whiteslaughter*, akin to our *manslaughter*). They say that, intuitively, "the actual English language should not become more racialized so as to mirror" this hypothetical language. Yes, I agree. Not every linguistic change is good. Some linguistic practices should be resisted. And, since some of these practices are revisionary, this shows that some linguistic revision should be resisted. And, conversely, some linguistic practices are good and should be preserved; and if these practices are revisionary, they should be encouraged. On this, I hope, we can all agree.

But our question is this: *Whether or not the Sex-Tracking View is actually true*, should we preserve or encourage the practice of tracking sex with our pronouns? Should we resist the attempt to speak in a way that doesn't track sex, or in a way that tracks gender, whatever exactly gender is, or in a totally gender- and sex-neutral way? To answer this, we'll first consider reasons in favor of abiding by the Sex-Tracking View. Then, we'll consider some arguments against that practice. I conclude that there is good reason to adopt or maintain a Sex-Tracking use of pronouns, no conclusive reason to abandon the practice, and there is good reason not to compel those who use pronouns in the traditional, Sex-Tracking way to violate their consciences and adopt a revisionary use of pronouns.

Reasons to Track Sex

What reasons are there in favor of using pronouns in a way that the Sex-Tracking View describes? First, the distinction between males and females is socially important: in general, biological males exhibit a greater disposition to violence than females do. And this is particularly egregious when the violence is directed against females, especially children. Groups of humans do well to keep tabs on males, to regularly refer to them in ways that imply that they're males, for general safety, but especially in order to help ensure the safety of sex-segregated spaces (in our era, spaces like bathrooms, prisons, women's shelters, and sports teams). Pronouns are one way of doing this. Surely this would reduce violence, especially against the most vulnerable. This is a reason in favor of keeping track of people's sexes, and even embedding reference to sex into the very meaning of our third-person singular pronouns.

There is also the importance of mating. Though cratering birth rates suggest it's "less of a thing" these days, sexual reproduction remains an important part of the human experience. Well, if humans generally have an interest in reproduction, this adds pressure in the direction of tracking sex, in order to find a suitable partner for sexual reproduction, if that's what you're into. One might also appeal to our penchant for genital preferences, for example, how the sex and sexual orientation of users are often listed prominently on dating apps. Those are salient pieces of information, given the interests of the users of those apps, and tracking sex via pronouns would facilitate humans matching up in ways that satisfy their genital preferences. Insofar as that's a worthwhile goal, tracking sex with third-person singular pronouns makes sense.

Finally and, I think, most importantly, consider that many kinds of acts, including speech acts, can pragmatically convey approval or disapproval. During the Edo period in Japan, under the Tokugawa shogunate (1603–1868 A.D.), Christianity was outlawed, and suspected Christians were forced to step on *fumi-e* (literally, "picture to step on"): tablets with Christian images of Jesus, the Holy Cross, or Mary, etc. If the suspected Christian refused, the punishment was death. Clearly, this act of stepping on a Christian image was chosen because of what compliance would communicate: stepping on the *fumi-e* tablet would convey a willingness to dishonor something considered sacred by Christians. The act would therefore communicate a rejection of Christianity. Refusal to step on the *fumi-e* was taken to communicate deep respect for what Christians consider sacred, even at the cost of one's life, and therefore adherence to Christianity. This act was chosen because performing it would pragmatically convey rejection of Christianity, and refusing to perform it would pragmatically convey approval of or adherence to Christianity.

In a similar way, at the time of the martyrdom of St. Polycarp (approximately 155 A.D.), Christians were persecuted by the Roman Empire. Often, suspected Christians were required to swear an oath, for example, "Caesar is Lord," or they were told, "Swear by the genius of Caesar; repent and say, 'Away with the atheists'"—meaning away with the Christians, who were considered atheists for their rejection of Roman popular religion—or to offer incense to idols or statues of Roman gods (cf. Lightfoot 1907, 205–6). As with the *fumi-e*, these acts were chosen because performing them would pragmatically convey rejection of Christianity, and refusing to perform them would pragmatically convey approval of or adherence to Christianity.

Examples are, unfortunately, easy to multiply. So, it seems clear that it's possible for acts to convey our approval or disapproval of religions, ideologies, political parties, or whole views of the world. And if such a statement would be a serious violation of one's conscience, of one's deeply held beliefs, then one has a strong moral reason *not* to perform that act. Let me give a couple of examples. Suppose you found yourself surrounded by Neo-Nazis, who insist that you swear allegiance to their cause by performing a Nazi salute to an image of Adolf Hitler. I think it's pretty clear that you have a strong reason not to do this, even if they threaten you with serious harm. Or suppose that you find yourself in North Korea, under the brutal, repressive regime of Kim Jong Un. The citizens around you habitually refer to Kim Jong Un using one of his many propagandist titles, for example, "Banner of All Victory and Glory," or "Peerlessly Great Man." Should you participate in this practice? I think it's clear you have a strong reason not to.

Consider another example. It is common for Muslims to use the phrase "peace be upon him" after any mention of Mohammad (and, to refer to him as the *Prophet* Mohammad). Muslims do this out of respect for Mohammad, and they would greatly prefer it if everyone else joined the practice. Given that I don't believe that Mohammad was a true prophet, should I participate in the practice of calling him 'Prophet'? I don't think so. More to the point for our purposes: even if I generally wish peace upon everyone, including Mohammad, should I participate in the practice of saying "peace be upon him" after any mention of Mohammad? Again, I think not. At least, I have strong reason not to. The reason is not that, by my lights, I would be saying something false or wishing something immoral upon him. No, the literal content of my utterance would be simply that I wish peace upon him. But—and this is the crucial part—what would be pragmatically conveyed by my use of "peace be upon him" is that I approve of Islam, or even adhere to Islam. I would be participating in a distinctively Islamic practice. And, given that I believe Islam is false (and, frankly, harmful), I have a strong reason not to signal my approval or participate in this way.

So far, I've chosen rather inflammatory examples. But I believe the same goes in less extreme cases. Should non-Catholics refer to priests as 'Father'? Should non-Buddhists refer to the Dalai Lama as 'His Holiness', or should non-Mormons refer to the LDS President as 'The Prophet'? Suppose your friend group adopts an obscene but affectionate nickname for your friend, who likes the name. Should you use that nickname?[6] Rachel Dolezal—who is Caucasian by ancestry but who identifies as black—would prefer that you refer to her with her new name, 'Nkechi Amare Diallo', and that you say that she is black. Should you participate in those practices? I think it's clear that the answer to all these questions is 'no', and especially clear that one is not *obligated* to participate in these practices which violate one's conscience, or one's deeply held beliefs. Even if one would, strictly speaking, not be asserting anything false by adopting Dolezal's proposed Igbo and Fulani names, one has strong reason not to approve or participate in a view of the world that one repudiates.

And the same goes for pronoun use and contemporary gender ideology. Whether or not pronouns actually track biological sex, when one is asked to participate in pronoun-sharing rituals, or to use *she/her/hers/herself* pronouns of males who believe they are girls or women, or to use neopronouns, one is being asked to perform an act that pragmatically conveys approval or adherence to a particular view of the world, to a particular ideology. Though it's hard to precisely define the contours of this ideology, it is familiar enough. It's a view on which womanhood or manhood are psychological phenomena, determined by one's "internal map" (cf. Jenkins 2016) or one's sincere self-identification (cf. Bettcher 2017, 396). It's a view with implications for social organization: sports teams, prisons, bathrooms, universities, and the like should be segregated not on the basis of sex, but on the basis of gender identity. It's a view with implications for the permissibility of medical interventions, for example, puberty blockers for children and surgical interventions for both children and adults.[7] Robin Dembroff (2018b) considers "nonbinary identity to be an unabashedly political identity." If so, no doubt many people would repudiate this political agenda and would have strong reason not to convey approval or adherence to it.

For many people, then, pragmatically conveying approval of contemporary gender ideology would constitute a violation of conscience. Performing actions that convey such approval, then, would involve willing what one's reason proposes as immoral. Such conscientious objectors have strong reason, therefore, not to perform any actions that would convey that approval, including using pronouns in the way preferred by trans activists.

George Sher (2023, 134–5) recently shared similar thoughts on the alleged duty to defer to the pronoun preferences of those with non-standard "gender identities," that is, non-standard attitudes about the sexes, including one's own. Speaking of someone asked to defer in this way, Sher says:

> [T]he more important problem is that the pronouns that he would have to use are ones that encode an ideology that many do not share. To refer to people in ways that reject the traditional binary view of gender is to imply one's acceptance of a radical recasting of a fundamental category of human existence, and there are many who find this recasting unwarranted and objectionable. If someone takes this position, then any requirement that he nevertheless use the novel pronouns to refer to those absent others who prefer them (or, *a fortiori*, to refer to everyone) will be just as intrusive, and will be intrusive for just the same reasons, as the requirement that he profess fealty to a cause in which he doesn't believe.

Yes, just so. What Sher characterizes as actions that "encode an ideology" and "imply one's acceptance" of that ideology, I would characterize as actions that pragmatically convey approval or even adherence to the ideology. Forcing a conscientious objector to perform these actions is, as Sher says, requiring that he "profess fealty" to a cause he doesn't believe in, and to violate his conscience.

So, we've seen three reasons in favor of using pronouns to track biological sex, and to resist the sort of linguistic practice recommended by trans activists, according to which pronouns track gender, or gender identity, whatever precisely those are: tracking sex is useful for preventing harm by violent males, it's useful for facilitating procreation, and participating in such a linguistic practice may violate one's conscience by pragmatically conveying approval or adherence to an ideology that one considers false and/or harmful. But reasons for a particular action can be trumped by reasons against it, so let's consider reasons on the other side, reasons not to use pronouns as the Sex-Tracking View describes.

First Reason Not to Track Sex: Gender Affirmation

One objection against the Sex-Tracking use of pronouns is that it occasionally fails to conform to people's preferred pronouns. That is, occasionally people who are male prefer that others use pronouns besides *he/him/his/himself* when referring to them, and similarly for people who are female. In this way, it is said, the Sex-Tracking use of pronouns fails to affirm the gender identities of some people, and this is taken to be a reason against tracking sex with our pronouns.

Why think this is bad? As philosopher E.M. Hernandez (2021, 619) put it recently, "Moral reasons to engage in acts that gender affirm derive from the commitment to give and express loving attention to trans people as a way of challenging their marginalization." And why is this loving attention morally significant? According to Hernandez (2021, 623), "the moral value of gender affirmation is rooted in loving attention, in the sense of perceiving someone on their own terms." (See also Hanna et al., 2019).

The first thing to say in response to this bit of reasoning is that, on the Sex-Tracking use of pronouns, pronouns communicate information about *biological sex*. So, unless gender or gender identity just are the same as biological sex—which I take it Hernandez and others do not want to say—pronouns are not gendering (or misgendering) anyone at all, on the Sex-Tracking use.

With regard to allegations of "misgendering," then, the Sex-Tracking use of pronouns can plausibly plead not guilty. Robin Dembroff and Daniel Wodak make a similar point in response to Hanna et al., and in defense of their proposed policy of using *they/them/their/theirs/themself* for everyone, when they say (2019), "It is wrong to misgender others. But it is not generally important to gender others correctly, as long as we do not gender others incorrectly." If *they/them* pronouns convey no information about gender, Dembroff and Wodak say, these pronouns cannot misgender anyone. And the same goes for the Sex-Tracking use of pronouns, since in this use, pronouns convey no information about gender, unless gender is identical with biological sex. (And, in that case, a male who believes he is a girl or a woman is not misgendered by *he/him/his/himself* pronouns, but rather is accurately gendered thereby.)

But the fact remains that the Sex-Tracking use of pronouns fails to align with some people's preferences; Sex-Tracking fails to, as Hernandez might put it, perceive some people on their own terms. This is true. And perhaps, *other things being equal*, it is good to perceive people on their own terms. But oftentimes, other things are *not* equal, and it's permissible—or even obligatory—not to perceive people on their own terms.

Consider some examples. A few years ago, the white English influencer Oli London wished to be seen as non-binary, and... *Korean*. With respect to the claim to be Korean at least, it was morally permissible not to affirm him in that way. It may even have been morally *obligatory* not to affirm London on this, in at least some circumstances. To borrow an example from the previous section, Muslims wish everyone would say, "peace be upon him," after any use of 'Mohammad', and such use would be a way of perceiving Islam on its own terms: namely, as individuals following a prophet of Allah. Yet, even if this would count as "loving attention" to our Muslim brothers and sisters, non-Muslims need not affirm them in this way. Similarly, Orthodox Jews prefer that we not say or spell the name of God, opting instead for 'Adonai' or 'G-d'. Again, doing so would be a way of perceiving Judaism on its own terms, and granting "loving attention" to our Jewish brothers and sisters. Yet, again, those of us who are not ourselves Jewish need not oblige on this. Many devout monotheists prefer that you capitalize 'God' and use masculine pronouns when referring to Him. Yet Dembroff and Wodak (2021, 369)—who advocate that we abolish the use of gendered pronouns for one another—condone using 'god', as well as feminine pronouns to refer to God as a subversive use that (allegedly) undermines sexist oppression. This is a failure of "loving attention," a failure to perceive this brand of monotheism on its own terms. Yet it's permissible, according to Dembroff and Wodak, and likely also to many of those advocating for the use of preferred pronouns. These examples show that, however good "loving attention" is, it is by no means a conclusive reason to abandon the Sex-Tracking use of pronouns.

Second Reason Not to Track Sex: Sex-Tracking Is Exclusive

While arguing that we should abolish the use of gendered pronouns—and instead use *they/them/their/theirs/themself* for everyone—Dembroff and

Wodak raise this objection to the Sex-Tracking use of pronouns: using *he/him/his/himself* for males and *she/her/hers/herself* for females leaves people out, namely genuinely intersex people. They say (2021, 367), "regardless of whether we interpret gender-specific language in terms of gender identity or reproductive features, a binary encoded within gendered language excludes and marginalizes those who do not fit that binary."

There are two things to say in response. First, it's not at all clear that anyone is excluded by Sex-Tracking's use of pronouns. Second, even if it were true, this is not a conclusive reason against Sex-Tracking. First things first: What is biological sex? As we've seen in Chapter 3, a male is an organism with the function of producing sperm—that's something it evolved to do. A female is an organism with the function of producing ova—that's something it evolved to do. And, of course, something may have a function without actually fulfilling that function. Like your windshield wipers, when they become too old to effectively remove water from your windshield. Their function is to wipe water away, even when they can no longer fulfill that function.

The vast majority of conditions commonly called "intersex" are such that, upon reflection, the question of biological sex is actually rather clear. For example, individuals with Complete Androgen Insensitivity Syndrome (CAIS) have XY chromosomes, and have bodies directed toward the production of spermatozoa, yet which, due to insensitivity to androgens (especially testosterone), do not realize this capacity. (Individuals with partial AIS may produce some sperm.) These are males. As another example, many individuals with Congenital Adrenal Hyperplasia (CAH) have XX chromosomes and have bodies directed toward the production of ova. Yet, due to the adrenal glands producing an androgen precursor rather than cortisol, these individuals are virilized, resulting in ambiguous genitalia (cf. Mulaikal et al. 1987). Nevertheless, these individuals are female, many of whom are fertile.

But it is true that being male and being female are not exclusive, and not exhaustive. If being male is having a body with the function of producing sperm, and being female is having a body with the function of producing eggs, it's certainly possible for an organism to be *both* male *and* female. This is the simultaneous hermaphroditism of your local garden snail and many other organisms besides. It's also possible for an organism to be *neither* male *nor* female—bacteria, for example. So, while it's conceptually possible for a human to be both male and female, or to be neither male nor female, it's controversial whether this has ever actually happened, and, if it has, it has happened only extremely rarely. So, if the Sex-Tracking use of pronouns leaves out some humans—namely, those who are neither male nor female, or those who are both—this will be a vanishingly small segment of the population.

And is it necessarily wrong to adopt a linguistic practice that is not exhaustive, that leaves some people out? May we permissibly use pairs of terms that leave some people out? Evidently, yes. It's morally permissible to describe people as tall or short, strong or weak, as mothers or fathers, brothers or sisters, etc. It's permissible to speak of mountains and valleys, day and night, etc. We needn't abandon these distinctions just because they're not exhaustive, just because some people may be neither mothers nor fathers, and dusk is neither day nor night. Even those who have revisionary attitudes toward gender should agree on this, since the neo-gender categories that are often proposed may well leave people out. There's no guarantee that everyone will be covered even if Dembroff (2018a) is correct that "the scope of gender identities outside of male and female is vast and effectively unlimited," and even if this includes "genders" like gendertrash, in-betweenie, polygenderal, and the shrug emoticon ¯_(ツ)_/¯ (cf. Ashley 2021, 35, 38). Still, it's possible that some people will be left out of these novel categories. So, even revisionists should admit that non-exhaustive distinctions are not necessarily wrong.

And the same goes even for our pronouns. Some languages mark a formal versus familiar distinction in their pronouns—they encode honorific information—such that one uses different pronouns depending on whether the referent of the pronoun is familiar to oneself or unfamiliar. Of course, some people will be "left out" of this practice, namely those occupying the hazy borderland between familiarity and formality. This doesn't entail that such a practice is immoral, and the same goes, I'd say, for our practice of tracking information about sex in our third-person singular pronouns.

Third Reason Not to Track Sex: It's an Invasion of Privacy

Dembroff and Wodak (2021, 368) put the objection like so:

> You have every right to privacy and autonomy about what's in your head and what's between your legs; everyone who uses third-person pronouns to describe you isn't entitled to know, or assume, information about either. Indeed, the point is arguably stronger if we think of gender in terms of reproductive features. It is at best inappropriate and arguably a form of sexual harassment to be forced to disclose or deceive others concerning one's own or another's genital status, much less to be forced to do constantly. But this is the fact of the matter in most contexts, where terms like 'she' are code for 'has-a-vagina' and terms like 'he' are code for 'has-a-penis'. Basic considerations of privacy weigh against using a language that forces us to perpetually communicate information about what's between people's legs while conversing.[8]

So, the idea is that a Sex-Tracking use of pronouns forces people regularly to disclose—or deceive others about—one's own or other people's genitals. And that's because, allegedly, 'she' is "code for" 'has-a-vagina', and 'he' is "code for" 'has-a-penis'. This compulsory invasion of privacy is inappropriate and perhaps even sexual harassment, and, therefore, we shouldn't do it.

In response, we should note that, on the Sex-Tracking View, 'he' is definitely not "code for" 'has-a-penis', and 'she' is not "code for" 'has a vagina'. On the Sex-Tracking View, these pronouns track biological sex, which is at best *imperfectly correlated* with genital structures. It's certainly not part of the meaning of 'he' that the referent has a penis, nor would that bit of information be presupposed as not-at-issue by the use of 'he'. Take the rooster who lives next door to me. He is a source of great irritation, but he—like most male birds—has no penis at all. And similarly with 'she': the nearest female spotted hyena is unusual in that she has a pseudo-penis in place of a vagina.

Even among humans, it's quite possible for a human male to lack a penis, due to injury, a disorder of sexual development, "gender nullification surgery," and the like. This imperfect correlation is relevant to Dembroff's and Wodak's objection, given the elusive nature of knowledge (cf. Lewis 1996). Knowledge can be defeated by even a small possibility of error, at least if that error is relevant in the right way. A member of a firing squad can't know that *his* bullet killed the criminal if he knows that at least one member of the firing squad was given a blank, and that might have been him. I can't know that *my* lottery ticket is a loser, even if there's a very high chance that it is. I can't know that *this* prisoner participated in the riot, even if I know that 99% of the prisoners participated. In a similar way, you might think, I can't know the genital status of *this* person if all I know is that he's male, even if I know that, say, 99% of (human) males have penises. As soon as I consider the question of his genital status, the salience of the no-penis possibility precludes my knowledge of his genital status.

Still, though, it's a pretty safe bet. And perhaps that's enough grounds for Dembroff and Wodak to complain about the Sex-Tracking use of pronouns: it regularly forces people to disclose information about others—namely, their biological sex—that significantly affects probabilities about their genital status. And this is an invasion of privacy, or maybe even sexual harassment. In any event, we shouldn't do it, you might think.

But do we really have "every right to privacy and autonomy about... what's between [our] legs"? Given how good humans are at identifying the biological sex of other humans—for obvious evolutionary reasons—one might think that we have *no reasonable expectation* of privacy in this regard. We are absurdly adept at identifying the sex of other humans by looking at their faces (Bruce et al. 1993; Cheng et al. 2001), the movement of their bodies (D'Argenio et al. 2020), their voices (Pernet and Belin 2012), etc. I suppose that, if one wished to remain indoors and out of sight, that might be within one's rights (depending on one's obligations to others). But as soon as one ventures out into the world, moves, speaks, and shows one's face, one cannot reasonably expect other people not to notice whether one is male or female. And—importantly for our purposes here—it is not immoral for others to notice this. That's the nature of public spaces.

Another consideration is that whatever right one has to privacy can be outweighed by other considerations. In the event of a pandemic, for example, one may be forced to disclose one's health or vaccination status. Given the vulnerability of air travel to terrorist attacks, citizens with a right to free movement are subjected to rather invasive screening by the Transportation Security Administration. And, of course, we couldn't reasonably expect "privacy and autonomy about… what's between [our] legs" if what's between our legs is a holstered firearm and we're headed onto an airplane. Speaking of firearms, even outside of air travel, in many states, one cannot legally conceal and carry a firearm anywhere on one's body without informing the government, and I imagine many opponents of the Sex-Tracking View think that's all as it should be.

So, if male violence were a pandemic, so to speak, it's now easier to see why we might notice and share information about one another's biological sex, and even encode this in our language as an extra safeguard. If it's legitimate to segregate spaces by sex, and there's grave danger in allowing males into female-only spaces, then one might think not only that we have no reasonable expectation of privacy about our biological sex, but that we have no right to that privacy in the first place.

Fourth Reason Not to Track Sex: You Will Be Canceled, or Worse

Something that bears mentioning is that, from the perspective of those in power, who have the ability to coerce others on matters of behavior and language, it's only natural that they would view their use of this power as morally legitimate. Of course, they don't think of themselves as the Neo-Nazis asking others to salute Hitler, or as North Koreans asking others to use honorific titles for Kim Jong Un, or as Muslims asking others to honor Mohammad. No doubt they'd think of themselves using other, more flattering analogies: perhaps as Abolitionists asking others to stop speaking in terms of masters and slaves, or as opponents of the caste system in India, asking others to stop speaking in terms of Untouchables, or as defenders of democracy asking others to use the title of "President" for one duly elected.

Surely, in these cases, wielding the power of the state to force compliance seems inevitable, if not downright righteous.

And the same goes with regard to our current topic. I do not doubt that those who advocate for revising (and compelling others to revise) our use of third-person singular pronouns have good intentions and sincerely believe that it is a mistake for their opponents to see this as a violation of conscience. Though in recent years the momentum behind revisionary uses of our pronouns has waned, there remain serious consequences for those who would resist this revisionary moment. People have been formally disciplined (like Nicholas Meriwether at Shawnee State University), have lost their jobs (like Peter Vlaming under the West Point School Board), and have been embroiled in lengthy and expensive lawsuits for refusing to abandon their Sex-Tracking use of pronouns.

A brief response: Life is short; character matters. Naturally, one's opponents will view themselves as "on the right side of history"; nevertheless, one has strong reason *not* to violate one's conscience. I mentioned above the martyrdom of St. Polycarp. He was asked to "swear by the genius of Caesar" and to renounce Christianity, under threat of fire and death. His response is worth meditating upon (Lightfoot 1907, 206–7): "Thou threatenest that fire which burneth for a season and after a little while is quenched... But why delayest thou? Come, do what thou wilt."

We rightly admire when one suffers for his deeply held principles. Too often, we wanderers under the Moon cannot see clearly which causes are just and which are unjust until well after the fact. And, until then, what better can we do than abide by the dictates of our consciences? To the degree that one disagrees with the politics and philosophy of the contemporary gender movement, one has strong reason to continue the Sex-Tracking use of our third-person singular pronouns.[9]

Notes

1. See also Alex Byrne (2023), as well as Sally McConnell-Ginet (2020, 199), who puts it this way: "English speakers learn very early to use *she* (and the rest of the paradigm: *her*, *hers*, and *herself*) for specific individual (presumptively) female referents and *he* (and *him*, *his*, and *himself*) whenever speaking of those we take to be male."
2. When pronouns are "bound," their referents depend on the meaning of another phrase (cf. Sudo 2012, 12). For example: "Every boy brought his lunch today." Here, the referent of 'him' depends on the domain of the quantifier 'every'. In this chapter, I'll be concerned primarily with unbound or "free" use of pronouns.
3. For the conventional implicature view, see, for example, Greenhall (2007). For the presupposition view, see for example Heim and Kratzer (1998, 244–5), Büring (2011), Sudo (2012, 22ff), and Dembroff and Wodak (2021). As Sudo (2012, 23) puts it, "presuppositions are pieces of information that are assumed

to be already true or at least uncontroversial in the conversational context." And the view is that the sex of the referent is one such piece of information when we use third-person singular pronouns in English.
4 In this way, the example would be like the following: "If this horse is a colt, I will take him to get gelded" (cf. Sudo 2012, 33 and Byrne 2023, 5). In that sentence, 'colt' implies information about sex, and so 'him' is appropriate in the consequent, even though the commitment to sex disappears in this embedded context.
5 What characteristics typical of females do *ships* have, which might explain the use of *she/her/hers/herself* pronouns for ships? Probably the answer is obscured by the mists of time, but one might speculate that the custom is related to our use of 'mother ship' to communicate the nurturing or carrying capacity of a ship, like unto a female's role in procreation.
6 If you're not the type to balk at obscenity, make the nickname sexist or racist.
7 See, for example, Andrea Long Chu (2024), who says, "We must be prepared to defend the idea that, in principle, everyone should have access to sex-changing medical care, regardless of age, gender identity, social environment, or psychiatric history."
8 More recently, the American Civil Liberties Union (2025, 14) used the same general reasoning in order to argue that a policy requiring the disclosure of one's sex on passport documents would violate one's privacy: "That is a profoundly private piece of information in which [one has] a reasonable expectation of privacy."
9 A reviewer rightly notes that the Sex-Tracking use of pronouns may encode an ideology that others find fraught, and wonders why the Sex-Tracking view should win by default. In response, let me clarify that I don't mean to argue that we all have conclusive reason to adopt or maintain the Sex–Tracking use of pronouns. I have argued only that there is good reason to do so, and good reason not to compel those who use pronouns in the traditional, Sex-Tracking way to violate their consciences and adopt a revisionary use of pronouns.

References

American Civil Liberties Union (2025). Orr v. Trump, "Class Action Complaint for Declaratory and Injunctive Relief." https://www.aclu.org/cases/orr-v-trump

Ashley, Florence (2021). "'X' Why? Gender Markers and Non-binary Transgender People," in *Trans Rights and Wrongs: A Comparative Study of Legal Reform Concerning Trans Persons*, Isabel C. Jaramillo and Laura Carlson (eds.) (Cham, Switzerland: Springer).

Bettcher, Talia Mae (2017). "Through the Looking Glass," in *Routledge Companion to Feminist Philosophy*, Ann Garry, Serene Khader, and Alison Stone (eds.) (New York, NY: Routledge).

Bruce, V., A. M. Burton, E. Hanna, P. Healey, O. Mason, A. Coombes, . . . A. Linney (1993). "Sex Discrimination: How do We Tell the Difference Between Male and Female Faces?" *Perception* 22: 131–52.

Büring, Daniel (2011). "Pronouns," in *Semantics: An International Handbook of Natural Language Meaning*, Vol. 2, Klaus von Heusinger, Claudia Maienborn, and Paul Portner (eds.) (Berlin/Boston: De Gruyter).

Byrne, Alex (2023). "Pronoun Problems," *Journal of Controversial Ideas* 3 (1), 5: 1–22.

Cheng, Y. D., A. J. O'Toole, and H. Abdi (2001). "Classifying Adults' and Children's Faces by Sex: Computational Investigations of Subcategorical Feature Encoding," *Cognitive Science* 25: 819–38.

Chu, Andrea Long (2024). "Freedom of Sex: The Moral Case for Letting Trans Kids Change their Bodies," *New York Magazine*, March 11th, 2024, https://nymag.com/intelligencer/article/trans-rights-biological-sex-gender-judith-butler.html, accessed October 23, 2024.

D'Argenio, G., A. Finisguerra, and C. Urgesi (2020). "Motion and Gender-typing Features Interact in the Perception of Human Bodies," *Frontiers in Neuroscience* 14: 277.

Dembroff, Robin (2018a). "The Non-Binary Gender Trap," *New York Review of Books*, January 30th, 2018, https://www.nybooks.com/online/2018/01/30/the-nonbinary-gender-trap

Dembroff, Robin (2018b). "Why be Nonbinary?" *Aeon Magazine*, October 30, 2018, https://aeon.co/essays/nonbinary-identity-is-a-radical-stance-against-gender-segregation

Dembroff, Robin, and Daniel Wodak (2021). "How Much Gender is Too Much Gender?" in *The Routledge Handbook of Social and Political Philosophy of Language*, Justin Khoo, and Rachel Sterken (eds.) (New York, NY: Routledge), 362–76.

Dembroff, Robin, and Daniel Wodak (May 30, 2019). *We Should All Use They/Them Pronouns ... Eventually*. Retrieved from Scientific American: https://blogs.scientificamerican.com/voices/we-should-all-use-they-them-pronouns-eventually/

Greenhall, Owen (2007). "Pronouns and Conventional Implicature," Paper presented at the *Fifth Barcelona Workshop on Issues in the Theory of Reference*.

Jenkins, Katharine (2016). "Amelioration and Inclusion: Gender Identity and the Concept of *Woman*," *Ethics* 126: 394–421.

Kirk-Giannini, Cameron Domenico, and Michael Glanzberg (2024). "Pronouns and Gender," in *The Oxford Handbook of Applied Philosophy of Language* (New York: Oxford University Press), 265–92.

Hanna, Alex, Nikki L Stevens, Os Keyes, and Maliha Ahmed (May 3, 2019). *Actually, We Should Not All Use They/Them Pronouns*. Retrieved from Scientific American: https://blogs.scientificamerican.com/voices/actually-we-should-not-all-use-they-them-pronouns/

Heim, Irene, and Angelika Kratzer (1998). *Semantics in Generative Grammar* (Oxford: Blackwell).

Hernandez, E. M. (2021). "Gender Affirmation and Loving Attention," *Hypatia* 36 (4): 619–35.

Hofstadter, Douglas (1985). "A Person Paper on Purity in Language," in *Metamagical Themas: Questing for the Essence of Mind and Pattern* (New York: Basic Books), 159–72.

Lewis, David (1996). "Elusive Knowledge," *Australasian Journal of Philosophy* 74 (4): 549–67.

Lightfoot, J. B. (translator) (1907). "The Martyrdom of Polycarp," in *The Apostolic Fathers*, J. R. Harmer (ed.) (London: Macmillan and Co.), 185–211.

McConnell-Ginet, Sally (2020). *Words Matter: Meaning and Power* (Cambridge: Cambridge University Press).

Mulaikal, R. M., C. J. Migeon, and J. A. Rock (1987). "Fertility Rates in Female Patients with Congenital Adrenal Hyperplasia due to 21-Hydroxylase Deficiency," *New England Journal of Medicine* 316 (4): 178–82. doi: 10.1056/NEJM198701223160402. PMID: 3491959.

Pernet, C. R., and P. Belin (2012). "The Role of Pitch and Timbre in Voice Gender Categorization," *Frontiers in Psychology* 3: 23.
Recanati, François (2005). "Literalism and Contextualism: Some Varieties," in *Contextualism in Philosophy: Knowledge, Meaning, and Truth*, Gerhard Preyer and Georg Peter (eds.) (Oxford: Oxford University Press).
Sher, George (2023). "Too Much Morality," *Public Affairs Quarterly* 37 (2): 125–37.
Sudo, Yasutada (2012). *On the Semantics of Phi Features on Pronouns*, Ph.D. thesis, Massachusetts Institute of Technology.

7
CONCLUSION

We have long segregated spaces and activities by sex: sports, prisons, restrooms, dorms, scholarships, entire colleges, and the like. Recently, disputes about the nature of the sexes have sown confusion and controversy about these spaces and activities. On one side, many argue that sex is excessively complex, and wield this Complex View to argue that sex is not binary. Others use the Complex View to argue that, among the constellation of things that 'male' and 'female' might refer to are what they call "gender identities." And so, they conclude, having a "male gender identity" is a legitimate way of being male, even if the person is male in no other alleged sense of the word.

Upon investigation, we have seen that the Complex View is false. There's no good reason to deny that sex is binary, or that it's nearly so complicated as the Complex View would have us believe. Rather, we have seen that the Gamete View is true. Our sex terms are univocal—at least when used as adjectives and said of organisms—and the sexes themselves are comparatively simple. To be male is to have the function of producing sperm, and to be female is to have the function of producing eggs. Our investigation has revealed something deeper about the nature of the sexes: they are activated higher-order functions had by organisms, functions to develop and maintain biological components with the function of producing anisogamous gamete-types.

We've also seen that, if gender really is defined in terms of the sexes, then a more accurate understanding of the sexes should also help us make better sense of—and perhaps significant progress in—contemporary debates about gender. As we've seen, there are a variety of things one might be referring to when using the word 'gender', but all of these many things are significantly or even wholly constituted by the sexes. I have also defended an attitude of deference to biologists when it comes to theorizing about the nature of the sexes, and we've provided reasons to doubt that a project of conceptual engineering our sex terms can be successful, even on its own terms. In chapter 6, we extended this discussion of conceptual engineering to third-person singular pronouns in English, and defended the claim that such pronouns *in fact* track sex, and that there is good reason to *continue* using them in this way.

With some luck and a great deal of effort, the deeper understanding we've gained of the nature of the sexes will help us sort through ongoing controversies about both sex and gender, in a way that respects the biological reality of males and females.

INDEX

Pages followed by "n" refer to notes.

Aatsha, P. A. 49–50
AHOF account 49, 60–1, 67, 76–8, 80–1, 92, 116, 120, 137, 147
Ainsworth, C. 4, 35
Ambiguity Hypothesis 11, 15–20, 37–8, 41–3
American Civil Liberties Union 5, 93, 152
anisogamy 2–3, 14, 37, 60, 67, 77, 85, 115–16
Aristotle 110–12, 117, 125, 125n1
Arvan, M. 17, 41–2
Ashley, F. 99, 101–2
asexual reproduction 2

Barnes, E. 101
Beauvoir, S. de 4, 77, 97, 106
Bettcher, T. M. 35, 121, 144
Bigelow, R. P. 3, 6, 43, 83, 86
Boghossian, P. 14
Boyd, R. 39, 44
Briggs, R. A. 100, 106
Brison, S. J. 106
Bruce, V. 150
Burgess, A. 126
Büring, D. 151
Butler, J. 11–2, 40–1, 86

Byne, W. 35
Byrne, A. 13–4, 42, 53–5, 83, 93, 104, 106, 151–2

Cappelen, H. 126–7
Casas, L. 60, 86
Cheng, Y. D. 150
chromosomal sex 11, 15–7, 35, 37, 42, 76–7, 114
Chu, A. L. 152
Coleman, E. 99
Complex View 4–5, 10–1, 15, 34–5, 38
conceptual engineering 110, 119–24, 126–7
Contextualist Hypothesis 11, 33–4, 38
Cosker-Rowland, R. 101, 107, 126
C. elegans 40, 43, 56
Cummins, R. 64–5, 84
Currah, P. 49

D'Argenio, G. 150
Dea, S. 10, 86, 107, 126
Dembroff, R. 99, 101, 130–1, 140, 144–6, 148–9
developmental pathway view 49–55, 60

Diaz-León, E. 39–40, 44, 126
DiMarco, M. 40, 82, 85–7, 114–17, 124–6
Dolezal, R. 143
Doryteuthis opalescens 1
DuBois, Z. 119
Dupré, J. 4, 6, 84, 87, 105
Dworkin, A. 17, 41

Edwards, B. 79
Eitel, M. 3, 36, 44
Encyclopaedia Britannica 83, 86

Fausto-Sterling, A. 4, 15–6, 35, 41, 112–13
female (definition): AHOF account 60, 67, 76–8, 80; Complex View 4–5, 10–1, 15, 34–5, 38; Gamete View 49–59; gender norms 94–5, 97–8; pronouns 130–49
Fine, K. 85
Fisher, R. A. 5
Franklin-Hall, L. 3, 5–6, 50–4, 60, 81–3, 86
function: activated function 61–4, 67, 76–9, 116, 137; AHOF account 60–1, 65–7, 76–80; biological systems 58–9, 61–6; gender identity 92; higher-order function 60–1, 65–7, 76–8, 92, 116–17, 120; pronouns 147
Fusco, G. 78, 83, 86
Futuyma, D. 6

gamete production 3–4, 6, 35, 37, 40, 43, 49–52, 56–60, 67, 76–7, 92, 116, 120, 147
Gamete View 4, 10, 37–8, 40, 49–60, 85–7, 92, 115–16
Garson, J. 3, 37, 58–60, 66, 84–6, 110
gender: as synonym for sex 93–5, 97–8, 103–4; distinct from sex 92, 103; gender identity 5, 10, 17, 41–2, 93–4, 98–3, 107, 119–21, 131–2, 144–6; gender norms 94–5, 99–103, 107; gender roles 94–5, 99, 103, 105; masculinity and femininity 93–5, 97–8, 103–4
gender affirmation 145–6
Gender-First View 131–3, 135–6
Gennerich, A. 84
Ghiselin, M. T. 5

Glanzberg, M. 131–6, 138
Godfrey-Smith, P. 67, 84
Goymann, W. 6
Greenson, R. R. 105
Griffiths, P. 5, 41, 56–8, 60, 83–4, 86, 117, 125

Hacking, I. 14, 40–1
Haslanger, S. 17, 41, 93, 105, 118, 120, 126
Heinämaa, S. 106
Hempel, C. 84
hermaphroditism 3, 5, 43, 52–3, 55–6, 60, 77, 83, 86–7, 114, 117, 147; sequential hermaphroditism 52–3, 55–6, 60, 76, 79, 147; simultaneous hermaphroditism 55–6, 60, 77, 147
Hernandez, E. M. 145
Hill, G. 5
Hine, R. 6, 86
Hofstadter, D. 140
Hoover, S. E. R. 87
hormonal sex 11, 15–7, 35, 37, 42, 114
Hurley, A. C. 1

Indeterminacy Hypothesis 11, 34–8
intersex conditions 76–7, 147–8
Ivy, V. (McKinnon, R.) 5, 126

Jenkins, K. 5, 99, 107, 119, 121, 144

Kirk-Giannini, C. D. 131–6, 138
Kirkpatrick, K. 106
Kitcher, P. 84
Kripke, S. 96, 106
Krohs, U. 84

Laskowski, N. 113
Lawford-Smith, H. 105
Lehtonen, J. 3, 85
Lennox, J. G. 84
Leonard, J. L. 5
Lewis, D. 127, 149
Li, J. 79
Li, J. 80, 87
Li, Z. 87
Lightfoot, J. B. 142, 151

MacLaughlin, D. T. 85
male (definition): AHOF account 60, 67, 76–8, 80; Complex View 4–5,

10–1, 15, 34–5, 38; Gamete View 49–59; gender norms 94–5, 97–8; pronouns 130–49
Martin, J. 2
Maung, H. H. 77
Mayr, E. 65, 84
McConnell-Ginet, S. 151
McGinn, C. 39
McLaughlin, J. F. 4, 85
Mikkola, M. 95, 105
Millikan, R. 64, 84
Minelli, A. 78, 83, 86
Minot, C. S. 3, 6
Money, J. 16–7, 41–2, 105
Moutos, C. P. 3, 53
Mulaikal, R. M. 147

Nagel, E. 84
National Library of Medicine 59, 83
Neander, K. 84
Nelson, R. J. 61, 84
Newman, H. H. 83, 86

Oakley, A. 95, 105
Ohya, I. 3
Özdemir, M. 87

Parker, G. A. 3, 6, 43, 83, 85–6
Parvin, S. 87
Pernet, C. R. 150
Placozoa 3, 36
Plunkett, D. 126
pronouns: gender-first view 131–3, 135–6; sex-tracking view 130–45, 149–51
Property-Cluster Hypothesis 11, 38–40, 44
Prum, R. 84, 86

Quine, W. V. O. 105

Recanati, F. 139
Reece, J. 61, 83, 86
reproduction 1–2, 14, 49–52, 67, 113, 131, 141
Richardson, S. 33, 112, 118–19

Rifkin, M. 3, 37, 58–60, 66, 86, 110
Roughgarden, J. 4–6, 37–8, 61, 86, 105, 114
Ruse, M. 84

Saborido-Rey, F. 60, 86
Sadler, T. W. 50
Sainsbury, R. M. 111, 123, 127
Saul, J. 113
Schroeder, M. 127
sex eliminativism 114, 124–6
Sex-Tracking View 130–45, 149–51
Shattuck-Heidorn, H. 119
Sher, G. 144
Slack, J. 85
Smiley, K. O. 4, 85–6
Srinivasan, A. 12–3
Stock, K. 38–9, 93, 104, 106–7
Stoller, R. 93–4, 97–8, 103–4
Stone, A. 38–9, 44
Stryker, S. 95, 97, 105
Sudo, Y. 130, 151–2
Swyer Syndrome 78

Takahashi, M. 79
Takeuchi, T. 3
trans issues 5, 41–2, 99, 101–2, 119–21, 133–5, 144–6
Trump, D. 92, 104, 111–12, 118
Tye, M. 111, 123, 127

Vale, R. D. 84
van Anders, S. 35, 113, 125
Velocci, B. 17, 40, 112, 114, 124–6
Venter, J. C. 80

Walsh, D. 84
Watkins, A. 40, 82, 85–7, 114–17, 124–6
Wodak, D. 130–1, 140, 144–6, 148–9
Wright, C. 6, 42

Yan, G. 85
Yu, F. H. 84

Zhang, S. 78, 87

For Product Safety Concerns and Information please contact our EU representative GPSR@taylorandfrancis.com
Taylor & Francis Verlag GmbH, Kaufingerstraße 24, 80331 München, Germany

www.ingramcontent.com/pod-product-compliance
Ingram Content Group UK Ltd.
Pitfield, Milton Keynes, MK11 3LW, UK
UKHW020628290825
462375UK00006B/89